The Victory Album

The Victory Album

Reflections on the Good Life after the Good War

PHILIP D. BEIDLER

THE UNIVERSITY OF ALABAMA PRESS
Tuscaloosa

The University of Alabama Press
Tuscaloosa, Alabama 35487-0380
uapress.ua.edu

Hardcover edition published 2010.
Paperback edition published 2015.
eBook edition published 2013.

Typeface: Caslon

Manufactured in the United States of America
Cover art: © Bill Bogusky / Fotolia.com
Cover design: Todd Lape / Lape Designs

∞
The paper on which this book is printed meets the minimum requirements of American National Standard for Information Science–Permanence of Paper for Printed Library Materials, ANSI Z39.48-1984.

Paperback ISBN: 978-0-8173-5845-7
eBook ISBN: 978-0-8173-8714-3

A previous edition of this book has been catalogued by the Library of Congress as follows:

Library of Congress Cataloging-in-Publication Data
Beidler, Philip D.
The victory album : reflections on the good life after the good war /
Philip D. Beidler.
p. cm.
ISBN 978-0-8173-1684-6 (cloth : alk. paper) 1. United States—Civilization—1945- 2. United States—Social life and customs—1945–1970. 3. United States—Social conditions—1945- 4. World War, 1939–1945—Influence.
I. Title.
E169.12.B35 2010
973.918—dc22

2009025780

To my brother, Garry, and my sister, Deborah

Contents

Acknowledgments

Many people helped me with this book, including Donald Anderson, Louel Gibbons, Laurence Goldstein, Fred Hobson, Jerome Klinkowitz, John Northrop, Michael Robbins, Merinda Simmons, Bill Ulmer, Dan Waterman, and Heather White. I hope the dedication page acknowledges a familial history of love and support from the best brother and sister a person could possibly have. Closer to home, I further wish to thank, as ever, the wonderful Beidler women, Ellen and Kat.

Acknowledgment is made for materials published in *Michigan Quarterly Review, Military History Magazine,* and *War, Literature & the Arts.*

The Victory Album

Introduction

After the Good War

On May 8, 1945, General Dwight D. Eisenhower, supreme commander of the Allied forces in Europe, having accepted the surrender of Nazi Germany, made the following announcement: "The mission of this allied force was fulfilled at 0300, local time, May 7th, 1945."*

On August 15 of that year Admiral Chester W. Nimitz, commander of the Allied forces in the Pacific theater, having confirmed the surrender of Imperial Japan, sent the following message to all units: "Orders have been issued to the Pacific Fleet and to other forces under the command of the Commander in Chief US Pacific Fleet and Pacific Ocean areas to cease offensive operations against the Japanese." With such terse, unadorned, workmanlike communications, American commanders told the world that the great task had been accomplished. The Axis threat had been ended, and final victory had been achieved. Now it was time to go on with the future.

V Was for Victory. This was the title John Morton Blum chose for his classic study of the World War II American home front. The past tense is telling. One feels the sense of completion and closure. For Americans on all fronts it was time for life to go forward; and go forward it would, as Lewis Lapham has written, into new dimensions of national possibility undreamed even by the most visionary of the founders: "In 1945,

*Albert D. Chandler, ed., *The Papers of Dwight D. Eisenhower* (Baltimore: 1970), vol. 4, 2696.

the United States inherited the earth," wrote Lapham; and "what was left of Western civilization passed into the American account." Further, "the war had also prompted the country to invent a miraculous economic machine that seemed to grant as many wishes as were asked of it. The continental United States had escaped the plague of war, and so it was easy enough for the heirs to believe that they had been anointed by God."*

In one form or another, such were the basic majority of attitudes for Americans of the postwar era where the new visions of promise attending the great triumph became portals to an ever-extending future, a golden age of American peace and plenitude that to a great degree has never ended. To be sure, for large numbers of post-1945 Americans the idea of the Good Life after the Good War remains decidedly problematic; most notably for blacks and women, it was hardly a uniform or even a majority experience, then or now. Nor, it might be added, even on the part of white males of the victory generation, can one avoid at significant moments a sense of the almost unbearable sadness of postwar American life in general as represented, for instance, in domestic novels by returned veterans such as James Jones's *Some Came Running*, Richard Yates's *Revolutionary Road*, or Joseph Heller's *Something Happened*. Still, the concept continues to shape both personal memory and cultural reflection. To put it simply, many Americans who, like me, came of age during the second half of the twentieth century will always find it difficult to think of themselves as anything but inheritors and beneficiaries of the post–World War II culture of victory. For us the facts will remain that, in outlook, education, and security, in moral energy and social and political opportunity, a lot of us had a head start on the rest of the world. To cite the reflections of a friend and contemporary I read recently, we all felt somehow as if we had been "part of a great triumph." Accordingly, the world of our formative experiences seemed imbued with a "pervasive sense of calm, confidence, and relief."† He gets it just right, I think. The world had been saved somehow. The future was ours to build. And we all knew who had laid the foundations for us. It was our parents and aunts and uncles—

*Lewis Lapham, "America's Foreign Policy: A Rake's Progress," *Harper's*, March 1979. Quoted in Studs Terkel, *The Good War* (New York: Pantheon, 1984), 8.
†John Northrop, executive director, Alabama School of the Fine Arts, Birmingham, AL, *ASFA Applause Newsletter*, Nov. 2007, 2.

our postal carriers and electricians and teachers and bookkeepers—the people who had fought and won the Good War and in the process had earned for themselves the title of the Greatest Generation.

Along with them, in spirit and energy, we felt the glow of victory in World War II as a kind of beacon, the light of a moment in which Americans' attitudes toward themselves and the world seem to have been endowed with a certain clarity and generosity of purpose. At home we all felt ourselves to have been given a gift of peace, prosperity, and security, a style of living and a quality of life unprecedented in human history. Abroad, in the annals of power, no other combatant nation had ever emerged from a major war with potentialities so great for a larger, global good. If we were advantaged by the affluence and power accrued in our great victory, we were also obligated by them. We felt in them a new purpose and a new duty to make our world, if not perfect, at least better and, further, to make it better not just for ourselves but for everyone.

Moreover—with frequent reminders at mealtimes, on shopping trips, and nearly anytime else a lesson in uprightness seemed in order from our parents or other elder relations—we were schooled to see ourselves as working with a compounded inheritance of strength, forbearance, sacrifice, and self-discipline from the years before the war. That is to say, as is frequently overlooked by Americans growing up after midcentury, the people we thought of as the adult generation of World War II remembered themselves equally as the youth generation of the Great Depression. And they never let us forget that either. In their own understandings of post-1945 America, to borrow the phrasings of Studs Terkel, the great chronicler of both epochal passages in the national experience, the vision of the Good War could never be separated from the memory of Hard Times. Before the trials of Pearl Harbor, Bataan, Anzio, and the Battle of the Bulge, before meat and gas rationing and the dreadful anticipations and arrivals of War Department telegrams about loved ones killed and wounded, there had been bank failures, crop disasters, plant closings, enormous migrations of the displaced and unemployed; losses and foreclosures of farms, businesses, family dwellings; breadlines, bonus marches, labor riots, political arrests, and lynchings. The other side of making do had in fact been doing without. The war had surely been a case of do or die. But no one had ever forgotten the other, earlier decade of fear, the classic Roosevelt formulation notwithstanding, that really had been something close to fear itself.

Now they desperately wanted to put all of it in the past, the years of shortage and want, threat and menace; and, if not vouchsafed the endless future envisioned by their children's generation at least granted the just satisfactions of getting on with a long-deferred present. The larger postwar world menaced and haunted. In their eyes the vast human suffering amid the ruined cities and blighted landscapes of Europe, the Middle East, Asia, and the Pacific (former allies and former enemies alike), hunger, unemployment, poverty, domestic suffering, and disease, they saw specters of new disorders and hardships out of which they had somehow, barely, if miraculously, been lifted by the war. Even by the most optimistic assessment, the books and movies of the war counted what had been lost as much as all that had been won. Coming out of the shadow of censorship, cutting through euphemism and popular sentimentalism, novels especially were quite grim. The specter of totalitarianism dominates *From Here to Eternity, The Naked and the Dead, The Young Lions, The Caine Mutiny.* Hard-boiled writing and bleak existential allegory fed into Hollywood film noir and political scare-fables of the McCarthy era. In politics, beyond the Marshall Plan for helping war-torn Europe rise from the rubble and the MacArthur shogunate bringing democracy to Japan, it was hard to see what Americans and the world might assess as having been truly gained in 1945, with quondam allies now the new enemies. The Soviets, after a wartime embrace as a necessary antifascist partner, resumed status as a regime every bit as monolithic, repressive, and murderous as any in history, launching new aggressive plans for totalitarian world domination. China—throughout the war a weak, corrupt, foundationless, pseudodemocracy—once the Japanese had been expelled, came down like a house of cards, with the Nationalist regime supplanted by a new, aggressive, Asian Communist monolith. Western allies such as Britain and France dealt with political and civilian economies teetering on the brink of collapse, meanwhile shoring up the remnants of prewar empire. Central European states fell one by one under Soviet-dominated dictatorships. Fragile coalition governments in France, Italy, Greece, and Turkey, attempting to reassume status as operating democracies, stood always on the edge of dissolving into anarchy or of succumbing to socialist or communist governments.

At home, Red Scare America fearfully scoured the nooks and crannies of national life for the enemy within. Conspiracy theories abounded about who ought to be watching whom. Big Brother had to be somebody, somewhere, as posited by George Orwell's classic novel *1984,* the title of which everyone knew to be a simple inversion of "1948." Not that there wasn't plenty to worry about. In 1948 the Alger Hiss–Whittaker Chambers case shared headlines with the fall of Czechoslovakia and the Berlin Airlift. In 1949 Poland and China went communist, and the Soviets exploded their own atomic bomb.

In the latter development came to be concentrated the postwar fear presiding over everything else, the worst specter of all: that of nuclear annihilation. Here the great achievements of victory culture were compounded into the most dreadful of all ironies. Ironically, the greatest of all the war's American production miracles had been the atomic bomb. Ironically, the Americans, at the forefront of the crusade for freedom, peace, and justice against murderous, utterly inhumane military totalitarianisms, had used the bomb on enemy civilian targets—not once but twice. Ironically, now, suddenly, it was equally plausible that the astonishing peace and prosperity of postwar American life could end tomorrow in the cauldron of fire rising under a host of similar monstrous mushroom clouds.

A great popular icon of hope for new geopolitical comity in the postwar era was the United Nations. Installed in its fancy, futuristic, glass-walled headquarters along the East River in New York, it got a lot of terrific publicity with its various global relief activities and its general assembly sessions generating reams of documents on human rights and new frameworks for international understanding and cooperation. With its sky-blue flag and trademark logo over the speakers' podium and visits by foreign plenipotentiaries in national costume, it may have been a great place for school trips, where kids in headphones could sit and be part of the miracle of simultaneous translation, but its work was largely a toothless internationalism, rendered ineffectual by the quarreling and obstructionism of major-power members of the Security Council. The only reason a U.N. force could be committed to the defense of South Korea after the 1950 Communist invasion from the North lay in the brief absence of the Soviet Union from that body, which it had decided temporarily to boycott.

The actual situation in geopolitics could be more accurately measured in the rise of the post–World War II "Third World"—the developing nations. In Africa, South America, the Middle East, South Asia, and around the Pacific Rim insurgencies destabilized fragile new postcolonial and nationalist coalition regimes. The global roster of Communist-bloc states threatened increase at every turn. Against this, according to American policies of "containment," "Free World" governments became increasingly identified as a dismal panoply of tin-pot dictatorships and authoritarian hellholes. Cast up as mirroring Tito's Yugoslavia, Gomulka's Poland, and Gottwald's Czechoslovakia were Chiang Kai-shek's Formosa, Syngman Rhee's South Korea, Ngo Dinh Diem's Vietnam, Alberto Salazar's Portugal, Francisco Franco's Spain, King Farouk's Egypt, Reza Pahlevi's Iran, Juan Batista's Cuba, and Anastasio Somoza's Nicaragua. In the new world order of nonstop geopolitical crisis, the only things getting better for anybody, anywhere, seemed to be improved nuclear weapons and more effective delivery systems.

Meanwhile, equally dispiriting for those willing to look them in the eye were the hard facts of American domestic politics, down with the oily gears and the working parts. David Halberstam was right. They were mean times: full of haters, dirt collectors, list makers, self-aggrandizing demagogues, creeps, and liars; of witch hunts, loyalty oaths, blacklists, race murders, spy executions, illegal surveillance, and censorship in the popular information and entertainment media.

One understands the built-in irony of entitling in countless retrospective studies. Emblazoned on the title pages one finds such grand phrasings as *American High: The Years of Confidence, 1945–1960* or *A Dream of Greatness: The American People, 1945–1963.* Underneath, one prepares to read of stifling conformity; smug materialism; stubborn anti-intellectualism; and bland, middle-of-the-road tastes in music, movies, television, and literature. Formula phrases about the times elicit a similarly axiomatic response: the Good Years, the Baby Boom, the Eisenhower era, the Fabulous Fifties, Happy Days. The idea of mainstream

America over these years has come to be deeply discredited: a nation out there in the heartland reading Norman Vincent Peale's *The Power of Positive Thinking,* subscribing to *Reader's Digest,* watching Charlton Heston in *The Ten Commandments,* and laughing at *I Love Lucy* on the boob tube. This also is the middle America retrospectively caricatured through the domestic upheavals of the 1960s, Vietnam, civil rights, the counterculture, and the endless succession of profound disappointments and disillusionments to follow—the manipulations of the Nixon-Agnew era, with its great "silent majority" opposed to "nattering nabobs of negativism." Against this it is hard to maintain that there was once a real place called post-1945 middle America and that, if it was not a good place, it tried to be, or it promised to try hard to be.

The argument allows no place for revisionary nostalgia or nostalgists—devotees of commemorative volumes, golden oldies record collections, restored classic cars, ducktail haircuts, poodle skirts, sock hops, TV dinners, drive-in theaters. Most of these remain relics of a world that largely didn't exist in the experiences of everyday Americans, save in ads or TV shows and movies; or if it did, it certainly did not shower its promised blessings on large numbers of actual people beyond the white middle class. Even in popular social commentary the idea of American promise being written about was frequently that of promise betrayed. The most respected cultural critique of the age was that of a theologian, Reinhold Niebuhr, entitled *The Irony of American History.* Other titles went more directly to the point: Richard Hofstadter's *Anti-intellectualism in American Life* or William J. Lederer's *A Nation of Sheep.* Before the 1960s discovered them as popular purveyors of Freud and Marx, Norman O. Brown in *Life against Death* and Herbert Marcuse in *One-Dimensional Man* had laid down the terms of essential critique. The "happy consciousness," Marcuse called it. The spirit of the times had become encapsulated in the insulating, narcotizing, self-hypnotizing belief that "society delivers the goods."

Abroad, the attitudes of other nationalities could be summarized as envy mixed with substantial fear and loathing. The only country in history to have used atomic weaponry on its enemies in a war now seemed to have set itself up as the world policeman, the self-appointed benevolent cop on the block. Old allies marched to the American beat. No matter what the cultural origins of any new aspirant state, American friendship and assistance required cultural reshaping in the type and image of the American way. America became the arbiter of acceptable structures of moral, social, economic, and political relationship, spouting democratic platitudes and professing democratic goodwill to former colonial peoples of developing nations, frequently non-Western and nonwhite, while practicing total racial segregation in every sphere from the bathroom to the ballot box and enforcing world peace abroad with the H-bomb, the B-52, and eventually the ICBM.

At the same time, one must not play false with the nostalgia of countercultural critique. The facts cannot be controverted that, for certain categories of Americans, the good life after the good war may have remained the not-so-good life. Where happiness prevailed, there was also plenty about it that remained dour, bland, insular, conformist, pedestrian, and joyless. The happy consciousness, such as it may have existed, was frequently restricted to a world of small pleasures. For young people this included learning and doing things in school (science, literature, mathematics, foreign language, and extracurriculars: sports, music, art, field trips). For their parents it included the daily regularities of work; a steady job; participation in school, church, service organizations, or other forms of community involvement; reading the hometown newspaper; an evening of TV; Sunday dinner and a nap. At the same time, one experienced a rich sense of earned satisfaction, a genuine and palpably experienced enjoyment of common life. People built houses, bought cars, went to movies, watched TV, played records, hummed advertising jingles for the simple pleasure of being part of the world they had made for themselves and their children. An immense avidity for things conjoined with a larger spirit of cultural curiosity and appetite for knowledge. It was the heyday of the great, mass-circulation magazines—of tables overflowing with *Time, Life, Look, Newsweek, Collier's,* the *Saturday Evening Post, Popular Mechanics, Sports Illustrated, Field and Stream, Boy's Life, McCall's, Better Homes and Gardens, Redbook, Ladies' Home Journal, Reader's Digest* (the latter likely on the toilet tank, maybe with *Guideposts*). There was also a tremendous book culture, abetted by flourishing subscription programs such as the Book-of-the-Month Club, the Literary Guild, and *Readers' Digest* Condensed Books. Here, and elsewhere, as is too often forgotten, the general abundance of things frequently expressed itself in astonishing variety. The idea of the planned community now suggests in retrospect the faceless, dispiriting, anonymous, homogenous, suburban housing development. But little houses made of ticky-tacky were simply and flatly not the rule for anyone growing up in any American town or small city. Rather, one recalls the plenitude of architectures—Cape Cod, Tudor, ranch, colonial, fieldstone, stucco, wood, brick; houses with front doors, back doors, front lawns, side lawns, backyards, sheds, shops, garages, porches, breezeways, balconies, attics, basements; good houses, built strongly and sturdily by people who knew their tools and equipment and thought well of their trades and vocations—carpenters, plumbers, masons, electricians; houses full of well-made mechanical equipment and appliances, from power drills and washing machines to vacuum cleaners and lawn mowers, regularly maintained and serviced. Much will be said here about TV, movies, music, magazines, advertising, cars, housings, clothing, fads, hobbies, and sports; about dumb pleasures like Friday night fights, Little League baseball, picture windows, frozen-custard stands, and swimming pools. But for anyone who was alive at the time, it is also still hard to gainsay the sheer, unselfconscious, tasteless exuberance of it all sometimes—and in images of anything but a desperate, barren, humdrum gaiety: the Big Bopper singing "Chantilly Lace," Domenico Modugno doing "Volare," or, before anybody ever heard the word *remix,* a stupid novelty record like "Flying Saucers" borrowing snippets from Fats Domino, Elvis Presley, Little Richard, and the Platters; Bill Veeck sending a dwarf to the plate in a Chicago White Sox game to draw a walk; Ernie Kovacs putting new meaning into the word *bop* with the cool sounds of the Nairobi Trio. People may have learned to eat "ethnic" or "foreign" food through grotesque mass-production mockeries—pizza from a Chef Boyardee box and Chinese from cans of La Choy or Chung King. In most cities at least they could wash it down with five or ten good local brands of beer. And say what one might about cars, there will never be another Nash Metropolitan or Packard Clipper, a Chrysler Town and Country Sedan or Lincoln Continental Mark II. On TV there would never be anything again like the shameless, mad effrontery of Uncle Miltie, *Your Show of Shows, The Honeymooners,* until maybe *Saturday Night Live, The Simpsons,* or *South Park.* In the era of Harry Potter, *The*

Lord of the Rings, and *Spiderman* (I, II, and III) nothing is so outrageously over the top as *Invasion of the Body Snatchers, Adventures of Davy Crockett,* or *Demetrius and the Gladiators.*

In politics, Republican or Democrat, young or old, blue-collar or white, heartland patriot or urban sophisticate, most people really did like Ike—and I emphasize the word *like.* Not "love," but "like": *like,* that is, as a word never conjoined with a possible opposite such as *hate* or even *dislike,* which in the case of Eisenhower was largely inconceivable. I say that with the authority of a teenage kid who grew up sitting a few rows back from him on Sunday mornings at the Gettysburg Presbyterian Church and on one memorable weekday afternoon shagged golf balls for him at the local country club; but I also say that as an American who can now truly remember him as the last American president no one ever hated.

Whatever world all that was, it is now somewhere behind us, somewhere between comic books and computer-generated screen heroics. In 1925 it was Jay Gatsby's dream, a green and golden dream of wonder lost somewhere "back where the dark fields of the Republic rolled on under the night." In 1950 the more apt analogue would be the world of the black-and-white TV Superman—Clark Kent, Lois Lane, Perry White, Jimmy Olson, Kryptonite, Metropolis, the *Daily Planet*—as an abstract or epitome of the times. If there was such a thing as an American superhero, in the age of Jim Anderson or Ward Cleaver, he would of course be in real life a bumbling, funny guy with glasses, knocking things off the boss's desk and never quite being able to say the right things to the swell girl he is secretly in love with. In the age of Dwight Eisenhower he would, of course, have spent a normal, unprepossessing, small-town boyhood steeped in the values of the heartland American family. As a new American urbanite, if he needed to put on his Superman suit, he would, of course, be able to change clothes in the nearest phone booth. Such happy TV credulity about this Strange Visitor from Another Planet, faster than a speeding bullet, more powerful than a locomotive, able to leap tall buildings in a single bound, really could couple with an honest belief in the worthiness of a never-ending struggle for Truth, Justice, and the American Way. For a nation attempting to conjoin unprecedented, almost science-fictional, superpower status with the espoused values of a basic working democracy, the ideal was, in a word, *citizenship.* It was once the kind of thing they taught in junior high school and gave merit badges for in the Boy Scouts and Girl Scouts, but it also meant something truly worthy and profound: the exercise of opportunity and obligation in a civil society and the attempt, where possible, to extend such right of exercise to other inhabitants of the globe. To be sure, other usages of the era both marked and mocked its anxieties and evasions. Civil defense was a reminder of unresolved geopolitical confrontation and omnipresent nuclear terror; civil rights taunted members of the body politic as the grossly unmet goal of racial liberty and comity. That both phrases now sound strangely archaic is a direct result of the energy, optimism, hopefulness, and, yes, magnanimity that helped Americans of the era aspire to making better the worst of times for someone, somewhere in the world, both at home and abroad.

Nearly everyone now dates the world after 1945 as the age of *Pax Americana.* After the great twentieth-century wars abroad, World War I, World War II, the cold war, the wars of national liberation, the current war on terror; and after the upheavals of the Kennedy and King assassinations, the tumults of the Vietnam War and the 1960s' counterculture, Watergate, the ensuing cycles of endless political scandals and economic bubbles and meltdowns at home; if anything, America is even richer, more militarily dominant, than ever before. In inexplicable proportion, for someone particularly of the post-1945 era now beginning to get old, one feels a distinct, overt, aggressive new meanness afoot in the land. Consumerism has evolved into a manic, trend-spotting acquisitiveness. Current-events curiosity has become a lust for celebrity scandal and media overload. A shared sense of religious, social, economic, geopolitical conviction, translating itself into a commitment—however misguided at times—to the global sharing of the values of a free society, has been reduced to a nasty insularity and self-righteous certitude. A cultural acceptance of massive economic inequities has been matched with a willed scientific ignorance and environmental shortsightedness. People will eventually get cloned; while they are waiting for that to happen, they can now choose a computer avatar.

A single material-production analogy from the recent histories of American wars may suffice for the moment. From the perspective of the post-1945 American generation who still remember images from both the assembly line and the battlefront, the machine that won World War II will be most likely identified as the Jeep—light, cheap, nimble, simple to build, easy to fix. The vehicle currently prowling the streets of Baghdad, Mosul, Fallujah, and all the other places where Americans and Iraqis are likely to get blown up this week is the Humvee—heavy, expensive, lumbering, prodigiously complicated to operate and maintain; or, in its domestic incarnation, the Hummer, the ultimate icon of hulking, metallic, gas-guzzling excess, America's way of expressing to the world its flamboyant recalcitrance and defiant unconcern for the human problems of lesser mortals elsewhere. Pride in the American Way of Life, indeed, here and elsewhere is measured for many of us by how far we seem to have traveled away from an older, but still-remembered, national capacity for goodwill and basic generosity of spirit. A lot of bad wars and sad lives later, it still may be the gift of memory that we can give.

I
Reds

Not a single major account of post–World War II American life and culture omits discussion of the Red Scare—as the phenomenon, alleged to have become a major preoccupation of many citizens during the late 1940s and early to mid 1950s, is now familiarly termed. Accordingly, chroniclers of the era attempt often to depict a great atmospherics of fear permeating the culture from top to bottom, within and without, and everywhere in between. This supports a certain strain of ideological argument, but thematically it never quite comes off. The effect is something vaguely humorous—like the panicked crowds of a city fleeing from space aliens or a movie monster, or of kids going fitfully to sleep at night while worrying about evil creatures under the bed. I suspect that, like me, many who came of age at the time read historical studies of it with a recurrent sense of disjunction between political accounts of the era and the recollection of how particular political moments—frequently spotlighted as nodes of scandal or crisis—were really experienced by most Americans.

For a young person such as myself growing up in post-1945 America, the Reds were certainly represented as the enemy, and in substantial degree, we were encouraged to believe, the enemy was everywhere. Most visibly, the Reds were the Russians, or, more properly, the Soviets, bent on communist world domination. Forget about the brave World War II ally, fighting for Mother Russia against the Nazis in the great patriotic war; about Stalin, the Big Three partner, along with Roosevelt and Churchill, the little father of the Russians, Uncle Joe. The Soviets became the relentless expansionists of the Communist bloc, the ruthless masters of the Iron Curtain countries, with their puppet governments. By 1949 they had the atomic bomb; as things quickly turned out, they had gained important parts of the technology through a system of spies within the United States capable of infiltrating the most secret of projects and security systems.

After 1949 the Reds also included the Communist Chinese, the new masters, under Mao Tse-tung, of the great Asian mainland; concurrently, they also extended their reach into Korea and Indochina, with the first, a communist dictatorship under Kim Il-sung, openly attacking southward in 1950 and precipitating a three-year war against U.S.-led U.N. forces; and the second, a revolutionary regime under Ho Chi Minh, waging a successful guerilla conflict against the French and eventually the United States. A notable feature of the two "anticommunist," "hot" wars Americans would actually fight, both in the latter precincts of Asia, would be that primary "communist" sponsorship could never be determined as predominantly Russian or Chinese.

On the world landscape, and in American minds, such sudden postwar reconfigurings of friend versus enemy required a certain hasty, parallel logic of geopolitical substitution. The Nazis and the Japanese were still back there in memory, to be sure, but their imperialist designs and heinous deeds were quickly fading from real-life history—good enough still for villains in war movies, comic books, and other popular-culture celebrations of Allied heroism but no longer part of the official calculus. From 1945 on, as a strategic bulwark in Europe, we needed the Germans almost immediately. Documentation of the death camps was downplayed. Some small mention of state terror against civilians was rendered at the Nuremberg Trials, but the focus of the tribunal was on war crimes in the military sense. As symbolic figures, Hitler, Goebbels, Himmler, and, eventually, Goering did the Allies the favor of committing suicide; by 1947 second-line members of the Nazi hierarchy were nearly all imprisoned or executed. "West" Germany and, to a similar degree, "free" Austria, both demilitarized and democratized under Allied occupation, became key strategic pieces in the puzzle of Western defense against the Soviets, interchangeably known as Russia and the Iron Curtain countries or the Communist bloc. They were also proclaimed as exemplary new "free world" European nations, showpiece Western-style democracies and capitalist market economies. As against the menace in Europe and the Mediterranean of thriving Communist parties in the political mix of France, Italy, and Greece, the Germans in particular were quickly rehabilitated in the American mind into a nation of the defeated and misled, suffering, bombed-out veterans and their families, starving and dispossessed, propagandized and lied to, who had been ignorant of the enormity of the Nazis' crimes. Repenting of their militarism, "West" Germans became freedom loving, fervently democratic, committed to full citizenship in the community of nations.

In Asia we turned out quickly to need the Japanese very badly as well. Hiroshima and Nagasaki had changed everything, conferring immediate, colossal victim status. As with the Germans, reimagined as a people preyed on by their ruthless leaders, the Japanese were deemed largely unwitting parties to imperialist designs for Asian domination. Tōjō and a handful of war criminals were tried and executed. The emperor, strategically retained, was himself re-enshrined as peace-loving, misled by militarists in government, at the end indeed the only figure resolute enough to brave a coup and even possible assassination by assenting to Allied demands for surrender. American catastrophes, such as Bataan, Wake Island, or Guam, and POWs and captured fliers, in their sufferings and tortures, got left to war movies, as did suicidal, crazy, Jap soldiers and kamikaze pilots, somehow no longer representative of the peace-loving Japanese people. Also played down, as with the Nazi mass murders of Jews and other conquered peoples, were Japanese war crimes against the Chinese. Played up instead, in the latter case, were ideological warlord rapine and murder, with the Communist Chinese never to be confused with the Christian, freedom-loving, Chiang Kai-shek Nationalists. Under the MacArthur shogunate, for five years, Japan itself became the great Asian laboratory of American-style capitalist free enterprise and democracy. Like a rehabilitated Germany teeming with U.S. military bases, soldiers, and weaponry, and war-destroyed industries up and running, in short order Japan became the great American bastion of freedom and economic productivity in Asia.

One may be surprised more than a half century later at the alacrity with which the postwar American mind undertook such overnight reorganizations of geopolitical consciousness, the sudden revisions of recent history and redistributions of friend and foe, ally and enemy, according to the new Red specter, the plot of Communist world domination. At the time, one now sees, perhaps only the instatement of a "plot" requiring such bizarre reimaginings and reinventions may have seemed an adequate response to a set of new political developments, actions, and events, at home and abroad, so putatively orchestrated, monolithic, unitary. It is frequently forgotten, for instance, that it was President Dwight Eisenhower who proposed the "domino theory" as a model of communist operation and that although the reference was to Southeast Asia, the idea seemed at the time (1954) to involve a natural and justified logic by extension from a constant atmosphere of Red crisis among Western nations where any location of the globe could suddenly spawn a pattern of communist takeover activities. In fact, before World War II had formally concluded, things were taking a bad turn, with the February 1945 Yalta conference of the Big Three allies being distinguished by obstructionist tensions between Stalin and Roosevelt on one hand and Roosevelt and Churchill on the other. By August 1945 at Potsdam, with Stalin facing off against Truman, replacing the dead Roosevelt, albeit not privy to many of the latter's previous agreements, promises, concessions, and with Churchill participating initially, already somewhat toothless as British representative, but shortly to be voted out of office and replaced by Atlee, the cold war began early and openly. At the meeting itself Truman was able to announce detonation by the U.S. of an atomic bomb; Stalin, apace, casting off the cloak of wartime antifascism, engineered a complete replacement of any spirit of allied cooperation with a climate of postwar distrust and deception. Bitter quarrels took place over divisions of Germany, Austria, zones of occupation, reallocations of territory, spheres of postwar influence, regional alliances. Refusals of comity or cooperation, when not achievable through constant obstructionism, escalated into threats of open hostility. Meanwhile, toppling regimes blotted great regions of the globe. In 1946 Poland was subjected to communist takeover, and in 1947 Hungary and Romania were as well; in the same year, China's Communist and Nationalist factions erupted into mass civil war. In 1948 a communist takeover in Czechoslovakia was accompanied by the near-victory of Communists in Italian elections; the blockade of Berlin by the Russians was followed by the highly publicized Berlin Airlift, bringing relief to the residents of the allied zones of occupation; direct U.S. intervention, under what came to be called the Truman Doctrine, was required to defeat a communist insurgency in Greece; larger U.S. strategic interests in Europe were evidenced in the creation of a full-blown military alliance, the North Atlantic Treaty Organization, or NATO. In Asia the Communist Kim Il-sung was installed by Russians as dictator of North Korea; to the South, on the Indochinese peninsula, open war began between the French and the communist Viet Minh.

Two catastrophic developments occurred in 1949: Russia successfully tested an atomic bomb, and mainland China fell to the Communists. Then, in 1950, came the Korean War, launched by a Communist invasion of the South and eventuating in an initial rout of U.S. and South Korean forces. The military situation became stabilized late in the year, with a countermarch northward, in turn culminating in a new catastrophe, Chinese intervention. The first hot war of the cold war, as things came to be termed, would continue for another two years, petering out into a bitter contest over terrain, position, and jockeying for endgame advantage.

As a source of geopolitical fear, then, the rise of global monolithic communism, at whoever's instigation wherever, certainly seemed real enough. In Europe a distinguishable Communist bloc commanded a solid center of East Germany, Poland, Czechoslovakia, and Hungary. To the south lay Rumania and Bulgaria, along with Tito's maverick Yugoslavia, comprising the former Balkan states, and on the Adriatic, strange, isolated Albania. To the north were the reclaimed Baltic lands of Latvia, Estonia, and Lithuania. Concurrently in Asia, an enormous new Chinese Communist state, with an overnight ascendancy to great-power status comparable to that of the Soviet Union in Europe, controlled the mainland, with the remains of a Nationalist government reduced to saber-rattling offshore on Formosa and a handful of buffer islands. In North Korea a bristling militaristic dictatorship separated from the South by a demilitarized zone required—in a defense responsibility increasingly considered parallel to that in Europe—a permanent U.S. commitment of active military forces. North Vietnam lay firmly in Communist hands, with an ascendant insurgency in the South and concomitant menaces visible in Laos, Burma, Malaysia, and Indonesia. Only Japan, Formosa, South Korea, South Vietnam, the Philippines (where a postwar Communist Huk insurgency had been barely put down), and various smaller Pacific island bases remained available as toeholds in Asia. Again, it now seems striking that the idea of "containment" as a major U.S. political doctrine for halting the spread of communism has become largely associated with efforts in Asia. At the time, it was known to be the intellectual brainchild of the government's most highly respected young Kremlinist. The fact was that communist expansionism had become essentially ubiquitous, a matter of East and West, as well as an experience being repeated across what was coming to be known as the Third World. "Nonaligned" nations of all sorts began to look as if they were leaning definitely elsewhere, with major entities as diverse as Tito's Yugoslavia and Nehru's India seeming to make independent, leftist turns. U.S. vigilance and promotion of "Free World" values wore themselves thin keeping the numbers and balances in line in Central and South America, Africa, and the Middle East. Even in the allied camp, France and Italy retained significant, legal Communist Party influence in their national politics well into the late cold war era. Meanwhile, disparate efforts at intervention in places as diverse as Greece and Turkey, Guatemala and the Dominican Republic, the Ivory Coast and the Congo were endlessly pursued to prevent nations from slipping into the "wrong" camp. Today, it is nearly impossible to recapture the stunning effect on Americans a half century ago, almost exactly, of finding that communism was in Cuba, ninety miles offshore.

To such a pattern of relentless, palpable, external threat, what seemed an orchestrated, monolithic, grand strategy of communist world domination, there came easily to most Americans a concomitant logic of internal networkings, infiltrations, and subversions aimed at the heart of American domestic political culture. In retrospect, this may now seem historically quaint; at the time, it was hard for politically informed Americans to ignore, emotionally and psychologically at least, what seemed a set of domestic parallels to menacing international developments. Threads, tendrils, conspiratorial networks of a global plan for communist world domination were clearly identifiable as at work in the great world beyond; if America stood as the chief bulwark of such an insidious plan for democratic overthrow, devised by such an unrelentingly creative and dedicated enemy, surely some must have been planted with the intent of their growth within the institutions of U.S. democracy itself. A suddenly victorious nation arrived overnight at superpower status—itself so late arriving in the war out of a hubbub of ideological conflict, New Dealers, internationalists, conservative isolationists, homegrown fascists, pacifists, America Firsters, socialists, leftover 1930s communist intellectuals and fellow travelers—was ripe for a domestic Red Scare. And when it happened, it was not the Reds who came out from under the bed but rather an aggregation of some of the most unsavory demagogues and right-wing opportunists in the history of the Republic. Some, such as Congressman J. Parnell Thomas and Senator Joseph McCarthy, in due time got their nasty comeuppance; others, such as Richard Nixon, parlayed Red-baiting celebrity through a political ascendancy eventually taking him to the highest office in the land. Preying on old ideological antagonisms and unresolved isolationist/internationalist quarrels interrupted by the war, and drumming up a series of widely publicized scandals and crises, along with assorted official inquiries and contrived political events extending over roughly a decade from 1947 or 1948 onward, they engineered a completely irrational turn in American politics. Anticommunism and virulent fear-mongering eventuated in what frequently seemed bizarre American parodies of the communists' own staged political dramas, investigations, show trials, and purges.

Of such stuff was the Red Scare, as it was called, with events themselves frequently captured under the generic phrasing of "Anticommunist Witch Hunts." For many of those alive at the time, it may be hard to recall who came off as more creepy and sordid—the inquisitors, their victims, or the assorted prosecution and defense witnesses and talebearers. There were shining moments. Ring Lardner Jr., one of the Hollywood Ten, a group of leftist scriptwriters hauled before the House Un-American Activities Committee (HUAC), surely got off the great, brave line of the era. Asked by HUAC head J. Parnell Thomas about Communist Party membership, he replied, "I could answer the way you want, Mr. Chairman, but I'd hate myself in the morning." But mostly, all around, one remembers it as just shabby, second-rate political drama waged often by small men for desperate purposes. Still, what must also be remembered is the cumulative effect at the time. As in a Joseph Heller, Kurt Vonnegut, or Norman Mailer novel, many of which responded directly to events and ideological conflicts of the period in question, it was precisely the spectacle of conspiracy scare and political circus, the generalized, omnipresent popular-culture drama of the absurd, however base and repellent, that somehow added up to a logic of paranoiac congruencies—somehow more real than any single version of any particular event. This was certainly true of the openings of the drama that included in 1947 an official U.S. government loyalty-oath campaign, eventuating in the dismissal of hundreds of employees from their posts, and concurrent hearings by HUAC on communist infiltration of the entertainment industry, resulting in the first "blacklistings" of public figures in the era, most notably the aforementioned Hollywood Ten. Also important in the same year was the passage of the Taft-Hartley Labor Act, which, among its provisions, explicitly prohibited communist participation in U.S. labor unions. In 1948, growing out of HUAC investigations, came the Whittaker Chambers–Alger Hiss controversy, the result of testimony by a seamy, devious, unstable former Communist, implicating a high-level state department figure, a card-carrying member of the eastern establishment, with a record of important postwar involvement in international activities, including the formation of the United Nations. Begun as a defamation lawsuit by Hiss against Chambers, and featuring high-profile involvement by figures as diverse as the dignified Secretary of State Dean Acheson and an aggressive young anticommunist member of the House from California named Richard Nixon, it ran on for another interminable three years, until Hiss was finally convicted and imprisoned on a perjury charge. Further domestic reverberations took place in 1949, with its great shocks abroad. Soviet revelations of A-bomb technology, clearly acquired through espionage at the most intimate levels of scientific secrecy, led to the 1950 Klaus Fuchs spy scandal, expanding to implicate Morton Sobell, David Greenglass, and Ethel and Julius Rosenberg. With immense consequences for future events in Asia, the "loss" of China led to purges of Far East experts in the State Department, involving everyone with any direct knowledge of the region with relation to language, politics, and culture. Amid such atmospherics, 1950 also brought the emergence into the Red-fighting pantheon of Wisconsin senator Joseph McCarthy, who claimed during a speech in West Virginia to have in his personal possession a secret list of fifty-two Communists in the State Department. As an extension of HUAC inquiries into the movie industry, the same year saw publication of a widely circulated pamphlet entitled *Red Channels,* revealing the names of 151 figures from the arts and entertainment communities suspected of communist leanings. More or less simultaneously, a renowned military fighter against communism, General Douglas MacArthur, gained nonstop headlines for his independent plan, as supreme commander of U.N. forces in Korea, to expand the conflict into a larger war against the Chinese. Relieved of his duties by the president for insubordination, he made a triumphant return in 1951 to ticker-tape parades and a wildly applauded speech before Congress. In the same year, the Rosenbergs were convicted of spying and sentenced to death in the electric chair. More dismal developments defined an increasingly surreal political scene during 1952. McCarthy was denounced finally by Truman; but Dwight Eisenhower, soon to be his successor, running for the Republican presidential nomination, shamefully elected not to repudiate McCarthy's slanders of Eisenhower's own patron and mentor, George Marshall. Meanwhile, Richard Nixon, his Red-baiting running mate, accused of misusing campaign funds for personal gain, was forced to make the Checkers speech.

In 1953 such matters at home seemed to reach a major conjunction of the planets with developments abroad. Eisenhower was inaugurated as president and, in keeping with a campaign promise, obtained a truce ending the Korean War. Along with the cessation of military hostilities in the latter, at a line basically where it had begun three years earlier, came the realization that a long era of dismal, far-flung military face-offs had probably begun. In the same year, Julius and Ethel Rosenberg were executed, concluding a notorious case in which the connections between external and internal forms of communist threat had been palpably cemented by atomic bomb espionage. As important—with the exception, perhaps, of the Eisenhower inauguration or, in a strange parallel, the coronation of the young Queen Elizabeth of England—1953 also brought the death of Stalin, the first great international media event of the postwar age. Television images, wire photos, and rampant newspaper and magazine reports fueled mysteries about the secret contests for power likely going on among rivals for the spot—or in some cases, it was assumed, for their lives. Shots of Kremlin dignitaries lined up on the reviewing platform in Red Square—Malenkov, Bulganin, Khrushchev, Beria—gave way to accounts of ensuing murderous intrigues. Beria, Stalin's executioner, was himself the first to go. In a shadowy succession Malenkov hung on for two years, before everything was swept before Nikita Khrushchev, in David Halberstam's phrasings, "a man who seemed to be the embodiment of the sheer animal force of the Soviet Union, its raw power and, perhaps many Americans feared, its irresistible will."*

Suddenly, things seemed to fast-forward into a more generally remembered and familiar cold war dispensation, a view of the conflict with the Reds existing at some point of convergence between the domestic and geopolitical. In 1954 the USS *Nautilus* was unveiled as the first U.S. nuclear submarine, with a capacity to stay submerged and appear anywhere desired. One last bout of hearings, involving the U.S. Army and a peculiarly seamy cast of complainants, resulted in the final discrediting and disgrace of Joseph McCarthy, who sank quickly into alcoholic oblivion. Dr. Robert Oppenheimer, among the chief architects of the U.S. atomic bomb, whose doubts about the moral use of such weaponry had caused him to be deemed a risk, was suspended from his security clearance. At Dien Bien Phu the French experienced a decisive military defeat in the Indochina War, with the country partitioned Korea-like, at the Geneva Conference that year, into a communist north and a democratic south. The Eisenhower government undertook a perfunctory defense of Formosa, sending the U.S. Seventh Fleet to quell artillery attacks by the mainland communists on the outpost islands of Quemoy and Matsu. Meanwhile, with the CIA, the U.S. engineered the overthrow of the Arbenz regime in Guatemala. At home, Americans learned to live with Civil Defense in the Nuclear Age, finding escape from their nerves in generally happy prosperity and golden age TV. They settled into acceptance of the cold war status quo. This was how it was going to be with the Russians and the Chinese, they thought. Eisenhower, a great military man who was also a good son of the great American heartland, was a security president, an anticommunist president in that he was prodemoc-

*David Halberstam, *The Fifties* (New York: Villard, 1993), 701.

racy. As part of the Pledge of Allegiance, "one nation indivisible" became "one nation, under God, indivisible." The religion being affirmed was that of a nation setting its face against godless Communism.

In 1955 Khrushchev created the Warsaw Pact—Soviet Union, Poland, Hungary, East Germany, Czechoslovakia, Bulgaria, Albania—to stand against NATO. The East-West standoff in Europe—in geography, ideology, diplomacy, weaponry—was official. In 1956 it came to increasingly hard-knuckle threat and counterthreat. The Soviets brutally suppressed the Hungarian Revolution. Without U.S. knowledge or sanction, the British and French allied themselves with the Israelis in a victorious surprise assault on Egypt in the Suez War, driving the latter and Syria into the Soviet embrace as part of the United Arab Republic. Closer to home, a band of Cuban revolutionaries under a guerilla leader named Castro began resisting the Batista dictatorship from the Sierra Maestra mountains of Oriente Province. Their model of regime change was that engineered by the United States itself with the overthrow of the Trujillo dictatorship in the nearby Dominican Republic. Their politics would prove otherwise. The 1957 Soviet success of *Sputnik,* the first satellite to be put in Earth orbit, launched the Inter-Continental Ballistic Missile era and a new generation of the cold war military race. The 1960 shooting down of a U-2 spy plane over Russia ruined plans for an Eisenhower-Khrushchev summit meeting. The 1960 presidential election victory of John F. Kennedy, over the old Red-baiter Richard Nixon, if anything accelerated the cold war game of geopolitical hardball. Powers great and aspiring faced off in nuclear brinksmanship and sponsorship roles in assorted wars of national liberation. It was a new age of cold war realpolitik, less ideological than simply strategically and militarily assumed, the province of technocrats and experts. Power was the issue, and problems awaited solutions in the responses of iron-nerved leaders, informed by their brain trusts of specialist advisers. Thought translated into calculated action: when a problem arises, don't waste time being scared; do something. Go eyeball to eyeball with the bastards. Call in the experts and send in the operatives. Don't form a committee; make a commitment. Don't fight a conventional war; send in a new breed of unconventional warriors. Don't worry about satellites; shoot for the moon. The embrace of such new attitudes became a measure of the relief with which the nation greeted Kennedy, along with his cool, lean, athletic anticommunism. As in the celebrated TV debates, where Nixon with his five-o'clock shadow and dreadful earnestness tried to square off against Kennedy with his finger-jabbing, intellectual, Harvard élan, Americans were smitten by the absence of nervous perspiration. In Norman Mailer's telling phrase, Superman had come to the supermarket. It was that kind of country.

Thus the evolving drama of ideological myth and countermyth, the argument of old versus new anticommunist dispensations, as things seemed to play out at the time, perforce now somewhere between memory and history. Whether things had actually taken that kind of turn, or whether people just thought they had, one still notes a great, vast wonder at how quickly the old Red Scare atmospherics vanished. Of nearly all the post-1945 cultural episodes, they now seem the most like ancient history, so strange, so far away. Possibly their replacement by global hardball just came as a form of collective emotional release after all the years of secret fear. Possibly the new-generation style of the Kennedy administration offered a way of shedding tired old post-1945 quarrels and bad political nerves. It is hard to recall now, when so much memory and so much history have intervened. After the upheavals of the 1960s and 1970s, the partisan hatreds and scandals of the 1980s and 1990s, the Soviets twenty-five years gone and China cloaked in the embrace of Western-style economic expansionism, with much of the world at large now plunged into a new age of fundamentalist Islamic terror—the great American Red Scare of the late 1940s to the mid-1950s plays like one of those strange, old, bad kinescopes from black-and-white TV: of Pinky Lee bounding onstage in his silly hat or the Eisenhowers and Nixons—Ike and Mamie, Dick and Pat—all holding hands and giving a big group wave at the Republican convention.

One thing remains certain though: they were ugly times. Patriotic crusaders and members of various investigative bodies provided a rogues' gallery of political bottom-feeders and heartland goose-steppers and flag wavers undreamed even by an H. L. Mencken. The resistance featured an odd mix of snide, condescending artists, intellectuals, and eastern establishmentarians along with leftover 1930s radicals, sentimental socialists, and fellow-travelers, jumbled in with Wobblies, Abraham Lincoln Brigade veterans, and other "premature antifascists." From the left the endless hearings and committee spectacles became America's version of Moscow show trials, with wheezing Midwestern pols in their ill-fitting double-breasted suits, gray little maleficent men looking not unlike typical Communist apparatchiks. From the right, the Rosenbergs, the Hollywood Ten, and the Red Channels subversives all represented the true enemy within. In retrospect the whole business may now be seen as a big, nasty, muddle of ideologies and ethnicities, of gender and class antagonisms—nearly equal in its collective virulence to the parallel drama of race playing itself out simultaneously. In the wake of the Holocaust it remained a delicate matter, for instance, that radical intellectuals old and new were frequently Jews or that, with the exception of Klaus Fuchs, the Rosenberg case, implicating the couple along with key figures such as Harry Gold, Morton Sobell, and David Greenglass, seemed to be a Jewish conspiracy. There had been genuine acts of espionage. This notwithstanding, for many people at home and abroad the Rosenbergs became the new Sacco and Vanzetti, with particular controversy arising over the conviction and execution of Ethel Rosenberg. The evidence of a capital offense was shaky; the interpretation of the law was far-fetched; and the execution in the electric chair was that of a wife, a homemaker, and a mother, leaving behind two children. Although not involving a capital crime, nearly as ugly was the incredulity of average Americans about someone as impeccably pedigreed as Alger Hiss as a possible communist agent, in a case reinforcing heartland suspicions while taxing explanatory powers of the eastern establishment. Nor were matters helped by the fact that his conviction and imprisonment came on a technical charge of perjury, with bizarre evidence and sweated testimony supplied by a possible homosexual and pathological liar.

In popular culture—books, movies, political rhetoric, popular advertising—one could not escape figures and images of bloblike agglomeration spreading contamination. Radiation sickness, monstrosity, and mutation presided over postatomic landscapes. Cancer was a political disease, a social metaphor of politics, a secret killer lurking within, growing, metastasizing.

The titles of popular memory constitute in retrospect a welter of ideological bombardment. On Broadway Arthur Miller's *The Crucible* was greeted as major art through its analogizing of the nerves and hysterias of contemporary politics with those of the seventeenth-century Salem witch trials. Out in the provinces, audiences were left to make what they might of *The Blob* or *The Invasion of the Body Snatchers.* Important figures got credit for brave, politically inspirational books they didn't write, including John F. Kennedy's *Profiles in Courage* and J. Edgar Hoover's *Masters of Deceit.* Things people didn't say got intellectually parodied and politically pilloried. Charles Wilson, the former president of General Motors, serving as Eisenhower's secretary of defense, was widely quoted as having declaimed, "What is good for GM is good for America." (Not least, so it was echoed, for instance, by Joseph Heller in *Catch-22,* where the multinational supply officer Milo Minderbinder makes such an assertion about M&M Enterprises.) What Wilson actually said was in direct answer to a question about his ability as a cabinet member to make decisions possibly adverse to his old company. He said he believed he could do so, although admitting to some difficulty "because for years I thought what was good for the country was good for General Motors and vice versa."* Things people did say became part of political legend. Eisenhower himself, in one of his last speeches before leaving the presidency, was cited as explicitly warning the nation against what he called "the military industrial complex." It was a hired civilian counsel for the U.S. Army, Joseph Welch, who is credited with precipitating the final downfall of Joseph McCarthy by spontaneously exclaiming, "You've done enough. Have you no sense of decency, sir, at long last? Have you no sense of decency?"

Everybody involved seemed to be corrupt or mired in some peculiar torture or derangement. J. Parnell Thomas, chair of the House Un-American Activities Committee, was eventually convicted of fraud, forced to resign from Congress, and imprisoned in a Danbury, Connecticut, facility with two members of the Hollywood Ten, one of them Ring Lardner Jr. By the end McCarthy, a raving alcoholic and pathological liar, was reduced to a last bout of hearings, involving the U.S. Army and a peculiarly seamy cast of complainants, including a left-wing dentist and an enlisted man, David Schine, whose welfare seemed a peculiar concern of the chief counsel, Roy Cohn. A more explicit, albeit no less virulent, strain of insinuation and innuendo became the currency

*Quoted in Halberstam, *The Fifties,* 118.

of everyday politics. Richard Nixon had gotten elected to Congress in the first place by accusing his opponent, Jerry Voorhis, of being "soft on communism" and then rising to the Senate by repeating the strategy with Helen Gahagan Douglas, dubbed "the Pink Lady," when both were nearly as anti-American as Norman Vincent Peale or *Reader's Digest.* As Eisenhower's running mate, he became the conservative hit man, denouncing Stevenson as "Adlai the Appeaser who got a Ph.D. from Dean Acheson's College of Cowardly Communist Containment." McCarthy's practiced slip of the tongue: "Alger . . . I mean, Adlai," found journalistic echo in Joseph Alsop's labeling of the Stevenson party as "eggheads." These may have been poor stuff as witticisms, but they certainly spoke to attitudes embraced in parts of the country where people watched Richard Carlson in *I Led Three Lives* and fluoridation of water and daylight savings time were regarded as communist plots. Norman Thomas was a socialist. He was a Red. Madelyn Murray O'Hare was an atheist. She was a Red. The Beats smoked pot, wrote poetry, hung out in coffeehouses, and expressed their love for other races. They were Reds. "Negro agitators," as they were called in those days, drew their civil rights strategies of resistance from the revolutionary example of oppressed peoples around the globe. They were Reds. If the Reds weren't under the bed, they might be some of the people who made the bed, or at least washed the sheets.

For the ones that got hammered, the Red Scare was real enough. In the 1947 Loyalty Oath campaign, 526 people lost government positions. The HUAC proceedings of the same year resulted in contempt of Congress charges against the Hollywood Ten; in 1951 renewed investigations resulted in around 320 more people blacklisted. In between, the Red Channels denunciations ran to a roster of 151. People went to jail, including the Hollywood Ten and, eventually, Alger Hiss. Two people were executed: Julius and Ethel Rosenberg. Fifty years later it is hard to see the death sentence of Ethel Rosenberg as other than a case of judicial murder.

In retrospect, the Red Scare era will always seem a grim little record of dwarves and mutants coming out of the woodwork from all sides at once. Grainy videos of McCarthy with his vulpine smirk, hectoring witnesses from his seat as committee chair, mix with photos of the Rosenbergs headed off to trial in a Black Maria, looking very much as they were, a drab, middle-aged, leftist Jewish couple, plucked from their cheap apartment at the Manhattan end of the Brooklyn Bridge. At the very least, in connected moments of crisis, it really seemed a kind of borderline schizophrenic world of paranoiac congruencies, with plots being whispered in subversive cells and loudspeaker blasts of sloganeering and propaganda alarm being broadcast in the streets. As to the politics of personal reputation, it was an ideological tangle elevating creepy people to the spotlight and scapegoating some of the noblest public servants of the century, not least General George C. Marshall. Indeed, the most immediate impression coming back to many of us will always be that of a collocation of caricatures and grotesques, the cockroaches of political hysterias, scavengers and bottom-feeders crowding in from the nightmare fringes of the national consciousness, its forbidden dreads and hates. As important to remember, however, is the degree to which the United States remained a country where, at the time, a lot of people were really more interested in Groucho Marx than in Karl Marx, in Charlie McCarthy than in Joseph McCarthy. Distractions and solaces of popular entertainment included golden age TV, the six o'clock news, top-forty radio, and Saturday nights at the movies. If anything, for Americans who may think we now live in uniquely troubled times, it seems a world not unlike our own: where celebrity homophobe pastors and congressmen get caught with male prostitutes; or where a U.S. president abrogates his responsibilities as commander in chief while distracted over matters of testimony about whether he solicited a blow job; or where for most people a missed cell phone message or the outcome of a TV reality show is more important than whether an administration can unilaterally begin a six-year (and counting) war with political lies and false intelligence.

Then as now, moreover, the manipulations of political fear were real, and they made people do bad things. And in retrospect, as above, one very real political legacy that can be identified, in something of the ascendancy of the current religious and political conservative right, was the bringing of reactionaries to real power in distinctly terrifying ways and instating them as would-be saviors of the Republic. And they were not just buffoons and lunatics. Indeed, the great right-wing danger in American politics of the late 1940s and early 1950s, it may now be suggested, was not McCarthyism but MacArthurism. Already in the last years of the Pacific War fancying himself a messianic conservative successor to the despised Franklin Roosevelt, Douglas MacArthur had become by the early 1950s a complete megalomaniac, the great man on horseback waiting in the wings, until his hopes for the U.S. presidency were finally dashed by Dwight Eisenhower. Another source of dire conservative threat to democratic processes and institutions lay with a formidable sibling pair, the brothers Dulles. The better known of the two, John Foster Dulles, serving as Eisenhower's secretary of state, became the autocratic engineer of cold war reactionary foreign policy—a rigid, dogmatic, blinkered, terribly limited man, a true religionist of the American way, his anticommunist missionary zeal compounded with an apocalyptic strain of Presbyterian ruthlessness. Meanwhile, America's spymaster was Allen Dulles, head of the CIA, compounding similar political fixations with utter professional ineptitude and allowing his agency to trump intelligence gathering with covert operations leading to one crisis after another. His own renowned secrecy, it turns out, amounted largely to the incessant covering of agency blunders with lies. Surely the most terrifying of all, however, remains FBI director J. Edgar Hoover, a closeted, self-loathing gay-male homophobe with a file on everybody. In a government less stringent in its legal and constitutional safeguards, one now sees, the country nurtured a secret police chief who would have not found Gestapo or KGB techniques uncongenial—the most glaring genuine psychopath, it might now be asserted, ever to hold major political power in America.

The most durable of all the Red Scare crusaders, however, was Richard Nixon, getting his start as a Red-baiting young congressional candidate and star member of HUAC, and continuing in the anticommunist limelight as the indefatigable pursuer of Alger Hiss. Having climbed over the bodies of political opponents to reach the Senate, and then the vice presidency, only to be defeated narrowly by the liberal democrat John F. Kennedy, Nixon survived endless cycles of defeat and humiliation, meanwhile undergoing constant reinventions and risings from the political grave. A complete political creation of the era that nurtured him, he now became the thing that wouldn't die, the old cold warrior as the new master of post–cold war endgame realpolitik, playing the Russians while bombing Vietnam back into the Stone Age, and then astounding Americans and both Western and Pacific Rim anticommunist allies by reopening relations after fifty years with China. It could only be in keeping, somehow, with the great, dark, garish political melodrama out of which he had sprung that Nixon was eventually taken from office in a gloomy, absurd welter of secret plots, break-ins, investigations, committee reports, judicial controversies, and congressional proceedings. Suborning the FBI and the CIA, using the White House as an espionage agency and a staging authority for covert operations, defying congressional subpoenas and Supreme Court orders, making enemies lists, ultimately provoking the most serious crisis of constitutional authority ever created by a president in our history, raving drunk at the end and talking to the pictures on the walls in the White House—Nixon came to represent the apotheosis of the paranoid style in American politics, born, like himself, in the age of the great American Red Scare.

Now Nixon is long gone, of course, and so are nearly all the Reds. Still, Americans have never quite gotten over being that scared in those kinds of ways. In fact, taste for such fear seems to run in the national blood, some need to manufacture one after another in an endless series of great Manichean crises in the great American journey toward ideological righteousness. As with so many other things about us, Alexis de Tocqueville got it right, a handful of decades into the hubbub of the brawling, infant republic: "For fifty years the inhabitants of the United States have been repeatedly and constantly told that they are the only religious, enlightened, and free people. They see that democratic institutions flourish among them, whereas they come to grief in the rest of the world; consequently they have an immensely high opinion of themselves and are not far from believing that they form a species apart from the rest of the human race."* Accordingly, when one enemy is vanquished, the gift for apocalyptic scare images becomes easily transferable to the next. The old masters of deceit, the new bad guys under the bed, although they may sometimes look like us, are probably gay, feminist, secular humanist; if they threaten physical violence, harm, injury, or death, at least they generally don't look like us, dress like us, smell like us, or go to our churches; still, we will do almost anything to keep them from living among us, hoarding their secret fanaticism, hijacking big shiny American passenger

*Alexis de Tocqueville, *Democracy in America,* tr. George Lawrence, ed. J. P. Mayer (New York: Harper, 2000), 374.

airliners and flying them into skyscrapers. We will police them around the world and put them in cells on a navy base that we still cling to, ironically, on a Red island in the Caribbean; and for good measure we will start a phony war in the Middle East that to date has killed four thousand young Americans and God knows how many Iraqis. In the post-9/11 age I still have bad dreams about fleets of Russian bombers coming over the hill behind our house. I should hope that my daughter, at least, will never feel that way about the Patriot Act. Abroad and at home, when we fix our eyes on those behaving at variance with American ways, we remain the scariest people in the world.

2
A Credit to Their Race

Colored People. This is what Henry Louis Gates, W. E. B. Du Bois Professor of African American Studies at Harvard, chose to call his autobiography of growing up black in post–World War II West Virginia. From one of the most celebrated cultural intellectuals of his generation, it is the case of a title speaking volumes, for an individual, a culture, and an era. *Colored People.* For right-thinking Americans at the time, white and black, the term conjoined polity with conventional politesse. It could even be said to have a pedigree, by racial consensus, in the official name, dating back nearly half a century, of the country's mainstream civil rights organization, the NAACP—the National Association for the Advancement of Colored People. W. E. B. Du Bois, after all, among the most progressive, even radical, of black thinkers and writers of the age, had been a founder, along with the crusading journalist Ida Wells Barnett; on the white side, it could count such respected cultural intellectuals and activists as Mary White Ovington and Oswald Garrison Villiard. Thus in general speech and writing, a popular euphemism made it mutually respectable for Americans of the two races to observe in words what continued to be despicable in political fact: that colored people went to colored schools, attended colored churches with colored preachers, and lived in the colored sections of towns.

The other phrasing that still alternated respectably with the first was, of course, *negro.* Among blacks themselves—intellectuals, educators, political and religious figures—it was the preferred racial term. Among whites, while operating similarly as a noun, it frequently came out as an adjective suggesting some kind of exceptional case or another—a negro writer, a negro intellectual, a negro professor. In some cases the reference could be more broadly generic—as in negro music or negro religion. In still others it continued to suggest some less than full qualification for belonging to the human race: as in a negro man or negro woman.

The signature of the latter term, among respectable people white and black, was the care taken in pronunciation. Nee-grow, one said; Neee-grow: so as to avoid guilt by glottal or political association. For members of the race there was the need to avoid "low" black speech. For whites matters were even more complicated. Of course, there was the need on one hand to avoid all possible contact with that word, whispered in jokes and available for classroom reading—and even then just barely—in Mark Twain's controversial classic *Huckleberry Finn;* but on the other hand, there was also the conscious public effort made, by anyone of progressive sentiments, to avoid the political echo of its semipolite stand-in among southerners, the genteel, almost courtly "nigra" favored by such segregationist pillars of the U.S. Senate as Richard Russell of Georgia and John Sparkman of Alabama—eventually to be recycled and spat out by successors such as George Wallace and Lester Maddox as a borderline obscenity.

When I was a kid, between the late 1940s and early 1950s, the polite phrasing I too remember most vividly was "colored people." In retrospect I find this not particularly surprising, growing up as I did as more or less a small-town contemporary of the boy they called "Skipper" Gates—with my formative experiences taking place in rural south-central Pennsylvania and his just across the Mason-Dixon Line in West Virginia. Perhaps it was a regional peculiarity. But it also involved ideas about race, I now see with disturbing clarity, even in our supposedly enlightened household that acknowledged no borders. Ironically, the evidence consisted in humorous stories, concocted and carried home to me by my father, a man genuinely beloved and admired of all who knew him, from his work as an executive of a large food-processing company that had a branch in Inwood, West Virginia. His route took him through a black community locally known as Darksville. There, he said, he had encountered a promising young black kid just my age with the improbable name of Snowball Jackson Brathwaite. A jocular threat, in response to any misbehavior of mine, was that I would be taken and exchanged for my black counterpart, he growing up thenceforth in my household and I in his.

Thus did post-1945 Americans grow up talking about race, if at all, in some strange midworld, as I remember it at least, in which certainly no civilized person said "nigger" yet essentially implied it even while resorting to its polite counterparts. Neither for black or white at the time did there exist any of the alternative terms arising out of the civil rights era and later-twentieth-century cultural intellectualism. W. E. B. Du Bois's *The Souls of Black Folk* or Richard Wright's *Black Boy* notwithstanding—or even John Howard Griffin's sensational 1961 popular exposé *Black Like Me*—"black" had to wait for the revolutionary cachet of the 1960s. Likewise "people of color" required rebirth as a postmodernist cultural studies formulation. The great in-between terms *Afro American* and *African American* were still out there trying to get devised along with *Native American, Asian American,* and the like. The only similarly hyphenated term for anything I can remember from the time, actually, was a brand of Italian food called Franco-American, a reference that even today I still don't understand.

The fact of the matter is, in word and image, my world was just astonishingly white. Colored people for me—even under that phrasing—were people to be seen in newspapers and magazines, heard about on the radio, or watched in movies or on TV. It is hard not to cringe just thinking about it. From Saturday morning reruns of *The Little Rascals,* I vividly remember Stymie, Buckwheat, and Farina. I recall *The Amos 'n Andy Show* on early TV as a short, unhappy run: the Kingfish with his fedora, his big fat cigar, his self-importance, his lazy drawl full of dialectal missteps; the sassy Sapphire and Mama; Lightnin', the shiftless janitor over at the Lodge; the lawyer, Algonquin J. Calhoun. Andy was a cab driver. Where was Amos? As I recall, nobody bothered to ask. (Nor did most of us learn until much later that the popular radio show from which the series originated had white people playing black characters.) From Broadway, by virtue of my father's fascination with the musical theater, there was *Porgy and Bess.* My acquaintance came by an early LP, which I understood somehow to be a bold attempt by the popular composer George

Gershwin to write a "negro" opera on life in the Deep South. *Showboat* was too old for me. Ditto Paul Robeson.

Although it seems nearly impossible to put back together now, in the twenty-first-century fields most visibly populated by black figures—sports and entertainment—all public negotiations of race of the immediate post–World War II era seem to have taken place likewise in some strange alternative universe. How quaint it now seems, for instance, that the first inroad made by a black player in big-time American sports began in 1947 with major league baseball. How often the story is told of what Jackie Robinson, having excelled as an athletic hero at UCLA and then as a proud, defiant U.S. Army officer fighting prejudice in World War II, had to go through to break the color line—albeit with the legend of his own courage linked to that of the white owner, Branch Rickey, who handpicked him for the heroic job. I was too young to remember much of that. But like any young fan with a drawer full of baseball cards, I knew everything at the time about Roy Campanella, Larry Doby, Don Newcombe, although again with the attendant circumstance that the first proved the most accepted of the group because he was of mixed-race origins—itself a fact distinctly ironic given popular taboos against interracial marriage. The offspring of a black mother and a white father, he was nearly always described as being "of Italian descent." The early players in turn opened the way to the first black baseball superstar, right up there with Mickey Mantle, as the comparison went, the supremely talented Willie Mays. Again, little remembered was how even Mays had labored in the old Negro leagues after growing up in the steel-mill outskirts of Birmingham, Alabama.

The most previously integrated popular sport, boxing, having undergone notorious racial upheavals earlier, made its way into the new television lineup with the *Gillette Friday Night Fights*, but as an American pastime it was on its way out. Joe Louis, after his much-heralded World War II service, was an anachronism, not unlike his epithet, "the Brown Bomber." His postwar successors would include more flashy personalities such as Archie Moore and Sugar Ray Robinson. What public interest remained got bound up in new politicizations of race. A European heavyweight, Ingmar Johanssen, appeared as a kind of Swedish great white hope. Floyd Patterson became every American's favorite polite black guy. Then came Ali. He probably was the greatest, but when he faded, so did boxing, racialized beyond recovery.

Meanwhile, the two great current black sports, college and professional football and basketball, lagged far behind the diamond—in both cases, as it turns out, with complex racial explanations. (This is now the case, one might add, concerning why baseball seems to be going in the opposite direction—with shrinking black rosters and new domination by players of white, Hispanic, Afro-Caribbean, and Central and South American origin. The simple answer for the professional game is simply the dominance of an affluent, mainly white, urban fan demographic. Meanwhile, in an imaging of generalized white flight in the educational sphere, the college and high-school sport has become almost completely white.) With football one could historically cite the northeastern, upper-middle-class college and university origins of the game: Rutgers and Princeton, Yale, Harvard, Columbia, along with the services academies and the prestigious men's colleges. Eventually the state schools came in, with the big Midwest and Pacific teams remaining segregated, ironically, because of the need to schedule traditional southern powers. Rutgers made a brave, grandstanding attempt at integration with the celebrated Paul Robeson. But for many years beyond, the post–World War II college game segregated itself, albeit increasingly along regional lines well into the 1960s. The names of the first black pro players of the postwar era now sound like living history: Tank Younger, Emlen Tunnell, Dick "Night Train" Lane. Great running backs began to emerge—Lenny Moore out of Penn State, Jim Brown out of Syracuse—followed by blockers, defensive players, and eventually linebackers. Far in the future remained the present array (with all attendant garish celebrity) of black megastar wideouts, flankers, receivers, and defensive backs. To the present, the prime "skill" position, quarterback, on the other hand, remains grudgingly white.

Twenty-first-century predominantly black basketball locates the origins of its corresponding racial saga with a late-nineteenth-century physical education teacher named James Naismith at a gymnasium in Springfield, Massachusetts. College basketball remained resolutely segregated until the late 1950s' and early 1960s' appearance of such big men (as centers were called in those days) as Bill Russell of the University of San Francisco and Wilt Chamberlain of Kansas. Ironically, in contrast to football, the pro game had paved the way with groundbreaking players such as Early Lloyd (Washington Capitols) and Sweetwater Clifton (New York Knicks). As for all-black basketball, in a kind of comedic imaging of the negro baseball leagues, there were also the famous Harlem Globetrotters—the brainchild of a Jewish impresario-entrepreneur, Abe Saperstein—who combined magical athletic ability and outrageous clowning with the contrived drama of a come-from-behind victory over "white" opponents. In the straight professional game, Russell and Chamberlain made it as prodigies of height and agility. The ball handlers and shooters would come later, eventually displacing the customary white "point guard" or "playmaker."

In tennis, about as white as a sport could get, Althea Gibson came to dominate the women's game until 1956. Similarly, a runner, Wilma Rudolph, became a women's track celebrity in the late 1950s and early 1960s. In both cases it seemed as if a gifted female black groundbreaker somehow seemed less challenging to the order of things in major sport.

In entertainment, post–World War II movies continued to feature such caricatured standbys as Bill "Bojangles" Robinson, Stepin Fetchit, and Hattie McDaniel. Walt Disney's astonishingly racist blend of live acting and cartoon animation, *Song of the South,* won a 1946 "honorary" Academy Award. Wartime movies had featured no black soldiers because the military services were segregated. In aftermath movies, accordingly, the problems of returning veterans and of home-front families were assumed to be those of white Americans. In dramatic film there was a near absolute absence of black actors. The closest race got to domestic roles came in a couple of melodramas about black women passing for white, with actress models including Lana Turner and Natalie Wood. Only in 1956 did a black actress (albeit of mixed-race origins), Dorothy Dandridge, appear in a serious film, a musical entitled *Carmen Jones.* Likewise no serious popular black actor preceded Sidney Poitier—himself a Caribbean black with his fine British accent, his striking good looks, and his impressive suitability for suffering nobility roles.

Post-1945 popular music likewise seemed to have traveled little distance from the age of Al Jolson and Eddie Cantor in blackface, the beautiful white-featured Lena Horne, or occasional black classical performers doing *Porgy and Bess.* Again, someone such as myself growing up in the era cringes to remember how thoroughly black music in mainstream popular culture was symbolized by groups appearing on the early TV variety shows—the Mills Brothers, for instance, or the Ink Spots. The singer Billy Eckstine, for all his gifts, came and went along with Señor Wences and Carmen Miranda. Nat "King" Cole, having come to prominence with his own instrumental jazz trio, became a famous crooner and, in 1957, the first major black celebrity to have his own TV variety show. Less known was that he had been assaulted during a concert the previous year in Birmingham, Alabama, in likely connection to the Montgomery Bus upheavals. Fearing a southern boycott, NBC pulled the TV show after less than a year.

In records, young people listened to black groups such as the Coasters, the Clovers, and the Platters. In contradiction, as will be seen, of the Elvis story about how "race" music joined with "hillbilly" to create rock 'n' roll—to this day a great provincial legend—in my memory of the 1950s at least, white kids everywhere listened to such black pioneers as Chuck Berry, Bo Diddley, and Little Richard as well. In the middle of the road was Harry Belafonte. Somehow the fact that he was a fine-featured Caribbean black made him OK, with his exotic, good-natured dialect songs about loading and unloading Banana Boats. ("Come mistuh tally man, tally me ba-naw-na.") Similarly, a curiosity appeal prevailed for someone such as Ray Charles (and a generation later, almost identically, Stevie Wonder), out of the conjoined traditions of spiritual and blues, black and blind, safe enough. In jazz Duke Ellington and Louis Armstrong offered counterposing signature styles, Ellington white and cool, Armstrong eye-rolling, sweating, oh-yeaaa. Benny Goodman, Gene Krupa, and Lionel Hampton became the first integrated combo. Blues figures such as Robert Johnson and Billie Holiday remained esoteric fascinations.

If one searched entertainment generally for an iconic 1950s white-black relationship, it is probably Jack Benny and Rochester—the latter actually named Eddie Anderson. A standing joke involved the latter's being the "valet" when he was really the "chauffeur." In the role itself this was like deciding whether he was Stepin Fetchit or Andy the cab driver.

"I'se res-gusted," he was in the habit of saying, Jeeves the Butler playing out the latest avatar of the coon.

In popular reading, figurations of black culture or history were stringently white-approved. Young people's literature confined itself to such favorite subjects as Tuskegee stalwarts Booker T. Washington and George Washington Carver—the former renowned for his gospel of accommodationism, the latter for his child-pleasing scientific discoveries regarding uses of the lowly peanut. No Frederick Douglass or W. E. B. Du Bois threatened such safe tokenism there or in an educational curriculum allowing at most sanitized versions of 1920s and 1930s literary figures such as Langston Hughes or Countee Cullen. In literature generally, Red-Scare America took its view of the vaunted Harlem Renaissance in versions thoroughly expunged of black nationalist or leftist social content. Richard Wright and Zora Neale Hurston (the latter with her own complex history among a mainly male cohort) were nonpersons. A Pulitzer Prize winner, as in a number of cases to come, with a woman perhaps less threatening in the popular mind than a figure of black male authority, was Gwendolyn Brooks. A National Book Award winner was Ralph Ellison's *Invisible Man,* albeit with its author elevated to the literary pantheon at the expense of its radicalism, with its racial formula of the underground man translated by way of Melville, Dostoevsky, Sartre, and others into the terms of the modernist-existentialist classic.

In the arena of what used to be called "current events," the U.S. Supreme Court's watershed school-desegregation ruling in *Brown v. Board of Education of Topeka, Kansas,* came and went in 1954 as far less visibly important or controversial than may be imagined in retrospect. Nor did its first test, two years later, in Little Rock, create all that monumental a sensation. To be sure, names such as Central High School and Orval Faubus made the news, but they did not make a great impression. A great, classic photograph caught the figure of one silent, expressionless black teenage girl, walking a mob gantlet, mirrored in the image of a white counterpart, screaming epithets, with a face contorted by rage and hate. But Arkansas for most Americans of the era was someplace else—as was Mississippi in the same year, and an incident, virtually unreported in the mainstream press, involving the torture and death of a visiting Chicago teenager named Emmett Till for the crime of whistling at a white woman.

All this registered little for most Americans in the world of workaday affairs, the world of what in the post-1945 era aptly came to be called middle America, a white, homogeneous, mainstream-culture life in which the dominant majority of Americans, however mistakenly, for good or ill, assumed their existence and basic patterns of experience to be not only normal but archetypal. In these respects the personal history of my own growing up became if not exemplary at least typical. A descendant of Quakers and Mennonites, I grew up in the English, German, and Scotch-Irish regions of south-central Pennsylvania with barely an African American in sight. In my consolidated school district I remember a single black student in continuous residence, with the rest, the sons and daughters of migrant laborers, working on farms mainly during the fall fruit harvest. The county seat, Gettysburg, site of the great 1863 Civil War battle and Lincoln's immortal speech, was nearly as white, with a small neighborhood of inhabitants who dated their origin to a community of free blacks formed before the war. Their descendants lived on Washington Street, dominated by an AME Zion church. They, too, for most white citizens, were largely invisible and, so it seems in retrospect, oddly accepting of such invisibility.

This was likewise the case with any other configuring of racially different or unusual status. Sometimes a person of obviously mixed parentage was deemed to be vaguely "Indian" or claimed to be so. Hispanics were limited to Puerto Ricans flown in seasonally or, in rare cases, kept on as year-round farm employees. Other ethnicities were nearly all random exotics—Italians, Greeks, Central Europeans, Jews. The hospital had some orderlies, DPs they were called (Displaced Persons), from the Baltic. Occasionally the board tried to hire a Chinese, Korean, or Filipino medical specialist on the cheap. One saw no Indians or Southeast Asians.

It was a world, simply, where colored meant black and where colored people so defined accepted definition as persons by carefully maintaining their social and political invisibility. The pied pipers of 1960s racial hate—George Wallace, Lester Maddox, and others—were phantasms of the future. So, prior to 1956 and the stirrings of resistance in Montgomery, Alabama, was the great Martin Luther King Jr. The message of race in my world and the world of my exact contemporary, Skip Gates, was the message of *Colored People.* If you want to get ahead in the world, get white people on your side. If you want to get white people on your side, be a credit to your race.

In the days of which Gates speaks—and of which I now, however imperfectly, try to recreate in corresponding image and echo—such a concept invoked a bare handful of celebrity names. The two most prominent of these in retrospect, surely, were Marian Anderson and Ralph Bunche.

Anderson was a celebrated Roosevelt-era holdover, with much of her pioneering work on behalf of racial progress in America completed before World War II. (In fact, combined with her sex, her relatively advanced age seems to have been integral to her postwar acceptance as an admired black role model.) Nearly everyone remembered the Constitution Hall concert incident of 1939, resulting in Eleanor Roosevelt's resignation from the Daughters of the American Revolution. Although a full decade intervened after the war, this was followed by her landmark performance of Verdi's *Un ballo in maschera* in 1955, making her the first African American to sing in a lead role at the Metropolitan Opera—albeit, it was noted, with the event marred by her diminished voice at age fifty-eight. Meanwhile, she had also been honored with service to the U.S. State Department as a patronizingly entitled "ambassador at large" and as an Eisenhower nominee to the Human Rights Committee of the United Nations, recently installed in its dazzlingly modern New York headquarters. Anderson sang at Eisenhower's inauguration, as she would at John Kennedy's and at the 1963 Washington March for Jobs and Freedom. A late-life recording career would branch Anderson out into religious, folk, and holiday favorites; meanwhile, "admired," "respected," even "beloved," she would continue to be trotted forth honorarily as a racial spokesperson, living on, almost unbelievably, until 1993.

The story of Ralph Bunche, following on those of historical male models such as the accommodationist Booker T. Washington on one hand and the radical intellectual W. E. B. Du Bois on the other, now seems at once more conventional and more complex. An orphaned child of working black parents, reared by his grandmother, Bunche was an academic prodigy, a star graduate of UCLA and the recipient of a 1934 Harvard Ph.D. in political science, with a prizewinning dissertation on postcolonial problems of developing nations. Major academic appointments followed, as did celebrated work in founding activities of the United Nations. These career achievements, all much heralded in the news and popular media, were further crowned by the awarding of the 1950 Nobel Peace Prize for work in cementing military truce agreements between Arab states and the new nation-state of Israel. He became a much-published writer on race matters at home and abroad. He also continued his work at the United Nations, rising to the rank in 1967, four years before his death, of undersecretary general.

For both of these figures the details of their celebrity careers seem quaint, vaguely heartwarming, frequently obscuring qualities of real genius and achievement. As a singer, for instance, Anderson was the real deal, praised by no less than Toscanini, who once told her "a voice like yours is heard once in a hundred years." In a parallel vein of prodigious achievement, Bunche was a cultural intellectual of the first order, not to mention a hardheaded strategic negotiator and prophet of postcolonialist internationalism. For both, the smarmy concept of the "goodwill ambassador" promoted by mainstream white culture and its popular media proved uniquely telling—figures sanctified in the name of racial amity at home while safely assigned vague government functionary status abroad, all in the name of generalized human uplift.

To be a credit to one's race, mainstream white approval was obviously the key criterion. In the immediate post–World War II era, a certain prewar venerability helped. Among the new agitations of black veterans and production workers who had manned assembly lines for the arsenal of democracy, E. Philip Randolph was counted on to replicate his work with Pullman porters: form a "negro" labor organization, but stay tractable, patriarchal, and parochial. An entertainment icon such as Lena Horne was to exploit dimensions of crossover appeal: emphasize the mature sultriness, but go easy on the blues. Eschew Billie Holiday for white standards like "Summertime" or "Stormy Weather."

Ascendant younger figures had to undergo character assessment in the public mind by the same standards of crossover acceptability. Professional accomplishment, preferably in sports or entertainment, was to be accompanied by personal probity and social respectability; this was all to be complemented, if possible, by a lack of publicly pronounced opinions on race matters or domestic politics generally. Even when such a personality could be newly identified, the general-interest media required of the candidate an extended trial period. The first post–World War II *Life* magazine cover photo of an African American celebrity, Jackie Robinson of the Brooklyn Dodgers, waited until May 8, 1950—a full three years after his integration into the national pastime. The second, of Willie Mays, who had entered the game in the early 1950s and achieved instant stardom, came a full eight years later, April 28, 1958, and was worked into his appearance as part of a motorcade marking the arrival of the former New York Giants in their new home city of San Francisco. (In the same year, to showcase American progressivism in collegiate athletics, while trumpeting prospects for upcoming Olympic victory, *Sports Illustrated* named as its 1958 sportsman of the year the decathlon world-record holder Rafer Johnson, who also happened to be, it was proudly noted, the black student body president at UCLA—a credit to his race if ever there was one.)

As the 1950s moved into the 1960s, the news focus on race passed unavoidably to civil rights, with a June 28, 1963, funeral picture featuring the widow and son of Medgar Evers. But even here, when possible, the racial celebrity spotlight tried to seek out the safer ground of sports—as in a March 6, 1964, cover feature on the boxer Muhammad Ali, post–Black Muslim conversion but pre–Vietnam War draft resistance. As late as 1966, cover shots came forth in the bizarre juxtapositions of images—a bright Hollywood shot of February 4 showing the entertainers Harry Belafonte, Sidney Poitier, and Sammy Davis Jr., followed at midyear by a July 15 black-and-white portrait of Black Panther youth—denoting in their jarring incongruities the popular representations of race in a culture of race holding on for dear life.

What was really happening in terms of relationships between black and white in America—the legacy of slavery and reconstruction; of segregation and of the great black migrations to the cities of the North and Midwest; and now, in response to long overdue civil rights initiatives and legislation at the federal level, the new southern counterresponse of massive resistance, frequently accompanied by mob violence and acts of intimidation and murder—was there for anyone to see and read about. To use a technological figure of the era, the nation was on a rocket sled hurtling toward racial crisis.

Yet incredibly, throughout even the late 1950s, for the average white American there prevailed the belief that this too could probably be averted—or at least, so it was assumed—somehow made good along with everything else amidst the business of partaking of post–World War II peace and prosperity. Never mind the sellout of the Democratic Party to the newer Dixiecrats in 1948. Nor were Eisenhower Republicans, albeit credited with the racial progressivism embodied in *Brown v. Board of Education* and federal intervention in Little Rock, more than grudgingly responsive. In the well-intentioned age of Norman Vincent Peale and the National Council of Churches, Ed Sullivan and Dale Carnegie, *I Love Lucy* and "See the USA in Your Chevrolet," there was simply the assumption that things would improve once average Americans got to thinking straight. Or, as Dwight Eisenhower himself was said to have remarked in an aside to a shocked Earl Warren of the good citizens of Little Rock, Arkansas, "These aren't really bad people. They just don't want a big buck sitting next to their little girl."

Meanwhile, events compounded. The 1955–56 Montgomery Bus Boycott was followed by an unsuccessful 1957 attempt to integrate the University of Alabama in Tuscaloosa. The same year marked the founding of the Southern Christian Leadership Conference. With the last two years of the Eisenhower presidency ticking down, the decade ended in a strange hiatus, a kind of tense breathing space, as if the nation were somehow readying itself for the struggle to come. Popular attitudes of mainstream Americans, young and old, were not unlike that of non-abolitionist northerners before the Civil War, waiting to be galvanized by something like the 1850 Fugitive Slave Law—as everyone from William Lloyd Garrison to Harriet Beecher Stowe completely understood—making the North actively and legally complicit in slavery. The general attitude of right-minded mid-twentieth-century Americans seemed to be analogous: that institutional racism, like slavery before it, surely continued to be bad business but not something to be dealt with overnight. In the event, for most people it was still somebody else's problem, that of a local citizen affected directly by the law or a federal or state official taxed with administering it. Those who deemed themselves enlightened on the matter were made to feel better with images of rabid segregationists, purveyed in journalistic and photographic caricatures, as cretins and Neanderthals—mean, scrawny, violent, inbred Tobacco Road and Sanctuary types. In contrast were the equally widespread depictions of noble, impassive black faces with their eyes on the prize. The problem got talked out at supper tables and community gatherings. "I've got nothing against colored people." "I just don't want one living next door to me." "How would you like your daughter to marry one?" "Think about the poor children." "Some of my best friends are negroes." "They're fine, just as long as they know their place."

As a new decade opened and the post-1945 generation came of age, events were at full throttle. Lunch-counter demonstrations in North Carolina in 1960, with images of neatly dressed black college students in a Woolworth's having Dixie cups of water poured on their heads, were followed by 1961 Freedom Rides in Alabama, accompanied by news photos in the national media of burning buses and civil rights activists being beaten senseless by white hoodlums. Scenes of resistance in the schoolhouse door dissolved into spectacles of campus riot. Images of fire hoses and police dogs in the streets of downtown Birmingham melded into Washington, D.C., vistas and grainy black-and-white news videos of the "I Have a Dream" speech at the Lincoln Memorial. By mid decade, television news audiences could flash between the spectacle of club-wielding state troopers charging into a crowd of marchers at the Pettus Bridge in Selma, Alabama, and helicopter shots of overturned police cars, dancing mobs of looters, and entire city blocks ablaze in the Watts district of Los Angeles.

If there was such a thing as the end of Victory Culture, a radical rupture of national life with some collective dream of post–World War II peace and prosperity, the case could certainly be made on the basis of the rapid movement away from the world of pre–civil rights era America. Indeed, for me, one of the most radical acts of reconciling memory and history in my youth concerns the astonishing emergence of race itself as a visible thing during the civil rights era—the experience of many average citizens such as those of my parents' generation and my own for the first time seeing race, thinking race, imagining race. Terms such as *mass demonstration, freedom march, voter registration, civil disobedience,* and *non-*

violent resistance suddenly became the common currency of American speech; as suddenly, it became nearly impossible for someone my age to remember a world before Rosa Parks and Martin Luther King Jr.; rapscallions like Adam Clayton Powell; trailblazers like Shirley Chisholm; martyrs like Michael Chaney, Medgar Evers, four young girls on a Sunday morning at the 16th Street Baptist Church; and God knows how many more whose names are now lost to us. And then, as quickly came the quantum evolutions, the watching and experiencing of it over and over again—the rise of the countertheologies of revolutionary violence and radical blackness, with their own internecine struggles increasingly a matter of flesh and blood. How nearly impossible it now seems to realize that Malcolm X was dead by 1965. How oddly quaint now seem such once radical contemporaries of ours from the post-1945 generation, Stokely Carmichael, H. Rap Brown, Huey Newton, Angela Davis, Eldridge Cleaver, all of them now 1960s relics, right up there with diehard Weathermen or Patty Hearst and the Symbionese Liberation Army.

Just as oddly, one of advancing age looks toward today's inheritors of the legacy of black political activism. A current generation of black politicians attempts to affirm ties with the civil rights past, meanwhile reconstructing themselves as new, living embodiments of the postracial future. The political and cultural legatees of King now become strange, apostolic stand-ins, as Jesse Jackson yields to Al Sharpton. Black Islam speaks from the margins with a dying Louis Farrakhan. As opposing exemplars, one now contemplates that once seemingly impossible thing, for most of us, as recently as twenty years ago: a prominent, powerful black Republican. Yet how can one not try to comprehend culturally the lives and careers of Colin Powell, the soldier-statesman son of Caribbean American parents, holding to the urban immigrant dream; or Condoleezza Rice, the polymathic prodigy with her upbringing amid traditional black social and intellectual elites. Now, in the latest dazzling evolution, Barack Obama becomes African American by reconstructing the term, for the first time in the history of race or of political celebrity of America, as completely outside the lexicon of conventional political definition. Not an African American at all in the common sense of the current cultural euphemism, he becomes on the other hand fully African American in the newest lexicon and orbit of immigrant political hyphenation—an African by his father's birth and racial and national origin and an American by his mother's birth and racial and national origin.

In the broader world of achievement and celebrity the professional golfer Tiger Woods, the son of a black American father, a retired U.S. Army Green Beret, and a Thai mother, becomes one of the greatest athletes in history in arguably the whitest sport ever invented. Oprah Winfrey, television talk-show host, actress, publisher, self-help adviser, reading-group promoter, and general middle-class entertainment entrepreneur, enjoys a cultural imprimatur without peer among living Americans.

In literature and the intellectual-academic canon, curricular reading lists feature the rediscovered and instituted riches of Frederick Douglass and Zora Neale Hurston. Ralph Ellison is rightly accorded the status of a Melville or a Thoreau. Among late-century authors, the recently deceased playwright August Wilson is unhesitatingly compared with such American giants of the theater as Eugene O'Neill, Tennessee Williams, and Arthur Miller. The novelist Toni Morrison has received the Nobel Prize, her 1977 masterpiece *Beloved* overwhelmingly chosen in a poll of writers and critics as the greatest work produced by a writer of American fiction in the twentieth century.

To put the matter directly: it is impossible now for anyone moving into late life in an America of history or memory just to imagine a world before Michael Jordan and Michael Jackson, Oprah Winfrey or Eddie Murphy, Toni Morrison or Tupac Shakur. O. J. Simpson now exists in a sequence of avatars: the all-American football hero, the television and movie actor, the sports broadcaster, the bloody murderer in the biggest celebrity trial in American history, the scumbag with the army of million-dollar celebrity lawyers who beat the rap, the bloated would-be tell-all pulp writer reduced to trying to sell his hypothetical confession in a bidding war that ultimately even the tabloids wouldn't touch, the convicted armed robber—as of this writing—serving a nine-year prison term. Puff Daddy becomes P. Diddy and then Sean Combs, moving effortlessly from hip-hop and rap to a fashion line and a big reputation for trend-spotting. Spike Lee makes movies the way Steve Jobs runs Apple. Richard Parsons is the president of Time-Warner, the old Henry Luce publishing empire in the age of the new media conglomerate.

But the big current cover story remains, of course, Obama, right up there with McCain, eyes on the prize. The question remains meanwhile how black he truly is. Does he have enough soul, the son of a Kenyan father and an American mother, raised in the multiracial environment of Hawaii and getting his Three Rs at Punaho, a prestigious private school, then at Harvard, where he has been president of the *Harvard Law Review? (The New York Times,* at least, does him the favor of a front-page feature on his fondness for blacktop basketball and the ability to throw a mean elbow.) The real question is the oldest one in the American book, the one that no one, black or white, ever wants to admit to. The question is not if he is black enough; it is if he is white enough.

Henry Louis Gates ends the account of his youth in *Colored People*—in a chapter entitled "Sin Boldly"—by quoting the last paragraph of the personal essay required as part of his Yale application; and by the terms so recalled, we catch the memory of the times (plural) in a way that makes us see how it certainly was time (singular) for a student at black Potomac State College, the Gates boy everybody called Skipper, to leave the world of colored people in Piedmont, West Virginia. "My grandfather was colored," he wrote, "my father was a Negro, and I am black." Defiantly, melodramatically, he went on, almost daring the admissions committee to have the courage to let him in. "As always, whitey now sits in judgment of me," he concluded, "preparing to cast my fate. It is your decision either to let me blow with the wind as a non-entity or to encourage the development of self. Allow me to prove myself." Gates says he regrets the rhetoric but stands by the sentiments. In retrospect, one agrees that, whatever the youthful bombast, he could not have gotten the historical moment or the language more accurately. Nor the challenge. He knew where he was going, and America with him. The nation is still catching up. The challenge is still open.

3
China Magic

When I was a grade school kid back in the early 1950s, I couldn't understand how one country—even a country as important as my own—could just make another—one of the biggest and most populated in the world, not to mention one of the most culturally rich and ancient—simply vanish from the earth. But that is basically what we did with China, starting in 1948 and 1949, and then carrying on for what now seems a nearly impossible twenty-five more years. It was a great geopolitical magic act—to this day, perhaps, the most astounding in our history, and with consequences as yet to be reckoned.

For someone coming of age during those years, it was all very confusing. As every American schoolchild was taught, Sun Yat-sen, the father of modern China, championing democracy over the imperialists and the warlords, had bequeathed his work to Chiang Kai-shek and the Nationalists; they in turn, while striving against Mao Tse-tung and the Communists, had fought against the Japanese to sustain and preserve democratic China as the great World War II member of the victorious Allies and to make possible its emergence as the representative Asian power in the postwar Big Four.

Suddenly, from around 1950 onward, everything was Formosa, with the name itself an index of the shabby, neocolonialism of the political fiction being instituted—an abridgment of the sixteenth-century Portuguese *Ilha Formosa,* or "beautiful island." (As late as the Vietnam War, it was still being thus listed as an R&R destination. Only in the 1970s did

"Taiwan" gain official currency.) Along with the names of offshore islands such as Quemoy and Matsu, intermittently shelled during the 1950s by mainland communist artillery, the word quickly became a touchstone of cold war–era current events reference in Asia. Everyone was comforted when the mighty U.S. Seventh Fleet threatened retaliation. Meanwhile new instruction was given to the effect that Taipei was the capital of the real China, not "Peking." It was that China, the one now called Nationalist China, and not the communist one, which had been awarded United Nations charter membership in 1945, as well as a permanent seat with veto power on the Security Council. Somehow, it followed, as of November 8, 1949, it was that China, along with all the good anticommunist Chinese people and their leader Chiang Kai-shek, which had been magically translated to this new place called Formosa. By mid-1950, *Time* magazine could adoringly describe a resolute, unbowed "Gimo," as he was still being called, short for his wartime title of "Generalissimo," proclaiming the mainland a Soviet Russian client state in revolution against lawful government.

Never mind that for a full twenty-five years before that—including all of World War II—the Chinese nation itself had consisted, if at all, largely of a Chinese civil war pitting the Kuomintang/Nationalists of Chiang Kai-shek against the Communists of Mao Tse-tung for control of the mainland, interspersed with sporadic but largely ineffective resistance to Japanese invaders occupying vast swaths of the country and population. Never mind that Formosa for the fifty years preceding the defeat of Japan had not been Chinese at all but a Japanese-occupied island fortress, or for centuries before that had been considered by the indigenous Taiwanese as a nation independent of China itself. Never mind that the new "nation" created overnight amounted to barely 2 million exiles superadded to a native population of 6 million, descended from aboriginal Malay-Polynesians, as opposed to the nearly 500 million mainland Chinese somehow erased from existence. To the tune of a half-billion souls, all the bad people had simply gone someplace where no one even had to pretend they existed. The geopolitical sleight of hand that willed into nonexistence Albania—the tiniest and most intransigent of post-1945 Communist nations of Europe—was likewise practiced on vast, teeming China. China became Albania.

As perplexing, in retrospect, was the degree to which all these developments furthermore required the erasure of a whole apparatus of golden-age American popular sinophilia that for the decades preceding had seemed so completely omnipresent in the mass-culture media. Unloaded, as if it were an attic full of worn-out trunks and suitcases with queer travel stickers and customs declarations, was a whole cultural baggage: the late-nineteenth- and early-twentieth-century mythology of a vast, striving, mighty China, democratic and Christian, rising out of its grand imperial history as the teeming ancient fountainhead of culture in Asia to become the new laboratory of Western values and ideas.

Carrying the literary banner between the wars was Pearl S. Buck, a daughter of missionaries reared in China, winner of the Pulitzer Prize for her novel *The Good Earth* and of the 1938 Nobel Prize for Literature. Other popular favorites included *Oil for the Lamps of China,* a 1934 fiction best seller by Alice Hobart Tisdale, and *The Importance of Living,* a 1939 work of armchair philosophy by Lin Yutang, a widely read popularizer of Chinese thought. Able Anglo European assists came from such respected novelists as Andre Malraux, in *Man's Fate,* a modernist chronicle of revolutionary-existential politics, and A. J. Cronin, in *The Keys of the Kingdom,* a missionary classic of love and Christian sacrifice, both set on a pre–World War II Chinese landscape of chaotic social and political upheaval.

But no one worked harder championing vast, suffering China than Henry W. Luce, like Pearl Buck, born and raised in China as the child of American Presbyterian missionaries in the first decades of the twentieth century. Identifying himself throughout life as a devoutly Christian, democratic, card-carrying "mishkid," as they called themselves, he had risen to become head of Time, Inc., publisher of *Time, Life,* and *Fortune* magazines, and, outside the movie industry and a few major newspapers, probably the single most influential shaper of American popular opinion. Indeed, as far as China was concerned, for Luce, the vision of the era he came to call the American Century could at times seem to consist of some grand missionary campaign of cultural countercolonization, a reengineering of history into a set of some of the most contorted claims of relationship ever established between major nationalities. Gone from the Luce narrative was the fact that the early romance of the clipper ships and

China trade—the commerce, as Thoreau and others called it, with "The Celestial Empire"—had quickly become a naked parlay of American political, economic, and religious interests, along with those other "advanced" partners in late-nineteenth- and early-twentieth-century imperialism: the smashing by German, British, French, American, and Japanese military forces of the Boxer Rebellion; the breaching of the Forbidden City and dynastic power; the destabilization of life in the cities and countryside into decades of anarchy and warlord violence. Gone was the memory of a vast inflow of Chinese domestic labor that had helped build the nineteenth-century American West—its great infrastructure of railroads, factories, public works—only to find utterly racist, xenophobic counterreaction in the Chinese Exclusion Act, to this day the only such immigration measure ever directed against the people of a single nationality. That was then, and this was now, the Luce publicity machine baldly asserted. Amid global economic crisis and the gathering of war in Europe and the Mediterranean, and against the claims of vast competing totalitarianisms both occidental and oriental, the Western defenders of freedom needed to embrace in Asia the hopes and aspirations of the Christian democratic capitalist Chinese represented by the brave, embattled, Nationalist regime of Chiang Kai-shek as fervently as they did their own.

To be sure, the Luce publications faithfully chronicled for their English-speaking readership events in Europe, Africa, and the Mediterranean: the travails of the League of Nations, the Spanish civil war, the rise of Mussolini and Italian conquests in the Horn of Africa, the ascendancy of Hitler and the crises of the Rhineland, the Anschluss, the Sudetenland, Munich, the Nazi-Soviet Pact. But both *Time* (founded in 1923), with its revolutionary news format, and *Life* (after its inception in 1936), with its stunning photojournalism, had simultaneously devoted unrelenting and graphic attention to Japanese aggressions and savageries on the mainland, covering their brutal conquest of Manchukuo, their atrocities in Nanking, and their ongoing campaigns in the south. Legendary *Life* photos included that of a crying baby, sitting burned and upright in the blazing ruins of a Shanghai train station and of civilians trampled and suffocated in a rush to shelters during a Chunking air raid. Also included were horrifying photographs of Japanese atrocities against Chinese prisoners and extensive coverage of the Panay Incident in which a U.S. Navy vessel was bombed by Japanese planes. Through the late 1930s and early in the new decade, to be sure, war coverage also kept up with concurrent European and Mediterranean events. But in early to mid 1941 a series of spotlighted personal contributions to *Life* by Henry Luce and his wife, playwright, journalist, and eventual wartime member of Congress, Clare Boothe Luce, kept the heat on. (By the end of the war, as the Nationalist leader, doggedly imaged and reimaged by the Luce publicity machine as the Asian counterpart of a Roosevelt, a Stalin, or a Churchill, Chiang would make at least six appearances on the cover of *Time* magazine alone.) Also *Fortune* between April and September 1941 saw fit to publish five major articles on China. Accordingly, when war finally struck Americans at Pearl Harbor, Luce, Inc., was ready to cement the terms of Holy Alliance with China, going so far as to publish in both *Time* and *Life* photo essays literally facing off Chinese physiognomies and body types against Japanese, complete with diagrams and pseudo-anthropological notation. "How to Tell Japs from the Chinese," read the first; "How to Tell Your Friends from the Japs," the second said. Although posing such analyses as supported by "science," no average person, the articles asserted, really had to get out the calipers or the measuring tapes. "Those who know them best often rely on facial expression to tell them apart," the *Time* researchers confidently asserted: "the Chinese expression is likely to be more placid, kindly, open; the Japanese more positive, dogmatic, arrogant."*

Throughout World War II Luce and his allies in the State Department and the Roosevelt circle kept the China fires burning. Meanwhile, the utterly abysmal military and political performance of the Chiang Kai-shek regime became a kind of black hole of Allied political, economic, and military commitments. The great "generalissimo," with his intriguing Wellesley-educated wife, spent as much of the war enriching himself and his courtiers and solidifying his domestic regime against the Communists as taking anything resembling concerted military action against the Japanese who had so thoroughly brutalized his people while occupying half of the Chinese landmass. (Churchill, for one, was ap-

*"How to Tell Japs from the Chinese," *Time*, 22 December 1941, 33.

palled by Roosevelt's blind spot for China, his naive sense of some Asian equivalency of the special relationship in the West between America and England, and his belief that in manpower and spiritual resources China's war effort paralleled that of the Russians against the Germans in tying down Japanese forces. In retrospect, Roosevelt was probably more right than Churchill about this, at least.)

In popular culture the attitudes that prevailed were those of the undisguised romanticizations of Hollywood. The noble, suffering Chinese, as in popular print, newsreels, and photojournalism, were invariably pitted against the villainous, bloodthirsty Japs—ironically, because of wartime internments, played by Chinese (Richard Loo), Koreans (Philip Ahn), or repellently made-up Anglo Americans (J. Carrol Naish). As brave allies of the Americans, the Chinese appeared in early films as diverse as *Flying Tigers* (1942), with John Wayne; *A Yank on the Burma Road* (1942), with Barry Nelson and Laraine Day; and *China* (1943), with Alan Ladd and Loretta Young. These were followed by wartime classics unstinting in their positive depictions: *Thirty Seconds over Tokyo* (1944), an account of the 1942 Doolittle raid on Tokyo and the ensuing travails of downed fliers on the Japanese-occupied mainland, with Spencer Tracy and Van Johnson; *The Keys of the Kingdom* (1944), taken from the A. J. Cronin missionary saga, featuring Gregory Peck; and *Dragon Seed* (1944), another Pearl Buck vehicle with Katharine Hepburn and Walter Huston reprising the 1937 noble yellowface impersonations of Luise Rainer and Paul Muni in *The Good Earth*.

Into the immediate postwar era, wartime propaganda about the new hopes and prospects on the geopolitical stage of a great Westernized, Christian, democratic China prevailed. The importance of China for Americans in the international policy dimension was marked by a 1946 special mission headed by General George C. Marshall, the wartime U.S. Army chief of staff and perhaps the most able and respected of all American leadership figures to emerge from the war. Marshall spent more than a year at his work, promising a continuation of wartime-level support to the Chiang Kai-shek government but coupling it with firm, if ultimately futile, insistence on genuine efforts to end corruption, disarm warlords, and take active military actions against Communists. Luce's unrelenting publicity shilling for the Nationalist regime continued apace—

despite massive and continuing evidence of its vast incompetence, corruption, and inaction. Meanwhile, the unholy conjunction of events in China with developments at home and in other crisis spots around the globe would dictate strange, composite formulations of U.S. cold war policy affecting American behavior in Asia for decades to come and with consequences at home and abroad that we are still trying to assess.

The eventual 1948 "loss" of China to the Communists, as it was roundly termed—as if it had ever "belonged" to the U.S. government in the first place—dovetailed with the House Un-American Activities Committee and McCarthy anticommunist witch hunts of the late 1940s and early 1950s and with the State Department's attendant purging of old China hands, as they were called—the latter being in many cases the last policy officials actually to have knowledge of Chinese language, culture, history, and spiritual tradition. The complete rejection of the *China White Paper* meticulously researched and articulated, laying the blame on Chiang and his bankrupt regime, accompanied the hardening of U.S. policy into a chronic refusal to support any form of Asian nationalism that could not be proven to be absolutely anticommunist.

Cold war developments from 1946 to 1948 didn't help the China situation. The endless Chinese civil war was eclipsed by events in Europe such as the Berlin Blockade and the descent of the Iron Curtain. By 1948 the world had learned that Russia had developed its own atomic bomb, investing the cold war with new nuclear terror; and in the same year the Arab-Israeli War marked the ascendancy of the Middle East as a site of persistent, intractable conflict. In Southeast Asia the French found themselves mired in a military effort to reinstate colonial rule in Indochina; nearby, Britain made its post-1945 farewell to a major empire by accepting the independence of India. Meanwhile, things in China were going completely to hell. Following a series of routs and hasty retrenchments, by 1949 the Chiang Kai-shek government had altogether fled the mainland, claiming new island dominion as a preposterous, in its way almost pathetic, shadow regime, with its real seat of government, as has been suggested, not in Taipei but in Washington, D.C. The China Lobby, as it was called at the time, remained in full cry, led by Luce, of course, but also containing such influential right-wing legislators as Styles Bridges, William Knowland, Pat McCarren, Kenneth Wherry, and others. The aging Chiang and his minions meanwhile continued to busy themselves with rattling secondhand U.S. weaponry and dreaming military nonsense about reinvasion and reconquest of the mainland.

Then, suddenly, in 1950 a new Asian complication of the domestic Red Scare, with its sundry fears about A-bomb espionage, subversives in the film industry, Communists in the State Department, was added in the form of the surprise invasion of South Korea by communist forces of the North Korean People's Army (NKPA). In the midst of this bewildering new development in the Far East, China wound up being nowhere and everywhere. Complex policy responses, based on virtually no knowledge of the attitudes or strategic goals of the Chinese communist leadership, attempted to factor in questions of Russian versus Chinese influence, or the likelihood of active military intervention by one power or the other in their calculations of Free World military response. These conundrums were not assuaged by the separate diplomacies of the U.S. Far East commander, the increasingly delusional Douglas MacArthur, working from his Tokyo American shogunate: in the first days of Korea, arguing for the commitment of a five-hundred-thousand-man Nationalist force as part of the United Nations military effort, or later, once an "invisible" army of thirty Chinese Communist divisions invading from across the Manchurian border had put his armies to rout, somehow imagining that the new introduction of such a Nationalist force might yet turn the tide, not just in Korea, but perhaps in China itself, by reinvading across the Yalu or even, possibly, by mounting their own landings across the Formosa straits.

In popular culture, as I recall it from the time, it was all very confusing—not least when, announced by bugles sounding the charge, three hundred thousand screaming foot soldiers of the Chinese People's Army actually did show up in North Korea during late winter 1950. My war comics filled up accordingly with hordes of infantrymen in quilted winter uniforms and cloth caps with red stars on them, all armed with tommy guns going "budda-budda-budda," in human wave attacks barely beaten back by pockets of brave, beleaguered marines and GIs. "Yonkee!" they screamed. "You die!" On the late show, regular reruns began to appear of *The Good Earth, Flying Tigers,* and *The Keys of the Kingdom.* Saturday morning TV still replayed Charlie Chan and his number-one son—a set of nearly thirty-odd films, the most memorable starring the redoubtable Warner Olan, spun off from the 1930s Earl Derr Biggers novel series about a Chinese detective in Honolulu. (Programmers often played these off in the rerun market against series featuring Charlie Chan's prewar Japanese opposite-number, Mr. Moto, played by Peter Lorre and derived from novels by John P. Marquand.) As if applicable to the new Red Menace in the East, in comics one could encounter Sax Rohmer's Fu Manchu, evil genius of the "oriental mind" (in Douglas MacArthur's melodramatic phrasing) incarnate; Flash Gordon's strange intergalactic nemesis Ming the Merciless; or, in *Terry and the Pirates,* the ever-charming, ever-dangerous Dragon Lady.

In feature film a new emphasis in representations seemed to manifest itself in a focus on the young, endangered, but somehow brave and resilient, Asian woman—frequently softened into the love object in a 1950s sentimental reprise such as *Satan Never Sleeps,* a missionary drama with William Holden, Clifton Webb, and France Nguyen; a classic star-crossed weepy such as *Love Is a Many-Splendored Thing,* featuring Holden again, along with Jennifer Jones, cosmetically orientalized through the magic of makeup as Dr. Han Suyin; or a charming artist-meets-hooker bedroom comedy such as *The World of Suzie Wong,* again with Holden and, in the title role, Nancy Kwan. (It is worth noting that in *The Bridges at Toko-Ri,* Holden yet again, as a Korean War navy carrier pilot—in fact an embittered, cynical World War II "retread"—on a last R&R in Tokyo among the utterly charming, hospitable Japanese, is paired for a doomed romantic good-bye with the exquisitely American Grace Kelly, accompanied by two gleaming children. Asian concubines, in this case, are reserved for the enlisted men.) Repeatedly, one saw China feminized and beleaguered, as was frequently the political case, and exiled to Hong Kong for intrigue and excitement. For charm, such nostalgist sinophilia could even be translated by the indefatigable Rodgers and Hammerstein to the Broadway stage (1957) and subsequent Hollywood musical (1961) in *Flower Drum Song,* about generational conflict among lovable Chinese immigrants in San Francisco: strange enough in its own right for being set in a former hotbed of anti-Chinese racism dating from the days of the Chinese Exclusion Act but also further notable for an original cast, carried to the movie, in which only the ingénue heroine, through some bizarre inversion of World War II ethnic casting protocols, Nancy

Kwan, was Chinese-born, from Hong Kong, and all the others—James Shigeta, Miyoshi Umeki, and Jack Soo—Japanese American. No less idiotic was the casting conceit pairing Ingrid Bergman in the early 1960s *The Inn of the Sixth Happiness,* with the aging German star Curt Jurgens, briefly abandoning the role of the likable Nazi, in truly bizarre prosthetic yellowface, as the dominating Chinese captain. Curiously, or not, the set of the latter was recycled for the early 1960s *Satan Never Sleeps,* where France Nguyen, of Vietnamese descent, has become a Communist rape victim.

For exotic intrigue and conflict, postwar China meanwhile provided the Hollywood backdrop of such early 1950s thrillers as *China Venture* and *The Shanghai Story,* both with Edmond O'Brien. In 1955 also came the thoroughly retrograde *Soldier of Fortune,* with Clark Gable and Susan Hayward, set in Hong Kong during the post–World War II Communist revolution. China also newly figured in garish costume drama, such as *The Conqueror,* with John Wayne as "Temujin," a.k.a. Genghis Khan, and Susan Hayward as the Tartar princess Bortai. Other period history pieces would feature Charlton Heston in *55 Days at Peking* (1963), set during the Boxer Rebellion, and Steve McQueen in *The Sand Pebbles* (1966), about the pre–World War II U.S. China Navy.

Films on the Korean War were filled with new bloodthirsty Asiatics—first North Koreans and later Communist Chinese—but depicted mainly as faceless members of onrushing hordes, indistinguishable as to nationality beyond generic classification as "gooks." In this connection, revealingly, the most memorable China-related movie of the Korean War decade—based on a 1959 Richard Condon novel, itself best described as a hybrid of sci-fi espionage and political thriller—may still be *The Manchurian Candidate,* a potboiler featuring a throwback, Fu Manchu–style Chinese evil genius and manipulator of minds, Jen Lo, leagued with North Korean intelligence and the KGB to reprogram a "brainwashed" American POW as a domestic political assassin. The 1962 film was withdrawn for twenty-five years following the murder of John F. Kennedy; a 2004 remake was in turn uprooted completely from cold war/Korean War/Chinese Communist origins.

As fictions go, however, not to mention their elaboration into geopolitical myth, no book, movie, or propaganda script will ever be written that is more preposterous than the basic U.S. policy fiction of the major cold war decades positing that Communist China simply did not exist: that the United States at home and abroad (as observed by David Halberstam in his last, magisterial text on the Korean War in its relation to post–World War II developments in Asia) should simply act as if the Nationalists had won the Chinese civil war, and the Communists had lost; that an instant creation of a "new" China as if on movie location—an island the size of Florida—was the real China, as opposed to some apparently "fake" China with a population of more than half a billion occupying the largest landmass in Asia. In the language of policy, the Republic of China was an official government entity; its opponents, the Chinese Communists or the Red Chinese, were not. And coupled with all this, with disastrous consequences for decades of U.S. political and military planning, was the insane but somehow irremovable strategic assumption, as noted earlier, that some future reinvasion of the mainland by Nationalist forces, on whatever pretext, might still lead to reconquest by the forces of democracy. Further, until that day there would likewise remain the intransigent insistence of the China lobby on barring the Communist regime from the United Nations, and continually reaffirming and solidifying as the bulwark of U.S. cold war policy in Asia the "permanent" great-power status of the exiled Nationalist regime, along with a seat on the Security Council. As is now known to students of the Korean War, militarily at least, any such actual pitting of "real" versus "phony" Chinese, in the ways posited by the increasingly erratic MacArthur, was wisely averted by Truman. In turn, Eisenhower, who was required by ongoing policy concerns to establish himself as a resolute defender of the Nationalist regime, met an ongoing pattern of 1950s China crises—mainly centered on Communist threats against offshore islands—with responses grounded in military and political symbolism that could satisfyingly be taken as such, and no more, by all parties concerned: demonstrations by large naval elements, infusions of castoff military hardware, or edicts by approved surrogates such as Richard Nixon and John Foster Dulles. In the early 1960s a new president, John Kennedy, quickly revealed that he, too, understood the China reality/unreality game. Responding to a remark by U.N. ambassador Adlai Stevenson, his former rival for the presidency, about the heavy responsibilities of the White House, he replied, "You have the hardest thing in the world to sell. It really doesn't make any sense—the idea that Taiwan represents China. But, if we lose this fight, if Red China comes into the UN our first year in town, your first year and mine, they'll run us both out."*

Accordingly, when American leaders shortly began to debate new military commitments to shore up South Vietnam against Communist aggression from the North, the willed blindness of a fervently anticommunist two-Chinas policy was compounded by a catastrophic ignorance of millennia-old Vietnamese historical attitudes toward China and the Chinese. At least initially, as a matter of facing down a new Communist aggression, the war was taken as largely a replay of Korea. As with the earlier conflict, serious debate raged on whether Ho Chi Minh's communist revolution was mainly Chinese or Russian-inspired, and on which power was a major supplier of weaponry and financial and advisory support. Again, the questions were the old ones. At what point could U.S. bombing of the North and sources of Russian supply and materiel provoke World War III? At what point, should the U.S. decide to cross into North Vietnam, might Chinese military forces enter the conflict? Only at some point years later did anyone note how Ho Chi Minh had made an utterly Vietnamese communist revolution, assimilating historical Marxism-Leninism to Vietnamese village culture, meanwhile playing off Russian patronage against Chinese support, but with the latter still backgrounded against a two-millennia-long tradition of Vietnamese resistance to Chinese cultural, political, and military domination. (Even when I was there in 1969, in the jungle regions around Saigon, one heard repeated stories from "up north" with the First Cavalry and the marines of Chinese advisers, of Chinese combat troops with NVA [North Vietnamese Army] units, of Chinese interrogators, or the discovery of Chinese KIA [killed in action] on the battlefield. It would take ten years more to put even that idea of military collaboration to rest with what is now called the Third Indochina War, in which an invasion by as many as two hundred thousand Chinese troops was bitterly repulsed by the People's Army of Vietnam.)

By 1971 the United States, playing an endgame in Vietnam, as in Ko-

*Quoted in David Halberstam, *The Coldest Winter* (New York: Hyperion, 2007), 650.

rea ten years before, found itself this time without even United Nations allies. Further, it found itself the last holdout in a larger Asian fiction about the "real" as opposed to the "make-believe" China as well. From thence, events began to go rapidly. In that year, with ground troops nearly withdrawn from Vietnam and U.S. international policies badly in need of renewed credibility, a Republican administration under Richard Nixon made a show of yielding to world pressure, refraining from opposition to a U.N. vote to unseat and expel the Nationalist Republic of China and seat the Communist People's Republic of China with membership on the Security Council. By 1973, with South Vietnam, after one last stopgap application of American firepower during the Communist Spring Offensive, left nakedly to its own fate, and with Watergate haunting the presidency like Marley's Ghost, Nixon and Kissinger made their famous trip to China, meeting with Mao and Chou En-lai. By 1975 both Chiang Kai-shek and Mao Tse-tung were dead. Over the ensuing decades new political leaders for both "Chinas" dispelled the cults of myth, personality, and history, concentrating on internal political, military, educational, and economic development. Taipei, along with Hong Kong and Singapore, became one of the great hubs of Asian economic power. In a kind of bad movie of history, Taiwan, while internally debating the role anticommunism should play in a new national nomenclature, ran full-page ads in the *New York Times* and the *Wall Street Journal,* lobbying for independent U.N. recognition and decrying its invisibility among the community of nations.

China, meanwhile, remained the Chinese People's Republic, at least in name. But it rapidly discovered its true power to be economic and, accordingly, allowed the unleashing of a rampant capitalism in virtually all sectors of development while hanging on to remnants of its own holy ideology in some vestigial fiction of communist government, the peoples' leaders somehow mingling uneasily with the new plutocracy—and executing the occasional commissar who seems to have been caught unlawfully snatching a bribe from the capitalist trough. In America suspicions of military and political threat were subsumed by political/economic love-hate, but mostly the scene was one of capitalist romance. Visions of burgeoning markets and proliferations of new, collaborative manufacturing opportunities jostled along with the more immediate concerns presented by a tidal influx of dubious consumer goods. Americans may say they feel menaced by the rise of China generally as the newest competing geopolitical power, in the sense that they once feared the Russians or now are fearful of Islamic terror or the rise of new nuclear states such as North Korea or Iran. But they surely are in it for the big economic game, whatever their concerns about lethal pet food, toxic toothpaste, and hazardous toys, not to mention bristling military might or pollution on a grand scale.

American politicians and policy makers find their own makeshift ways. They pillory China on human rights; they applaud Chinese help in negotiations to terminate the North Korean nuclear program. What they mainly see is an economic growth of 10 percent annually. Even the old real China, Taiwan, for all those querulous anti-U.N. ads decrying its unjust exclusion from the world, adjusts its reality picture accordingly. It does not now claim to be the real China. It just wants to get in, like Albania. Economically, it pitches bargain-basement investment in the Taipei stock market as an attractive competitor to those of Hong Kong and China proper, with stock prices in the former having doubled in the past two years and those in the latter having quintupled during the same period.

Meanwhile, on the mainland, even bigger, nearly earthshaking economic good news greets the 2007 meeting of the Chinese Communist Party for its seventeenth Congress. China now leads the world in the number of publicly traded corporations valued at more than $200 billion—with in fact eight of the top twenty, as opposed to seven for the United States, four for Western Europe, and one for Russia.

For the way China will shortly fill the horizon of American geopolitical reality, predictions for as near as 2025 might be said to at once dazzle and terrify. In sheer human demographics of a single nationality, mainland population will be 1.5 billion. Numbers of English speakers in China will exceed numbers of native English speakers in the world. Economically, the U.S. and China will have at least equivalent GDPs, with many predictions favoring the Chinese as substantially larger. In pure size of production measures China will undoubtedly have the largest economy on the planet. According to many political analysts, Taiwan will likely have become part of a larger Chinese confederation. The

United States will no longer have military bases in Korea or Japan. China and India, its powerhouse competitor, will have basically split shares of Asian influence, leaving the West to cope somehow with what amounts to Asia's whole new recolonization in terms of global power and production relationships.

Apace, for someone who grew up during America's great China hiatus, the world still continues to look much like a Looney Tunes/Merrie Melodies cartoon of the era, where a jar of "vanishing cream," rubbed on, makes a character instantly invisible and then, rubbed off, makes the character visible again—meanwhile raising all kinds of holy hell in the world populated by all the other characters in the manic, lurid, violent scene before the viewer's eyes. Historical China, then and now, will have always been too big and powerful for such cartoonish reduction. But one can still rub one's eyes sometimes, still say truly in retrospect that once upon a time in America, a geopolitical reality called China really did come close to being reduced to a lesser Rodgers and Hammerstein musical, food out of a can labeled La Choy or Chung King, and Hop Sing, the always irate yet somehow lovable cook for the Cartwright boys on *Bonanza.* With the opening of contemporary China to the world, and with the awakening of the world to the geopolitical prospect of an era many have already come to predict as the Chinese century, new images before our eyes are there to be seen from Chinese artists and filmmakers, and new texts are there to be read from major Chinese writers such as 2000 Nobel Prize Winner Gao Xingian and celebrated U.S. expatriate and National Book Award Winner Ha Jin (Jin Xuefei). Politically or culturally, this time, we may all rest assured, in the great American image factories of Washington, D.C., New York, or Hollywood, no leftover version of the old China magic will work.

4
A Tale of Two Task Forces

As a son of the World War II generation and an armored cavalry veteran of Vietnam, I find I cannot read or think about Americans in combat during the Korean War without a mixture of rage and horror, on one hand, at the utterly misbegotten way that war was conducted and of gratitude and relief, on the other, that I did not have to fight in it. It has been called the forgotten war, the coldest war, and the first hot war of the cold war. At the time it was not officially considered a war but a "police action," with the latter term justly adduced over the years as a measure of the distance between the horror of combat and the sanitizations of political discourse and popular understanding that would become a signature of post-1945 American military involvements. More properly one might see it as both the last conventional war and the first unconventional war, combining the slaughter and chaos of earlier large-scale wars with the strange new battlefield terrors and unknowns of a host of shadow wars to come. For soldiers and marines in the middle of it the misery was beyond naming, combining the worst features of twentieth-century mass-formation slaughter with the savage, small-unit, close-quarters combat of the patrol, the outpost, and the ambush soon to become the trademark of a new style of postatomic limited war. Further, as if this were not sufficient, it remains distinguished to this day by the combination of mischance and mismanagement that prevailed at every conceivable level of operation.

The barest summary of events evokes to this day a shifting nightmare scenario, offensive and counteroffensive, crushing advance and bloody retreat, overwhelming attack and desperate, last-ditch defense, a kind of black hole of military memory expanding and contracting before one's eyes. A massive July 25, 1950, cross-border invasion by six divisions of North Korean People's Army (NKPA), at the 38th parallel dividing the peninsula into post–World-War II communist and free world client-states, resulted in South Korean forces and hastily committed American units nearly being pushed into the sea. With U.S. and U.N. combat forces fed in to support collapsing South Korean formations, a desperate defense was mounted in the enclave known as the Pusan Perimeter. Beginning in mid-September, an allied counteroffensive, coupled with a high-risk amphibious flank maneuver at Inchon, then drove the North Koreans back the entire length of the peninsula to the Yalu River, marking the country's northern border. In turn, a late-November cross-border counterattack by new Chinese formations numbering in the hundreds of thousands pushed the allies with tremendous losses back across the 38th parallel into positions near the original defensive perimeter. After a surreal seven months of bloody march and countermarch, battle lines were restored roughly at midcountry. Twenty thousand Americans would be dead, and the most legendary warrior-general in the national history since Grant or Pershing would be dismissed from supreme command for insubordination. Two years of bitter, murderous stalemate would follow, during which thirteen thousand more American troops would die. When an armistice would be signed, the two armies would still find themselves facing each other at the 38th parallel. A spectacle of slaughter, rout, and capture, eventually subsiding into a grinding, inconclusive misery of attrition, the Korean War would remain among the strangest, most ill-fought, and least understood wars in American history.

In terms of the experience of the American soldier, Korea may now also be said to have encompassed a bizarre anthology of twentieth-century American wars, replaying in its opening phases nearly everything that went wrong in well-remembered World War II combat debacles before then going on to anticipate such bitter, inconclusive struggles as ensuing wars in Vietnam and Iraq. For those with the memories of 1941 to 1945 fresh in their minds, the opening rounds especially, with entire units committed to hopeless defense or plunged into fighting retreat, recalled dark images of catastrophe ranging from Bataan to the Battle of the Bulge. Whole formations suffered annihilation. Platoons, companies, and battalions, even in some cases regiments and divisions, simply vanished, ceased to exist in the face of a relentlessly advancing enemy. Two years would then follow of the equally bitter, savage, close-up war of the perimeter, the patrol, the outpost, and the ambush, the new world of limited war that would become the late-twentieth-century reimaging of the world of no-man's land—frequently with civilian and refugee noncombatants bleeding and dying in the middle.

As if a war of attrition was any less grinding, or the dead and wounded any less dead and wounded, victory and defeat in Korea simply became marked, as with new American wars to come, by the mounting dead and wounded. The country even possessed a climate to make it the worst of wars. Popular accounts frequently emphasize the astonishing cold. It is too easy to forget that it began in unbearable heat. For the soldiers and marines, from the ground up—the level of squad, platoon, and company, up to battalion, regiment, brigade, and even division—incessant, remorseless killing remained the order of the day on both sides. Toward the end much would be made of POW issues—on the allied side of "collaborators" and "turncoats" subjected to communist "brainwashing" techniques, and on the enemy's part, of an insistence on the involuntary repatriation of large numbers of unwilling Koreans and Chinese. The fact was that a relatively small proportion of those taken in combat by either side ever made it into captivity. In the big battles and the small in Korea, the watchword was annihilate or be annihilated.

This chapter represents an attempt to return to the Korean War in a way that honors the particular experiences of certain Americans who found early combat and sacrifice there: of one unit in a doomed, hopeless battle marking the beginning of American combat involvement in the war, and of another, a bare five months later, in an even more catastrophic battle arguably marking the beginning of the end, and to treat their stories as defining military moments in the first of the long line of twilight wars of American geopolitical intervention extending from 1945 to the present. My title states the focus simply. Here is told a tale of two task forces, two ad hoc fighting formations, both now designated in histories according to the names of their commanders and remembered according to the dreadful cost of dead and wounded. One, down near the southern tip of the peninsula, was to be the lead element of an American force envisioned as stopping and then quickly mounting a rapid counteroffensive against invading North Korean formations in the earliest days of the war; the other found itself unexpectedly a bare five months later—following a desperate defense, an inspired amphibious maneuver, and lightning advance back up the peninsula—at the lead edge of that counteroffensive far to the north, nearly to the Yalu River, only to be thrown into a fighting retreat against a massive new Chinese military invasion. Both were simply sent to their doom amid the chaos of the earliest of what we might now call the long, savage, bloody wars of American peace. The story of the first might now be seen as a testament of American unpreparedness and complacency, the second as a corresponding monument to the arrogance founded in assurance of victory—what might now be called the "mission accomplished" syndrome. Catastrophe in both cases became the measure of a strange hubris that would so often in later years bedevil similar American efforts: the chronic overconfidence, willful misreading of intelligence, ignorance of political circumstances, and generally faulty assumptions about the ever-changing nature of the enemy and the type of war Americans could be expected to fight amid the challenges of post-1945 geopolitical conflict.

The first unit memorialized here is remembered as Task Force Smith, named for Lieutenant Colonel Charles B. ("Brad") Smith, from the Japan-based Twenty-fourth Infantry Division, who arrived with his hastily deployed occupation battalion during the first days of the North Korean onslaught into the South. Near a place called Osan, already far to the south of the captured South Korean capital of Seoul, Smith and his troops would find themselves thrown into a hopeless scratch defense and would be quickly overrun in the earliest engagement of American ground forces with the invading North Korean People's Army. The force consisted of two companies of infantry (out of four) from Smith's unit, the First Battalion, Twenty-first Infantry, a two-gun 75-millimeter recoilless rifle platoon, two 4.2-inch mortar crews, and a battery of 105-meter artillery. The total number of soldiers came to around 540. They would be attacked by a North Korean division spearheaded by a tank brigade. Smith himself was a well-qualified and respected professional, part of the Twenty-fifth Division at Schofield Barracks on December 7, 1941, serving in combat with that division during the early Pacific War and earning the praise of the commander, Joseph Collins, commanding at Guadalcanal and, by the time Task Force Smith committed to action—now the U.S. Army chief of staff. Smith was an experienced enough officer to recognize that he was being cast into a suicide mission, even as he received the order to mount an ill-fated delaying action north of Osan. Arriving in Korea with mission instructions from his division commander, Major General John Dean, a figure who himself quickly proved to be something of an ill-informed martinet and glory seeker, Smith was supposed to block the North Korean advance as far north of Pusan as possible and put some backbone into a broken ally. "Sorry I can't give you more information," Smith remembered Dean weirdly saying; "that's all I've got." Specifics, he was told, were to be given by the general officer currently commanding on the scene, John H. Church. Those specifics consisted of the following memorable sendoff from the latter: "We have a little action up here. All we need is some men up there who won't run when they see tanks. We're going to move you up to support the ROKs [Republic of Korea troops] and give them moral support."*

Meanwhile, individual soldiers were encouraged to believe on their own part in some bizarre notion that the NKPA, on finding out Americans were engaged, would drop their weapons and skedaddle. As one corporal put it, Smith's pickup unit "figured to be a week in Korea, settle the gook thing, then back to Japan." On July 5, 1950, the reality of affairs revealed itself to Smith and his individual soldiers, newly deployed on a set of low hills bisected by the main route of attack southward, in the form of a column of more than thirty enemy T-34 tanks, the main Soviet battle tank that had proven to be one of the best of World War II. With one or two exceptions, these passed completely unscathed through the heaviest defensive fires Task Force Smith could muster. The 75-mm recoilless rifles and 2.36-inch rocket launchers proved completely useless. One gun in the whole 105 artillery battery happened to be supplied with a handful of antitank rounds; after knocking out two tanks of thirty-three in the column, this gun was destroyed by North Korean fire. Then, shortly, there appeared another tank unit, this one heading a column of trucks and, be-

*T.R. Fehrenback, *This Kind of War* (Dulles, VA: Brassey's, 2000), 65–66.

hind that, a column of infantry, in the words of one officer, "miles long." American units, including Smith's two infantry companies and command group, were quickly surrounded. Saying "this is a decision I'll probably regret the rest of my days," Smith gave the order to withdraw.* Individual formations trying to execute a fighting retreat through a series of delaying positions were attacked from all sides with devastating North Korean infantry fire while mortars rained down from overhead. The withdrawal quickly turned into a rout, with fleeing clusters of soldiers and individuals fighting for their lives. Soon it became every man for himself. Fleeing Americans abandoned their weapons, their helmets and equipment, sometimes even their boots. They ran, scrambled aboard trucks of other retreating units, hid in villages by day and stumbled back through paddies at night. Survivors who reassembled some days later numbered roughly a third. Seven days later, when the unit reassembled at Taejon, half of its officers and two-thirds of its men were still unaccounted for. The final figure of dead, wounded, and missing in action came to 185—a loss rate of 35 percent.

In the opening days of a war that would entail a desperate search for heroes, the legend of Task Force Smith, the first American unit to fight in the war, was quickly enshrined in popular lore. ("We were sent over there to delay the North Koreans," recalled one survivor, at the time a nineteen-year-old enlisted infantryman; "We delayed them seven hours."† Ironically, now, in retrospect, they are credited with delaying the NKPA at least three to four days—a time, according to certain historical opinion, that would prove crucial to the establishment of the successful Pusan Perimeter.) At the time, they became a byword for the epidemic of hopelessness and confusion that spread among early American units sent to stem the sudden military catastrophe into which showpiece American-sponsored Republic of Korea forces had been plunged. To soldiers on the ground they were pretty much the story of the early war—a soft, ill-equipped, disorganized half battalion in an even more ill-prepared and ill-organized division, rushed from Japan and doomed to annihilation in

*Quoted in Spencer Tucker, "Task Force Smith," http://korea50.army.mil/history/factsheets/tfsmith.shtml (June 16, 2009).

†Rudy Tomedi, *No Bugles, No Drums: An Oral History of the Korean War* (New York: Wiley, 1993), 8.

a defense where nobody, from Smith's perspective at least, was remotely in charge—and worse, where nobody seemed able to take charge. To the credit of the army, Smith himself was not scapegoated and continued in battalion command with a spearhead unit in General Walton Walker's Eighth Army. He would retire a brigadier general, living long enough to be interviewed for a 2007 account of Task Force Smith on the FOX TV show *War Stories* with Oliver North. Not nearly so professional a fate, one might add, would be bestowed on his superior officer, Twenty-fourth Division commander John Dean. At the Battle of Taejon, the latter was last seen running around taking on tanks with a bazooka—a bizarre abdication of command responsibilities even at the time not universally applauded by fellow officers. Wandering in no-man's land for a week until finally picked up by the NKPA, he remained a celebrity POW for the duration.

The second unit to be memorialized here, the even more grotesquely ill-fated Task Force Faith, got its larger and even more catastrophic fate written into history a bare five months later and is frequently overlooked in accounts of the hideous, confusing nightmare of attack and retreat—down and up and then back down the peninsula—comprising the war's opening stages. First designated Task Force MacLean, it came to be named for its ad hoc commander, Don Carlos Faith, a U.S. Army Seventh Division lieutenant colonel leading the First Battalion, Thirty-second Infantry, cast into command when his regimental-level military predecessor came to a quick and ignominious end within hours of the unit's formation when he was wounded in an icy ambush and hustled off into captivity, where he died within days. By now, the site was far to the north, on the other side of the Chosin Reservoir from the equally surrounded U.S. Marines, with the two forces fighting a bloody withdrawal to escape encirclement and annihilation by the newly invading Communist Chinese, part of an estimated 120,000 invading across the Yalu River against the U.S. X Corps, under Major General Edward Almond, by now separated without any hope of reinforcement from the equally embattled Eighth Army to the west. With seven hundred attached South Korean troops, Task Force Faith began its fighting retreat with thirty-two hundred men.

As for tactical control, again the focal figure was another young battalion commander in his thirties, in this case a stellar 1941 OCS (Officer Candidate School) graduate, the son of a brigadier, having survived uncounted brushes with death throughout World War II as an Eighty-second Airborne officer, serving as an aide to the fearless, lead-from-the-front Matthew Ridgway, himself shortly to become the savior of Korea. (Much admired and trusted by his troops, he was frequently seen walking the battlefield with a handsome cane rather than a weapon.) And again, as to general-officer idiocy from above, the event was preceded by the ground commander's encounter with a misinformed, glory-grabbing two-star giving ill-advised orders in complete ignorance of the real situation on the ground—in this case the X Corps commander himself, the much-despised MacArthur courtier and protégé, Major General Edward W. Almond. The latter had already been warned by his direct marine subordinate, Brigadier O. P. Smith, about dividing even his own substantial force during what became the race to the Manchurian border. "I told Almond we couldn't make two big efforts," Smith said. "Either we go to the Yalu by Chosin, or by the northwest route, but not both."* Now, with disaster striking in two places at once, Almond still persisted in flying in from his rear headquarters to forward army positions with bluster about being held up by "a bunch of Chinese laundrymen"; he had a pocketful of Silver Stars for on-the-spot "impact awards" as they are called in the armed forces—among his trademark gestures of motivation. One was given to Faith, one to a wounded lieutenant, and the third to a headquarters mess sergeant who happened to be walking by. As soon as Almond made his departure, according to several officers present, Faith ripped the decoration from his shirt and threw it in the mud.

When catastrophe ensued for Task Force Faith, just as surely as it had for Task Force Smith, it proved a hideous repeat performance of the chaos from the war's opening days in the south, of surrounded, overwhelmed units trying to make a fighting retreat; but this time it was on a far larger scale in both numbers and destruction, not to mention sheer duration of horror and suffering. Given the massiveness of enemy forces involved, for the proportionally overwhelmed American formations it became an endless flight, slipping in and out of panic, and punctuated by one combat

*Quoted in Max Hastings, *The Korean War* (New York: Touchstone, 1987), 147.

nightmare after another: roadblocks, blown bridges, murderous defiles, flank attacks along the length of the column, desertions by supporting Korean formations and embedded KATUSA (Korean Augmentation to the United States Army) infantry, wreckage of combat and transportation vehicles, frequently in the latter case involving trucks full of wounded. Early supply and ammunition drops fell among the Chinese; retrievable belts and clips were frequently damaged. An early napalm drop on a Chinese roadblock went astray, hitting the head of the mixed Korean-American column, sending its lead units reeling back in flames. Amid the screams and flash, an American NCO (noncommissioned officer) was seen shooting a burning comrade. At another point a halted segment of the column was overrun by Chinese who forced the able-bodied to dismount and then set fire to trucks containing many wounded. Here and elsewhere Faith himself was repeatedly forced to rally troops forward at gunpoint. To keep the column moving, he personally charged into roadblocks and enemy positions, frequently alone and wielding a .45 pistol, rallying stragglers, threatening to shoot them, and in fact summarily executing two South Korean KATUSA troops of an attached unit. When all hope disappeared of possible linkup with withdrawing marines, through an air liaison officer's radio link, Faith spoke for the last time to forward division headquarters at Hagaru. "Unless someone can help us, I don't have much hope anybody's going to get out of this." When told that no ground support was likely forthcoming, he replied, simply, "I understand."* Eventually separated from even a handful of lead elements, and badly wounded by a grenade fragment near the heart, like his predecessor MacLean, Faith too suddenly and simply vanished. As the road to Hagaru for a moment precariously opened and retreating forces made their way past dead comrades and destroyed vehicles, he was found further wounded, dying in the back of a bullet-riddled truck. He had to be left behind. His only memorial was a posthumous awarding of the Medal of Honor.

The percentage of survivors was shockingly small. Of roughly 2,500 U.S. soldiers fighting as part of Task Force MacLean/Faith, holding out for slightly more than three days and nights, only 1,050 would be found

*Quoted in Hastings, *The Korean War,* 156.

alive. By comparison, the far more heavily publicized marines fighting their way out of the Inchon Reservoir on the other side would suffer an admittedly ghastly 4,400 wounded out of 15,000, with 7,300 more non-battle casualties, mostly frostbite; but their death toll would number 730, or roughly 7 percent. Wounds, cold, illness, captivity, and abandonment to certain death were the more common fate of Task Force Faith. After five days of action, survivors of the withdrawal deemed fit for duty numbered 385. This time the numbers never improved with age. Task Force Faith lost 90 percent of its soldiers.

Complex military catastrophes are usually rendered large. This has been most frequently the case with Korea, and there has been plenty to say. In this case it can be done in brief, with the two ground actions themselves seen as bookending an endless nightmare of incompetence and mismanagement being played out at the highest levels of command. That means beginning at the top. And that in turn means the fabled MacArthur, flying in and out on highly publicized occasions between his palatial Dai Ichi headquarters in Tokyo and his embattled forces, engineering troop dispositions and making glorious pronouncements. In fact, between the start of the war and his eventual dismissal, MacArthur, as USAFA (United States Armed Forces Asia) commander, physically set foot in Korea six times, never spending a single night on the peninsula. Nor was the overall command situation helped by the more or less autonomous decision by the Joint Chiefs in Washington to entrust the newly formed Eighth Army to an immediately subordinate general of proven fighting abilities, a Patton protégé named Walton Walker, himself somewhat given to strutting and brass-hat dramatics. Never mind that Walker truly did prove worthy, through a full nine months of command culminating in his freakish death in a traffic accident, in not just one but two fighting retreats and successful defenses, a sequence of last-ditch, fire-brigade maneuvers, with holes left by overrun American and South Korean defenders barely filled by replacements rushed to the scene. Such abilities notwithstanding, his role remained in many ways predetermined, then and now, as a function of the MacArthur publicity apparatus—the barely competent goat, beneficiary of the great man's quasi-divine interventions, lordly visits, flying in to "restore the situation."

And of course, right in the middle of things there was the great Mac-

Arthur amphibious stunt, just at a time when allied forces around Pusan were themselves ready for a breakout against the heavily worn NKPA: Inchon. A dazzling strategic gamble, embellishing the legend of genius one last time by sending the First Marine Division ashore, in a flank envelopment with virtually no casualties, it was of course regarded as a masterstroke. Less appreciated, yet obvious to anyone who has tried to make decisions under the pressures of combat, was how likely it might have proved a piece of consummate idiocy—a completely irrational roll of the dice by a figure alleged to be the one living master of amphibious warfare whose knowledge and experience in the military art should have told him absolutely not to do it—not to mention fellow commanders who should have known better. As one naval planner put it, "We drew up a list of every natural and geographic handicap—and Inchon had 'em all."* Accounts of the crucial meeting where MacArthur stroked, speechified, bullied, and cajoled navy and marine commanders into participating are beyond embarrassing. It is painful to believe that a gathering of the most senior military commanders in the Far East could have bitten on such histrionics and bombast. Nor, in retrospect, should anyone imagine that the real genius of Inchon, for all the heroism of those who fought and died there, turned out not to be inspired generalship. It was just plain, crazy, roll-the-dice chance, dumb luck. Even Ridgway used the word. The odds were those that a second lieutenant should have rejected.

Meanwhile, besides nourishing MacArthur's megalomania, Inchon also had other very specific command consequences at crucial levels of military decision making, all of them further contributory to eventual disaster. One, frequently mentioned as a major error of the early war, was a decision to maintain the division of forces instituted specifically as an ad hoc measure for the Inchon Operation. The First Marine Division and Seventh U.S. Army Division, which had served in support, would become the basis of a new formation to be called X Corps, operating separately up the east side of the peninsula from Walker's Eighth Army on the west—comprising the bulk of U.N. forces, including eventually the U.S. Second, Third, Twenty-fourth, and Twenty-fifth infantry divisions—to which it

*Quoted in Halberstam, *The Coldest Winter,* 295.

would be technically subordinate but, for all operational purposes, tactically and strategically, as it quickly turned out, parallel and coequal.

Nearly as catastrophic, however, at least in retrospect, was a personnel decision bound up with this new operational plan: the installation by MacArthur, as commander of X Corps, of his own chief of staff, Major General Edward M. Almond—a man, according to one high-ranking colleague, who could create a crisis on a desert island with nobody else around. A courtier and protégé, known as "Iago" to his junior staff members, albeit not of the old Bataan gang, Almond had been initially detailed as provisional commander of the Inchon forces while still serving as chief of staff. There, living up to his reputation as a sour, imperious, aggressive personality, he had managed instantly to alienate the marine commander, General O. P. Smith, referring to the gray-haired marine brigadier as "son." Meanwhile, by his officious, bullying habit of presuming to speak for MacArthur in matters of operational command, he had already so thoroughly offended Walker, his official senior in rank and command, that the two were basically reduced to shouting angrily at each other on the phone.

Thus had occurred in the space of five months a near-disaster at Pusan, with American and U.N. forces very nearly driven off the peninsula, redeemed by a much-heralded amphibious end run that may or may not have been the miracle it was made out to be, followed by an ill-advised offensive northward, eventuating in a race to the Yalu, in complete defiance of intelligence about Chinese forces massing across the Manchurian border, with completely divided forces headed by commanders refusing to speak to each other. Under the Chinese assault would basically come a reprise of the opening catastrophe of attack and rout, with the horrific bloodshed amid the heat and stench of early summer now to be replayed, this time amid the mud, snow, and ice on the Chinese border. On both sides of the peninsula, whole units thrown into the path of six major, pounding, unstoppable Communist Chinese and NKPA advances would be basically wiped out. On the left, Walker's Eighth Army, with entire field commands vanishing into the new Chinese onslaught southward—including the whole Second Infantry Division—would be forced into basically a repeat of the Pusan Perimeter. On the right would come the ordeal of the Seventh U.S. Infantry division and the First Marines at Chosin. With Walker killed in a freak jeep accident, Ridgway would be brought in as Eighth Army savior. With MacArthur shortly relieved of command, Ridgway would be elevated to USAFA savior. After a combined fighting withdrawal and eventual counteroffensive of six months, mirroring in its own ghastly way the first six months of the war, the hardest sort of grinding combat would eventuate in a restabilization of the battlefront by mid-1951 at the midpoint of the peninsula. Two more years of fighting would follow. In 1953 the two sides would sign an armistice.

In this context the whole story of the war now seems not just once but twice foreordained from start to finish in the image of the two military disasters described above. Indeed, long afterward, a "distinguished Marine veteran" described by Max Hastings, recoiled at the bite of the dreadful phrasing. "Whenever I hear the words 'task force,'" he said, "I shudder." In Korea everyone knew what that meant. In Hastings's words it became "an apology" somewhere on the ground "for a makeshift collection of vehicles and men committed to disaster."*

It is in the nature of historical reflection generally to look at other people's wars and their blunders and idiocies on the grand scale. My purpose here, in this short space, has been to put a concentrated focus on the sheer suffering, hopelessness, and misery of those who fought in Korea from start to finish, to personalize in the name of individual soldiers its nightmare of folly, sacrifice, and abandonment. As various commentators have remarked on the sacrifice of the current volunteer forces fighting on their third, fourth, or fifth tours in the endless war in Iraq, "We do not deserve these people." The same could be said basically from the outset for the twenty thousand Americans who were basically mowed down in the first six months of Korea, and the subsequent fifteen thousand who died fighting until nearly two years later, with the signing of an armistice establishing the line between North and South Korea at the 38th parallel—exactly where the war began.

The second half of the war, taking slightly less than two years, proved a bitter stalemate, a nasty synthesis, if it can be imagined, of 1914–18

*Hastings, *The Korean War*, 156.

trench warfare on the western front, with the hit-and-run tactics of limited, irregular warfare. Although combat never became the war of the ambush or booby trap as in Vietnam, or even what came to be called there the battle of the latest trail bend, it remained mired in the pointless shedding of blood and anger over some disputed terrain feature, elevation, or tactical strong point bearing nasty names like Pork Chop Hill or Bloody Nose Ridge. In a closer prophecy of Indochina, while peace negotiations ground on interminably over details about truce protocols, POW treatment, exchanges, and repatriations, combat wound down to patrols or meeting engagements, with every American on the peninsula fervently seeking not to become the last man killed for an abandoned cause.

Popular attitudes evolved apace. The first year in Korea, give or take a month or so, was predictably front-page news. Headlines blazoned Communist aggression, quick and determined U.N. response, stopgap U.S. military defense, the Pusan Perimeter, the miracle of Inchon, the race to the Yalu, the new Communist Chinese offensives, the MacArthur firing, the arrival of Ridgway, the rumors of peace talks at Panmunjom. Popular memory tended to do a fast-forward on the sequence of disasters and concentrate on how long it took the whole thing to end, somehow suppressing early "oh, not again" photo and newsreel images of catastrophe and last-ditch heroism, and replaying movies eventually made about black-and-white small unit actions in DMZ-style position warfare or MIGs and Sabre Jets in dizzying, Technicolor dogfights. Images of combat faded into the latest news over Panmunjom truce squabbles, POW brainwashing and repatriation controversies, 1952 presidential politics, and the like.

After that the story trailed off. Nobody even seemed to care that Ted Williams left baseball and went back into the air force as a jet pilot or that military historian S. L. A. Marshall did another star turn with *Pork Chop Hill.* Comic books with titles like *G.I. Joe* or *Fighting Marines* made it generic in its cheap thrills, with brave U.S. infantry mowing down gook hordes in quilted uniforms, Russian-looking winter hats with fur earflaps and red stars on the upturned front, with burp guns going budda-budda-budda. Everybody seemed happy just to have it plain over. Meanwhile Panmunjom as a famous name was already being displaced in public consciousness by another faraway exotic trouble spot called Dien Bien Phu.

And then somehow that all got mixed up with a new American war and a movie and TV show called *M*A*S*H,* about an army medical unit where Korea somehow got interfused with Vietnam and everybody made jokes and plotted sex while doing meatball surgery. When I got back from Vietnam, I thought it was the unfunniest thing I had ever seen.

My earliest memories would always be of before the wars, both of them. From the first, I would hear from my family relation or the odd lawyer, doctor, or high-school coach National Guard officer who had been called up for service; but I would mainly remember the agriculture and industrial arts boys from the high school who eventually exchanged their FFA (Future Farmers of America) blue corduroy or black leather motorcycle jackets for their quilted, embroidered Korean "gook shop" specials—not unlike the ones I would see after Vietnam. This was not at all strange, for they would turn out to be versions of the same people I knew in Vietnam: a college kid from Kansas, a guy who dropped out of med school, a center fielder about to be called up by the Mets, a Guatemalan immigrant cooking in New Orleans, a petty criminal who chose enlistment over a jail sentence. Further, I would surmise that—now male and female—these would all look pretty much like the volunteer professional army, marines, navy, and air force, officers, NCOs, and enlisted persons, on their second, third, and fourth tours in Afghanistan or Iraq. In Korea they were not Douglas MacArthur's or Dean Acheson's sons. In Vietnam they were not William Westmoreland's or Robert McNamara's sons. In the current war they are certainly not George Bush's or Donald Rumsfeld's sons and daughters. They get up in the morning to go out and do the job with the latest task force. As in Korea, as in Vietnam, as in the long line of savage wars of American peace—a string of wars so nasty, bloody, dirty that it is hard to say which one is the most awful war—they go out and do the hard, dangerous work of combat. As with Task Force Smith or Task Force Faith, the least we can give our men and women serving us in war is a record of their personal example worthy of the commitment and endurance they reach deeply down and persistently find.

5
How the Holocaust Didn't Become Current Events

In my experience as an average, reasonably well-informed teenager growing up in the United States after World War II—small-town, middle-class, Protestant, the son of college-educated parents in a house with a television, daily papers, and many of the popular news and photojournalistic magazines of the era—I submit that I qualify as a case study in post-1945 American ignorance of what we now call the Holocaust: the Nazi Murder of the Jews. I do recall having a certain awareness that, among Hitler's evil deeds, a uniquely heinous crime had been carried out against the Jewish peoples of Europe and the conquered Eastern lands; yet even as I try to reconstruct such knowledge as I may have had, the attempt to fill in the blanks of both personal and cultural remembrance moves me to a retrospective emotion I can only describe as shame. Even now, more than half a century later, having received a privileged education amongst the nation's elite, having survived combat in my own generation's savage war in Vietnam, having returned to enjoy a university career as a teacher and writer, and, most important, having come to know through marriage and parenthood the intensities of love and familial loyalty, I still feel whatever evolution I may have undergone in consciousness is conjoined with a conviction of utter urgency in my need to dispel a legacy of disregard. After all the decades, as regards this particular monstrous, evil thing—unarguably the central dark deed of my century—I still find, precisely at the meeting point of individual and collective imagination, a haunted, ignominious ignorance, against which I piece together some stopgap simulation of knowledge. Further, it is an ignorance that seems always some dreadful extension of the crime itself.

What did I know? How or when did I come to know it? Through what evolving codes of information and cultural discourse did such an astonishing fact of history take shape for me over the years as a construct of memory? To what degree have such codings themselves now come to shape for me not only the forms of knowledge but also the terms of moral action, to condition not only what I know or think I know about the world, but also how I have ethically conducted myself as a person in history? In sum, what is entailed in the process of cultural remembering whereby an American of my era goes back and tries to come to terms with such a visitation of human monstrosity—described by Niall Ferguson as "the first and only industrialized genocide" and by Simon Sebag Montefiore as "without parallel the most wicked act in history"?*

As I look back to date my personal awareness, I now find it almost impossible, not surprisingly, to dissociate it from the forms of popular culture consciousness prevalent in the late 1940s and early 1950s golden age of what we used to call "current events": the generalized public knowledge of national and world affairs common in a country saturated with the popular media of the times—newspapers, magazines, movies, radio, television—but perhaps most characteristically embodied at the time in the mass-circulation news and information magazines. There just seemed to be piles of them thrown about the reading tables in our house and the houses where we visited—*Time, Life, Look, Collier's, Reader's Digest,* the *Saturday Evening Post.* The public schools mounted yearly promotional campaigns to sell them. They even held current events contests for student readers. I know because I won one, receiving as my prize—naturally—a volume of essays from Time-Life. To this degree, then, I think I may say that as a young person of the postwar generation, I replicated the knowledge of my parents and the parents of my classmates: people belonging not just to what were once called the business and professional classes—educators, civic leaders, ministers, doctors, lawyers,

*Simon Sebag Montefiore, "Century of Rubble," review of *The War of the World: Twentieth Century Conflict and the Descent of the West,* by Niall Ferguson, *New York Times,* Sunday Book Review sec., Nov. 12, 2006.

bankers, corporate managers—but also members of the relatively prosperous middle and working classes—farmers, factory workers, storekeepers, secretaries, and skilled tradesmen.

Such was the condition of being well-informed: possessed at least of a certain illusion of cultural coherence and, thereby in its way, perhaps, as far as reflective understanding was concerned, superior to that pieced together amid the incessant electronic bombardments of the present. To be sure, a lot of questions might have been asked. What were the ideological preconditions of the discourse? Who was managing the flow and thus dictating both the content and the contexts of information? But here such questions pale for me in the face of simple issues of fact, of what we did not know for so long about the greatest single horror of the age. What happened at Auschwitz, Belzec, Chelmno, Maidanek, Sobibor, Treblinka? Not only did we not ask such questions; for a great while we did not even know how to ask them. Where was, in a word, the Holocaust?

Part of the problem may now be said to turn on certain matters of naming. And I do not indulge here in some conceit of unspeakability. Rather I address the matter of an evolving historical language, the search among postwar nations and peoples for an all-comprehending term at once crossing and unifying cultural vocabularies. *Holocaust* is the word generally settled on, a term that now seems familiar. Fifty years ago it was nonexistent in its current role, although appearing incidentally in publications and speeches during the war era. As a general term for the Nazi murders of the Jews, it seems to have been brought into usage by Elie Wiesel and others; there seems to be agreement that it did not become widespread in the United States until the mid to late 1960s. Even now, at certain levels of cultural discussion, linguistic consensus is not complete. In its Greek etymology—*holo* meaning "entirety," and *caust* meaning "consumed in flame"—it seems to have been associated with religious sacrifice; and it thus remains invested for many Jews with a priestly significance, not to mention a dreadful, unintended pun on the idea of burnt offering, completely inappropriate to this unholiest of all acts. In practical usage there also continues to be disagreement over the extent to which the term should be applied to the mass Nazi murders of all peoples, with Jews constituting more than half but among which were also included homosexuals, gypsies, intellectuals, and religious and political dissidents. As to crimes against the Jews, the French have retained the precise *genocide.* On the other side, it is hard not to respond to the grim pull of the German *Endlösung*—Final Solution. Ironically, the term *Holocaust* only arrived in Germany in 1979, after an American television series. In Hebrew the preferred term would now seem to be *Shoah.* But this term is not without its own problems of religious derivation, signifying originally a punishment visited by God on Jews.

Beyond such large questions of cultural vocabulary, there also remain issues of concrete historical and geographical naming grounded in the fact that particular things happened at particular places with particular purposes. The names of the Nazi camps specifically built for exterminations of Jews are those I have given: Auschwitz, Belzec, Chelmno, Maidanek, Sobibor, Treblinka. In those very names this is how they must be distinguished always, in memory and history, even from Buchenwald, Bergen-Belsen, Dachau, Mauthausen, Sachsenhausen, or Theresienstadt. These latter, located in Germany and Austria, with some dating from the pre–World War II era, are places where Jews were murdered in large numbers but where the killing and burning of Jews was not a dedicated mission. The former were constructed by the Nazis in the conquered eastern territories of Poland as extermination centers. But even here the matter gets complicated. Of the former names, Auschwitz is likely now identified as the greatest of killing factories. Ironically, of the Jewish death camps, it is the only one that served as a mass labor camp as well.

For a decade and longer all such installations were referred to in print and common oral reference as "internment" or "concentration" camps—as if the killing chambers, crematoria, and warehouses of personal effects were incidental features of a larger totalitarian apparatus. And so the victims went largely undifferentiated in newspaper, magazine, and movie reports. People who had lost their lives in the Nazi camps became part of the endlessly photographed piles of rotting corpses; people who survived all became part of the silent spectacle of emaciated, ghostlike survivors looking out from behind the wire. For British and American civilians living in domestic witness to the gates of imprisonment bursting open all over the world, the panoply of victims came to include a ghastly mix of their own countrymen and countrywomen. Photos of Dachau and

Buchenwald merged with those of hollow-eyed stick Kriegies from the German POW camps; and to those were added new images of Brits and Americans liberated from their Japanese captors, survivors in some cases of the Bataan Death March or the fall of Singapore. (In testament to the obduracy of racism, even as the details of the Nazi genocide began to be revealed, according to surveys Americans still believed the Japanese to be the more barbaric of the Axis enemies.)

At some point, one imagines, the issue of what to call the dead of all such places just became irrelevant in a world barely able to deal with those still living. Especially in Europe and the East, captured combatants and political prisoners, internees and deportees, slave laborers and surviving members of groups marked for extermination now mixed in with an even more enormous general population of those uprooted from their lives, homes, and families as a result of the Nazi conquests. For this horde of survivors in faceless, homeless, identity-less, rootless, terrified flight, the going euphemism became DP, "Displaced Person." Every American of my age surely has some memory of the term or the recollection of such an individual. A deeply personal one sticks with me. At the local hospital, sometime in 1950, as a six-year-old going in for a tonsillectomy, I remember being carried to the operating room in the arms of a DP orderly. He was, I was told, a Latvian. Did he have a tattoo on his forearm? I didn't know to look. Was he a member of the wartime Communist underground? Was he a Baltic Nazi collaborator finding refuge from the returning Russians? No one at the time knew enough to ask.

Beyond even language at the time was a sheer numbingness of post-1945 human mathematics. The dead of the war were estimated at between 70 million and 100 million. Nations with the largest losses included the Soviet Union, with figures ranging from 16 million to 27 million, and the Chinese, of whom at least 20 million died. European deaths alone between 1939 and 1945 have been thought to exceed 36.5 million—equal to the prewar population of France. Of these, 19 million were noncombatants. It is generally not disputed that the Germans killed between 5 million and 6 million Jews. Across the camp system, however, they also took the lives of as many as 5 million others.

Those who survived became part of another set of numbing statistics. After the war the refugee population of Europe reached fifty million.

Thirteen million Germans alone were relocated from conquered territories back to the devastated homeland. (Jews came back as well—in the case of Germany, twenty-two thousand of a prewar population of six hundred thousand. After 1946 pogroms in Poland, returnees brought the total to sixty-two thousand—a tenth of the prewar number.)

In such a clog of facts and figures it is now possible to imagine any particular Anglo American consciousness of the Jewish Holocaust as adrift in some muddle of postwar inundation. This is an illusion of cultural memory to be resisted. While events were actually taking their course, we now know, particular information was widely available about the Nazi genocide, with the earliest evidence of mass murders, antedating the death camps, reported from the German occupation of Poland and the early campaigns of Russian war by the Jewish-American press, most notably the *Daily Forward.* By December of 1942, within ten months of the Wannsee Conference officially setting up the timetables and mechanics of the Final Solution, details of mass exterminations were being reported. (A prominent activist, Rabbi Steven Wise, president of the American Jewish Congress, supplied administration officials in late 1942 with copies of Nazi planning documents and organized support rallies for European Jews, including a Chicago meeting of mid-1943 at which one of the speakers was Senator Harry S. Truman.) With the camps working at full capacity, war leaders such as Roosevelt, Churchill, and Stalin knew what was going on and where, especially in the death factories of the east. With massive long-range air power at their disposal, Roosevelt and Churchill made specific decisions not to bomb any of the major killing sites or to destroy rail connections. Various justifications have been ventured: a refusal to compound the horror in the camps with more murder and suffering wrought by massed bombing, a strategic decision not to divert military strength from the main mission of defeating the Germans and thereby ending the terror as quickly as possible. Apace, American Jews, although much better informed than their non-Jewish countrymen on the Nazi exterminations, remained largely silent, hesitant to blazon the victim status of their European counterparts for fear of stirring the resentment of other Americans at the idea that their sons and daughters were dying to save the Jews.

As American armies rolled across western Europe, and Russians came from the east, the hideous "secret"—or so it was called at the time—of the Nazi concentration camps was revealed to the world. On the Anglo American side, that was only half true; again, the problem was a matter of both physical and moral geography. To be sure, in terms of the sites overrun by the western Allies, people came face to face overnight with graphic revelations about the Nazi concentration camps generally as reported in print, photographic, and newsreel media. Top American commanders including Eisenhower, Bradley, and Patton were shown amid the stench and rot of a place called Ohrdruf. (Patton was described as turning away from the photo grouping to vomit. Eisenhower was recorded as turning to a GI in attendance and asking, "Still having trouble hating them?"*) Subsequent publicity, even more horrific in its particulars, attended the American entry into Buchenwald and the British liberation of Bergen-Belsen.

The problem remained, as to identifying and assigning the peculiar evil of the Holocaust, that these were the western European camps, where, in fact, the murder of the Jews had been part of the extermination of various other populations of social and political undesirables—political and religious dissidents, intellectuals, homosexuals, gypsies; and however shocking the savageries revealed, even they could not be taken to represent the specialized, particular horror of the attempt to annihilate the Jewish people.

Vernichtung is the German word for "annihilation." This was the special province and discrete mission of the eastern camps. Many of these, the dedicated Nazi death factories for the Jews, had already been overrun by allied Russian armies advancing relentlessly from the east. The Russians reported their versions of such discoveries, but they also had no scruples about deflecting the truth about the particular deadly work of killing the Jews into accounts serving their own more immediate political purposes. Clearly timed to correlate with Anglo American publicity concerning the death camps, a major *Pravda* story appeared in May 1945, for instance, centering on Auschwitz—in fact, overrun by Russian troops five months earlier—as a center of Nazi war crimes. But the chief victims were alleged to have been Russian POWs, with only additional mention

*Quoted in Carlo D'Este, *Eisenhower: A Soldier's Life* (New York: Holt, 2002), 686.

of European peoples. Jews were never referred to. American journalism uncritically echoed such claims. "Reds Say Nazis Slew Four Million in Polish Camp," read a VE-Day headline in the *New York Herald Tribune.* In the accompanying story, almost impossibly, the word *Jew* does not appear. A competing story in the *New York Times* likewise forwent any focus on the Jews and went for a mournful listing of victims by nationality: "citizens of the Soviet Union, Poland, France, Belgium, Holland, Czechoslovakia, Yugoslavia, Hungary, Italy, and Greece."

Such was the extent, save for a few other rudimentary reports and photos that failed to achieve much distribution, of the publicity from the Russians, who had overrun the camps that had been the centers of Jewish extermination. Why? Partially, they wished to downplay the record of their own westward advance, constituting one of history's great campaigns of rape, plunder, torture, and murder, however justified in their own eyes. After all, they had lost 4 million soldiers—many of them POWs starved to death or dying from wounds and disease in captivity during the waves of Nazi invasion—and perhaps as many as 20 million more civilians. These were now debts of savage conquest to be repaid with interest.

Beyond lay their own wartime treatment of POWs and political prisoners—including, as Stalin laid his designs for a postwar Soviet empire, the murders of officers, teachers, intellectuals, writers, members of the professional classes. And beyond that lay the world's memory of Stalinist prewar genocidal terrors perpetrated on Russian people: the mass exterminations of peasants in the early 1930s famines caused by collectivization, with deaths estimated at 7 million; the great political terror later in the decade, claiming 4.5 million. The total of the Russian purges, forced hungers, removals, expropriations, and executions will never be known. It is commonly reckoned at between 11 million and 13 million, roughly the numbers killed in the Nazi camps. It is further set in relief by the existence of the Russian camp system. Even as the war ended, with dissidents and POWs transferred back to Russian hands, their own swelling Gulag teemed to the breaking point, estimated as housing in any given year between 1933 and 1960 between 10 million and 12 million souls.

Then and later, the silence that fell over American mass culture regarding the Holocaust may thus be attributed in part to cold war unavailability of information from the East. As to charges of totalitarian torture and murder, issues also became confused by reports of the new Red terror, which descended over much of Europe behind the Iron Curtain, and the stunning rapidity with which stories and images of Nazi "liquidations" were replaced by new revelations about their Soviet and Communist-bloc successors. American popular culture of the late 1940s and early 1950s was inundated with lore concerning communist purges, show trials, executions, internments, eliminations, secret consignments to the swelling Gulag of prison and torture camps. (Ironically, only later would it be revealed that after the war Stalin himself finally felt free to give his own deeply seated, racial anti-Semitism something like free genocidal reign. An enormous proportion of ideological enemies eliminated in the late 1940s and early 1950s purges turn out to have been Jewish in birth or cultural origin.)

Meanwhile, even with the former Reich still under four-power occupation, quickly countervailing images were set into place of a de-Nazified, democracy-loving, "free" Germany partnered with the postwar nations of the anticommunist West. The purgative drama of the Nuremberg Trials, with their grand but strategically unspecified theme of "crimes against humanity," was followed by a series of flashpoint "crises"—the 1948 Russian Blockade, the 1953 East German Workers' Riots, the 1961 erection of the Berlin Wall—in which Germany served as a new bulwark of cold war resistance to communist tyranny. The showpiece *Bundesrepublik* became proof of how thoroughly the image of a people could be cleansed of a criminal era just past.

As the West slid into a generalized cold war torpor, with every major European government struggling to deal with critical postwar shortages and social exigencies, Americans embraced comfort, prosperity, and a judicious reisolation from the troubles of former allies and the crimes of former enemies. Outside, just too many new fears and visions of geopolitical evil loomed for anyone to remember much about old ones. Specters of Communist World Domination were everywhere. Skilled agents—*Masters of Deceit* they were called in a best-selling 1958 book allegedly authored by the FBI director J. Edgar Hoover—threatened to infiltrate government and social institutions. Senator Joseph McCarthy made secret lists of "known" Communists and hectored endless victims in congressional hearings. Above hovered the bomb. Citizens practiced civil defense drills and invented *On the Beach* scenarios of nuclear doomsday.

In their domestic lives they embraced the much preferable dominion of what Herbert Marcuse—himself a refugee German Marxist Jew—called "the happy consciousness": "the belief that society delivers the goods."* Nurtured by an all-providing consumer culture, it also expressed itself vividly in popular media ranging from Broadway and musical recording to movies and TV—frequently, as I have noted, involving the work of Jewish artists, actors, and producers. The world so imaged and expressed was one of beneficent homogeneity. For many Americans the national life was imagined as a Rodgers and Hammerstein musical by way of a TV family sitcom, wherein all parents look like Ward and June Cleaver, and all kids look like Bud and Betty Anderson.

Explicit postwar popular-culture images and representations of the Nazi terror in literature and the arts confined themselves initially to movie Germans in uniform. Only in 1952 did a work finally appear concentrating on the Germans and the Jews, the first American edition of the narrative of Anne Frank, published under the title *The Diary of a Young Girl;* and even then the Nazi genocide seemed to take a thematic backseat to other concerns. To be sure, the heroine was identified as a hunted, persecuted wartime Jew, part of a family being protected by good Dutch Christians so that they would not be swept up by the German occupation and consigned to the camps. This is a central reality. At the same time, the thrust of the text—as signaled in an introduction by no less than Eleanor Roosevelt—seemed to lie in the direction of spiritual uplift. The qualities Americans were encouraged to admire in Anne Frank—even as she faced death under the Nazis—were the inspirational virtues of bravery, love, even undying hope. The most quoted line of the book goes thus: "Despite everything, I still believe that people are good at heart."

The book, an enormous best seller, was superseded by an award-winning 1955 Broadway play, starring Susan Strasberg. In turn, it was translated into a much-praised 1959 film, featuring Millie Perkins in her screen debut, with a supporting cast of Dean Stockwell, Shelley Winters,

*Herbert Marcuse, *One-Dimensional Man* (Boston: Beacon, 1964), 84.

Ed Wynn, and Joseph Schildkraut, the last reprising his stage role as Anne Frank's father, Otto.

In print, stage, and film versions, *The Diary* remained a postwar classic and a staple of American education. Yet as a holocaust text its identity continued to be subsumed under more palatable, heartwarming, positive, and audience-friendly American accentuations. Even a grim mid-1950s *Life* magazine addendum to the story, graphically and explicitly detailing Anne's removal to Auschwitz, and then to Theresienstadt, where she died of typhus, proved insufficient to deflect the original text's ongoing reputation as an inspirational classic, a testament of family loyalty, awakening love, and a young person's capacity for hope and belief.

From the standpoint of what might be called the big picture, a suggestively comparable popular-culture production of the era, the Stanley Kramer movie *Judgment at Nuremberg,* similarly backgrounds the Nazi genocide into more abstract issues of German guilt, punctuating its drama with affirmative testimonies of anti-Hitler resistance. Derived from the 1947 showpiece trials of major Nazi figures, the film takes as its specific pretext the prosecution of German civilian judges implicated in the state apparatus of legal terror and judicial murder. From the stand are heard case histories—Judy Garland as a victim of the Nuremberg laws concerning Aryan-Jewish intermarriage; Montgomery Clift as a survivor of Nazi sterilization and euthanasia campaigns to eliminate the mentally unfit. A part of the prosecution case involves the viewing of film from the camps. But once again, with Burt Lancaster as an American prosecutor played off against Maximilian Schell as an anguished German defendant—the script has the general effect of assimilating the specific experience of the Jews as objects of state violence into their generic reclassification among myriad other classes of victims.

Meanwhile, positive history for post-Holocaust Judaism was being marked for American Jews and gentiles alike through celebrations attending the 1948 founding of the new state of Israel. In popular culture the locus classicus for this would be Leon Uris's novel *Exodus*—a romantic blockbuster on a scale not seen since *Gone with the Wind.* And of course even bigger indeed would be the ensuing wide-screen Technicolor movie, the kind of docu-cameo epic usually reserved for such biblical sagas as *The Robe, The Ten Commandments,* or *Ben-Hur*—in this case with the action accompanied by the lush, soaring strains of popular piano duo Ferrante and Teicher.

On the domestic scene, meanwhile, cold war–related political developments fostered new strains of anxiety between gentiles and Jews. Distinctly troubling to American Jews was the notoriety of atomic spies Julius and Ethel Rosenberg, along with accomplices Morton Sobell, Harry Gold, and David Greenglass. As elsewhere in the world—always a winning combination for anti-Semites—Judaism found itself linked by deadly association with communist conspiracy. Nor, during the Army-McCarthy Hearings, did even the downfall of the nation's most virulent Red-baiter completely eclipse the shady prominence of such Jewish figures in the case as chief counsel Roy Cohn and David Schine, a favored army PFC (private first class) for whom he had sought preferential treatment.

On the Nazis and their crimes, a bizarre index of late 1950s and early 1960s popular-culture sanitizations was Rodgers and Hammerstein's *The Sound of Music.* A musical by America's most prominent Broadway team, both of them deeply assimilated American Jews, it focuses on the love between a young Austrian governess and a widowed former Austro-Hungarian navy captain, with his horde of intractable children, around the time of the Anschluss, Hitler's 1936 political and military annexation of the country. The Austrians are pious Catholics and impassioned patriots, given to dirndls, lederhosen, alpine scenery, picture-book cathedrals, and châteaus. (The song "Edelweiss," composed for the show and ardently sung by the father just before he leads his family over the mountains into neutral Switzerland, was at the time assumed to be the traditional Austrian anthem.) The Nazis are mainly officious, misguided, and quite incompetent as sleuths and trackers. One does not have to look far for the mid-1950s ideological matrix. Among the earliest Axis countries de-Nazified, Austria, although initially under four-power occupation, quickly found promotion as a progressive outpost of Western democracy surrounded by postwar Iron Curtain totalitarianisms. A poster child for the Marshall Plan, it became plucky Austria, bulwark against the Russians in Eastern Europe. Vienna, as if showing the way to Berlin, became with much celebration the 1956 capital of a free Austria; and within months the Hungarian Revolution gave it new luster as a refuge for those fleeing Communist tyranny across the border. Thus easily forgotten was how twenty years earlier a majority of Austrians openly welcomed the German annexation. Thus erased from history were the 1936 photographs revealing how quickly in Vienna, great, charming, cosmopolitan Vienna, they had Jews on their hands and knees scrubbing sidewalks and worse.

Almost as disturbing, on the stage and in movies, playing counterpoint to myths of inclusion and assimilation, were charming fables of ethnicity, often a combination of immigrant romance and shtetl nostalgia. Ranging from historical recreations such as *Fiddler on the Roof* or *Yentl* to stagy celebrations of immigrant urban culture such as *Funny Girl* and *Hello Dolly,* they were joined as late as the 1990s by cartoon epics of immigrant mice such as *An American Tail* and its sequel, *An American Tail: Fievel Goes West.*

Only at length did unavoidably newsworthy historical events compel the beginning of an attempt in the West to distinguish the Nazi murder of the Jews from the other mass killings of the war or the century. Here things made their definitive turn, it is almost universally agreed, in 1961. The occasion was the trial in Jerusalem of the Nazi war criminal Adolf Eichmann, recently captured but long identified as a major engineer of the Final Solution. Now, for the first time, in an Israeli courtroom, a trial was actually conducted about Nazi crimes committed while pursuing the industrial genocide of an entire people; at the same time, it became a reminder to viewers and readers around the world that this dreadful thing had been done by human beings, even so harmless looking a retired bureaucrat as the accusee in the dock. In finding him, bringing him to justice, and eventually executing him, the Jewish state had published his evil to the world and somehow perhaps exorcised that evil from the world, putting it before the bar of international justice and the judgment of historical memory. To be sure, even here postwar consciousness attempted to gain purchase against the particular horror, most notably through Hannah Arendt's introduction of the concept of the banality of evil, the suggestion that such Nazi operatives were average men, no better or no worse than most people, simply yielding their beliefs and wills to monstrous deeds under the pressure of ideology and political and cultural circumstances. This remained largely a matter of dispute among critical intellectuals. At bottom, it is hard not to agree that once and for all the world saw what Winston Churchill so vividly described in a letter to Anthony Eden: "There is no doubt that this is probably the greatest and most horrible crime ever committed in the whole history of the world," he wrote, "and it has been done by scientific machinery by nominally civilised men in the name of a great State and one of the leading races of Europe."*

The late 1960s in America saw the production of the landmark PBS documentary series *The Holocaust.* It was followed a decade later by the German-produced *Shoah,* to date still the most arresting composite personal history representation. Memoirs began to be available in translation such as Elie Wiesel's *Night,* Primo Levi's *Survival in Auschwitz,* and Jerzy Kosinski's *The Painted Bird.*

What accounted for the upsurge of Holocaust consciousness during this period? The answer, platitude notwithstanding, is that the times demanded it. Two major political developments proved especially important: the enlistment of many mainstream Americans for the first time in the struggle for civil rights, with its campaigns for political equality and social justice for the descendants of African American slaves; and the rise of the anti–Vietnam War movement, again bringing into the resistance increasing numbers of everyday citizens who eventually came to see a war of indiscriminate killing in Asia as reminiscent of the Nazi genocide. To these should be added a new political awareness of the nation's dark history regarding the removals and exterminations of native peoples. With such aptly titled texts as Dee Brown's *Bury My Heart at Wounded Knee* and Vine de Loria's *Custer Died for Your Sins,* the nation increasingly began to come to terms with its New World legacy of ethnic cleansing and elimination.

What might be called the current phase in American popular-culture representations of the Holocaust may be said to begin, for good or ill according to the observer, with William Styron's acclaimed novel *Sophie's Choice* and the Academy Award–winning film featuring Meryl Streep in the title role. To be sure, the horror of the Nazi genocide is present, with

*Quoted in Winston Churchill, *The Second World War,* vol. 6 (New York: Mariner, 1986), 693.

the title in fact a reference to the decision required of the heroine by an SS doctor on the station platform at Auschwitz as to which of her two children she will select to be preserved from the flames. Simultaneously, however, the conceit of Auschwitz is appropriated to more general novelistic and cinematic purposes. With a first-person southern narrator, much of the early part of the novel attempts to connect the Nazi camps with the inhumanities of American chattel slavery. At the same time, the concept of a specific crime committed against the Jews becomes broadened into various metaphysical ironies. Sophie, it turns out, is a Polish Catholic, with a father and husband who have been Nazi intellectual sympathizers. The manic Nathan, her doomed partner in love and eventually suicide, is an angry American Jew filled with a kind of self-hatred at his own survival and a loathing of his spoiled contemporaries—"yids," "kikes," "momsers," he screams at them.

The most recent extension of such popular Holocaust consciousness, of course, is yet another movie: Steven Spielberg's *Schindler's List,* adapted from a novel by Thomas Keneally and showing how the actions of a single industrialist in Nazi-occupied Poland saved hundreds of Jews from being killed at Auschwitz. Yet starting with a morally and intellectually compromised titular protagonist, here, too, everything about the project seems to carry its own baggage of popular adulteration. The novel is by an Australian, a popular hand at historical fiction, with the germ of the story, we are told in the preface, inspired by a visit to a Beverly Hills custom luggage shop owned by a Holocaust survivor. The film, in black-and-white, carries the Spielberg signature: a characteristic mix of graphic terror and wrenching sentimentality. A stunning performance is turned in by the British actor Liam Neeson in the title role, with support from Ben Kingsley and Ralph Fiennes. Music is by John Williams. At the end come touching interview-vignettes with Schindler survivors. Their descendants, we are told, outnumber by half the four thousand Jews still living in Poland.

Winner of the 1993 Oscar for best picture, in terms of sheer influence on Holocaust awareness, *Schindler's List* is indisputably a remarkable film by any cultural standard. Specific objections were raised at the time that the titular hero, somehow awakened to the call of moral duty, remains a collaborationist German gentile. As to the film's generalized moral tenor, as noted by Peter Novick, there was the corresponding suggestion that Spielberg had managed "to make a feel-good entertainment about the ultimate feel-bad experience of the twentieth century."* Such a backlash was probably inevitable given the fulsome self-congratulation only the American entertainment industry is capable of when it passes out awards to itself. "I'm a better person as a result of seeing *Schindler's List*," claimed Oprah Winfrey, for one. What she said was probably true for most Americans. In *Schindler's List*, book or movie, one finds a text of redemption grounded in horror and grief.

A final stage of awareness has surely been evinced in what might be called the rise of Holocaust museology, with major remembrance and education centers in America alone numbering around thirty and including such metropolitan sites as Dallas, Houston, Los Angeles, Miami, New York, San Francisco, St. Louis, and Washington, D.C. The attempts at recreation are intense, frequently combining graphic display with interactive visitor participation. By no surprise the flourishing of these institutions has been coincident with similar living history civil rights museums and museums of the American Indian, which in both cases they are now roughly equal in number.

The great living, breathing, flesh-and-blood memorial to the Holocaust in American cultural and political memory, however, will always remain the State of Israel. To put it simply, in the larger domain of post-1945 American foreign policy and political, military, and diplomatic commitment, the survival of the Middle East nation-state of Israel has remained sacrosanct. Foes of such a policy have cited an Israel lobby; defenders invoke the long-held commitments of a Middle East realpolitik. The fact is that for Americans, generally, the basis of such support remains simple, formed of an unstated but unwavering commitment of the preeminent victor among all World War II nations to say to the world, with the Jews of the world, "Never again."

Accordingly, in every military conflict involving Israel as a modern nation-state, beginning with the 1948 Independence War against Arab enemies and extending through the 1956 Suez Campaign, the 1967 Six-

*J. Hoberman, *The Magic Hour: Film at Fin de Siècle* (Philadelphia: Temple University Press, 2003), 133; repr. from "Schindler's Oskar," *Village Voice*, Dec. 21, 1993.

Day War, and the 1973 Yom Kippur War, there has been a bottom-line position of American popular support. No matter that official U.S. interests frequently lay elsewhere—from an Eisenhower administration blindsided and furious at secret Anglo French and Israeli collusion in the 1956 strikes against Egypt to later ones harshly critical of the occupation and administration of conquered territories including the West Bank and Gaza. All these have seemed, for most Americans with a memory of World War II, justified wars of Israeli survival, as have been military and political responses to Palestinian intifadas, with their countless suicide bombings, rocket attacks, and murderous incursions into border settlements. Thus was American response largely muted even regarding a recent punitive invasion of Lebanon to defang Hezbollah armies, resulting in massive Lebanese civilian casualties and destruction of homes and properties, as well as domestic infrastructure of roads and bridges.

Zionism. At various points this term has been used in America to describe the mission of various political, financial, and cultural interest groups working in support of Israel in particular and Jewish causes worldwide. Today it can as easily be applied to new Israel lobbies formed and financed by big-money American evangelicals who take time out from faith healing and media fund collection to direct the attention of believers to the importance of a reascendant Jewish nation in the fulfillment of end-times prophecies. The point remains that most Americans still practice a kind of cultural Zionism that will always, as long as there is any memory of World War II, be a cultural inheritance of the post-1945 World Order. Such a vision will always honor the Israel of David Ben-Gurion, Moshe Dayan, Golda Meier, Abba Egan—and it will dictate that none but the most vicious ideological anti-Semite can stand by while citizens of a Jewish nation are threatened.

This will continue to be the rule even as former cultural cosponsors among the Western community of nations drop away: the French, through revelations about a collaborationist past, combined with independent policy interests related to Islamic peoples in former territories and elsewhere, as well as heavy numbers of Muslims living within the national borders; the Dutch, having done their own chipping away at the resistance myth, along with corresponding problems with immigration; Italy, coming to terms with its own complicity in German roundups and murders and indictments of the World War II–era papacy. Likewise, even the deeply implicated Germans and the Austrians: they have built their Holocaust memorials; they have made their official pronouncements of national guilt and remorse; they have even created thought-crime categories for Holocaust denial. The fact is that they have now just found it necessary to attend to more pressing current problems. Alone, the Americans and the British now seem to be left with this legacy of World War II. Why? They are the two great Allied peoples that might have done something about the Nazi genocide. The only difference between them now is power. As Americans, we shoulder the responsibilities of geopolitical supremacy along with the self-assumed burden of Holocaust remembrance in all its aspects. We did not do more then. We were slow in the gaining of knowledge and the formation of popular memory. We will do anything now. This is the price, we tell ourselves, the West must pay—the victors of World War II still left standing. We will pay the price—in hate, in oil, in money, in blood—for what the Nazis and their collaborators did to the Jews.

For the World War II generation of Americans, and for their sons and daughters, who have grown up for the most part in periods of postwar peace and prosperity, this will always remain the great historical and cultural tie-in with the current war against terror. Many of our younger countrymen may be genuinely puzzled by the passion of current Islamic enemies whose hatred for us seems unfathomably murderous and fanatical. An earlier generation knows. It is our support of Israel. At the same time, the depths and the origins of such a commitment are exactly what our Islamic enemies fail to understand. Our motivation as a historical culture, that is, goes back to a vision of the Islamic world versus Israel, for whom their hatred is unfathomably murderous, hateful, fanatic, and genocidal. Whatever their names—Sunni or Shia; Taliban or al Qaida; Hezbollah or Islamic Jihad—militant Islam, even amid Muslims in nations and cultures worldwide with long traditions of cultural pluralism, carries for the West in general and Americans in particular the stigma of fanatic Jew hating and Jew killing.

Thus one details the long strange process whereby the Holocaust became current events in America and remains so, albeit perhaps in ways American memory and American history could not have anticipated.

Thus also one is impelled to remember the degree to which the past is always constituted by its relation to an ever-evolving succession of present ideological concerns expressing themselves through new syntheses of history and memory. What did we know, and when did we know it? Once we knew something or thought we knew something, what did we do about it or not do about it? What should we be thinking and doing now? These are deeply moral, human questions. For Americans they continue to come, as they have always come, at the intersection of individual moral memory and collective cultural myth. They are now more than ever, in the fullest sense of the term, global. But they still begin, for each of us, at home. As a descendant of Quakers on one side and Mennonites on the other who grew up a Scots Presbyterian, was I (am I) a cultural anti-Semite? To what degree do I remain a creation of the popular media of the late 1940s and early 1950s—the world of Time-Life, Technicolor movies, and TV? Whose problem was it that by the time I finished college—and only then, by remotest chance getting matched up through a last-minute housing match with a junior-year roommate—I had gotten to know one Jew in my entire life? In Vietnam, as an armored cavalry platoon leader, I fought off enemy attacks with maximum firepower, frequently calling massive artillery and air strikes. In trying to reconcile the traditional combat imperatives of mission and men, was I an accomplice in Vietnam to genocide? I know I wasn't an Eichmann—or a Calley. I certainly did use the word *gook* a lot. To what degree has my cultural awareness been shaped by its flow through a career at a university once notorious for its segregationist past, where my faculty colleagues have frequently been Jews? We are, after all, composites of personal and cultural memory.

So here I find myself, in my sixties, at most a walking current-events prize, still trying to find out the truth of things. I may have gotten the highest score. But I knew less than nothing.

How much less? This is perhaps measured best by a recitation of news items discovered at length concerning events taking place on the day of my birth, October 29, 1944, in Gettysburg, Pennsylvania. Simultaneously, I now find, at the far edge of eastern Europe, a final transport of fifteen hundred Jews were being gassed and cremated at Auschwitz, the vast Nazi death camp near the town of Oswiecim, in occupied Poland. Having been entrained the day before from a satellite facility, Theresienstadt, they were the last of between 2.1 and 2.5 million persons to be killed and burned at the Auschwitz complex. It is recorded that on the day after these concluding genocidal acts, German efforts to dismantle the camp and destroy the crematoria began. The reason? Believe it or not, they seriously seemed to think they might attempt to hide their crimes before the eastern territories could be overrun by the Russians.

Even in its malignant folly, here was a truly diabolical notion: the idea that destroying the physical archaeology of evil would make a difference in the world as long as language and memory survive. Yet what is to distinguish it from a recent conference in Tehran, officially sponsored by the Iranian government, promoting Holocaust denial as a plausible topic for serious intellectual discourse and concluding with the Iranian president's heralding of the day when Israel will be wiped off the map? For this reason alone the Holocaust should remain current events for every American, not to mention every person in the world who understands that memory and history must always be defended from those who think they have the power to erase them.

6
The War of the Generals for the Presidency

My point in this chapter about post-1945 American presidential politics is simple: Douglas MacArthur, beyond any high-ranking military leader in U.S. history before or since, hungered after the U.S. presidency in a way that outstripped mere ambition; he simply thought it was his personal destiny. Fortunately, Dwight Eisenhower—albeit himself hardly a person without ambition—became president, reaffirming in the post–World War II nation and world a legacy of American belief in government by civilian constitutional leadership and authority. This is also what might be called the moral of the story. The story itself is much more complicated.

In the early 1930s, Franklin D. Roosevelt, while still the Democratic nominee for president, identified General Douglas MacArthur—at the time the glamorous, highly decorated, boy-wonder U.S. Army chief of staff—along with the Louisiana populist demagogue Huey Long, as the two most dangerous men in America. The Kingfish, of course, would be assassinated before the decade was out. Roosevelt, after spending most of World War II trying to keep his Pacific prima donna generalissimo under some semblance of presidential control, was himself gone by 1945. In the postwar era, only MacArthur was left standing—and by then, I would further propose, had come into sole qualification for the menacing epithet bestowed on him by the president years earlier. *American Caesar:* this is how William Manchester aptly chose to entitle his definitive biography of MacArthur. And there is every reason to think that the titular hero spent much of a legendary life nurturing such a vision of culminating destiny. MacArthur truly thought himself the incarnation—and in fact had made a career throughout the 1930s, 1940s, and early 1950s of promoting himself as such—of the figure known to history as the man on horseback. As Washington had been the revolutionary Cincinnatus and Jackson the backwoods Napoleon at his country's bidding, MacArthur, in the role of self-anointed first consul, would have at any number of points ridden back in from the frontiers of the empire to rescue the Republic. He was, to his own thinking at least, truly the figure of Caesar or Charlemagne or Napoleon reborn as the ultimate, self-reliant, democratic great captain, in Herman Melville's phrasing, "a mighty pageant creature formed for noble tragedies." His fall would be spectacular in its might and rapidity; and at the heart of it would indeed be what the Greeks called hubris, overweening pride. At the end he was godlike and delusional in the same measure, the creation of his own fine megalomania.

As MacArthur's style was born of legend, so was his sense of familial destiny. To be specific, this most legendary of all American soldiers began life as the legendary son of a legendary father, a Union general who had begun his own career by winning the Congressional Medal of Honor, at age nineteen, at the battle of Missionary Ridge during the American Civil War. The son's meteoric rise began with a stellar cadet career at West Point, heroic exploits in the Philippines and Mexico, and an almost insanely brave performance in World War I, resulting in seven Silver Stars, the Distinguished Service Cross, and nomination for the Congressional Medal of Honor (out of which he always felt he had been swindled by Pershing), meanwhile earning him promotion to general and appointment as the youngest division commander in the AEF (American Expeditionary Force). Returning home, he became superintendent of West Point, where he conducted a thoroughgoing educational reform, and then U.S. Army chief of staff. There, he undoubtedly helped save the U.S. military between the wars from total disintegration. In a famous exchange with his commander in chief over budget cuts, MacArthur expressed his fervent hope that the dying curse on the lips of an American boy in the next war would not be "MacArthur, but Roosevelt." Rebuked by a furious Roosevelt for his insubordinate language, MacArthur vomited afterward on the White House steps. He also got his defense appropriation.

With no worlds left to conquer, so to speak, by the mid-1930s, MacArthur eventually resigned to become an adviser to the armed forces of the Philippine Islands. In turn, a second career phase, even more heroic, would open, wherein for a quarter of a century MacArthur would be exclusively associated with the Pacific and Asia. A doomed defense of the Philippines would end in a daring last-minute evacuation, along with his family and key staff members, by PT boat and B-17 bomber to Australia—a journey of escape for which, ironically, MacArthur would be awarded the Medal of Honor he had so long felt to be his due—and the beginning of the long way back to Allied victory, with MacArthur acclaimed for a grand Southwest Pacific strategy of bypassing fortified positions, using the combined strengths of army air and ground forces, and coordinating major campaigns with those of the navy and marines. In token of his strategic genius he would preside over the 1945 Japanese surrender ceremony aboard the USS *Missouri* in Tokyo Bay. That same year he would assume the imperial role of effectively overseeing the postwar reconstruction and democratization of Japan. With the surprise attack by North Korean forces across the 38th parallel in 1950 and the commitment to the defense of South Korea of a largely American United Nations military force under his command, he then returned to active military leadership, executing a breakout from the besieged Pusan Perimeter coupled with a brilliant amphibious maneuver at Inchon Landings, not only pushing the North Korean invaders back across the 38th parallel but pursuing them all the way to the border with Red China. This time his genius turned hollow, however. A counterattack by hundreds of thousands of Chinese troops, streaming across the Yalu River, pushed U.N. forces back to their original starting points and beyond. Another two years of the worst sort of grinding combat would be required in order to gain a negotiated peace, with the country divided precisely as had been determined in 1945. He had been made a fool of by the enemy and his own staff, who fed him only the intelligence and order-of-battle information he wanted to hear. In his anger and humiliation MacArthur turned to geopolitical bravado and threat, including warnings to the Communist Chinese of massive bombing and possible invasion, and unilateral discussions with the Chiang Kai-shek regime about the addition of Nationalist Chinese forces to the fight. Within weeks he was dismissed from command for insubordination, specifically for the refusal to obey the constitutional authority of the civilian commander in chief. Relieved, and forced to resign from the army, he was brought home. As he no doubt hopefully envisioned, the firing became a cause célèbre. He was greeted with ticker-tape parades and an unheard of invitation to make a dramatic speech before the combined houses of Congress, with the famous conclusion of histrionic refrain, "old soldiers never die; they just fade away." But this last flurry of political drama was brief and followed by a gradual fading into obscurity. The playacting had eventuated one more time into destiny, albeit in a way one imagines MacArthur himself may have been hoping against to the end. As the self-styled indispensable man, he had proven quite more easily dispensable than he or his worshippers could have possibly imagined. A quasi sinecure was his as board chairman of Remington Rand, as well as a suite at the Waldorf Astoria, to which politicians would repair for the odd campaign visit or policy consultation but mostly for the sake of the requisite photo. But mainly he was history.

Paralleling the quick rise and long fall of Douglas MacArthur, and mirroring it in many ways, was the steady ascendancy of Dwight Eisenhower. "Ike," everyone called him, from beginning to end of a career a long time in the making and crowned with everlasting military honor and affectionate political memory. In contrast to the great captain, convinced of the infallibility of his leadership and charismatic genius for authority, Eisenhower was what we would now call the ultimate team player in American military and political history. He was a company man from start to finish, a "consensus builder" if there ever was one. The scion of German Brethren who had migrated to Kansas, he grew up among four brothers. For the chance at a free education he basically worked his way into West Point, where his graduation biography suggests that his main interest, even after he had wrecked a knee, remained varsity football, with perhaps some time out for convivial drink hoisting. Disappointed that he missed out on a combat assignment in World War I, he embraced his stateside duties and gained a reputation, as commandant of a new tank-training installation at Camp Colt, outside Gettysburg, Pennsylvania, for his skills in operations and troop training. Along with George Patton—a slightly older, strutting, self-dramatizing brass hat in the MacArthur mold, renowned for both his erratic genius and his fire-breathing histrionics, who would become Eisenhower's World War II subordinate—Eisenhower became an early advocate of the new armored force. Meanwhile, between the wars, he patiently served, waited out the army system, husbanded his own burning ambition, and learned to accommodate it within the politics of the professional military. Along the way he pursued a series of protégé relationships, first during a tour in Panama with a visionary general named Fox Conner and then for a longer period—while stuck in decades of middling rank—with MacArthur, during the latter's chief of staff period and again in the Philippines, where pictures of him may be seen attending the great man during the Bonus March and at Manila palace receptions. Meanwhile, he acquired the seriousness and good sense to finish at the top of his class at the U.S. Army Command and Staff College at Fort Leavenworth and, as a result, receive concomitant recognition from the new mentor and career sponsor who would be the making of him, General George C. Marshall. Even this took a while. Standing out as one of the key figures of operational intelligence and leadership in the celebrated Louisiana maneuvers of 1940, and, with a new world war impending, assigned to line infantry command with the Third Infantry division, he found himself suddenly shifted to staff assignment in Washington under Marshall, where he too had a celebrated, and in this case career-altering, exchange. Although major combat assignment was on the horizon for many officers, Marshall was alleged to have said pointedly that, as an indispensable planning assistant, Eisenhower should not expect to keep up with his fellows likely to reach high general officer rank in field command. Fuming, Eisenhower attempted to leave the room but turned back at the last moment. "General, I'm interested in what you say," he told Marshall angrily but respectfully, "but I want you to know I don't give a damn about your promotion plans as far as I'm concerned! I came into this office from the field and I am trying to do my duty. If that locks me to a desk for the rest of the war . . . so be it!"* In response, Marshall cracked a rare smile; he somehow knew he had *his* indispensable man for what would become the ETO—the European theater of operations. As things turned out, Eisenhower found himself vaulted from a lieutenant colonel in 1939 to a lieutenant

*Quoted in Geoffrey Perrett, *Eisenhower* (New York: Random House, 1999), 150.

general in the 1942 North African invasion, where he and his American troops underwent their apprenticeship in facing the Germans. Two years later, with Operation Overlord in Normandy, he commanded the greatest military invasion force in the history of the world as Allied supreme commander. At the end of the war he was rightfully recognized as one of the grand architects of Allied victory in Europe, not least because of his gifts for managing the Allied coalition—at the top ranging from a set of difficult British personalities, Churchill, Brooke, Montgomery; and on the French side, Charles de Gaulle; not to mention his own meddlesome commander in chief, Franklin Roosevelt. Through interservice relations he further melded naval and air staffs, British and American—including such formidable figures as King, Cunningham, Ramsey, Arnold, Spaatz, Tedder, and Leigh-Malory—and kept in line an equally diverse lineup of operational U.S. Army subordinates such as Bradley, Clark, Patton, Hodges, and Simpson. No less than Winston Churchill himself recognized the manner in which Eisenhower had done all this while leading the western Allies to victory over Germany: "he supervised everything with a vigilant eye, and no one knew better than he how to stand close to a tremendous event without imperiling the authority he had delegated to others."* An abstract or epitome of the personal style through which this was accomplished could be read in the message he sent back to Washington on the day of the German surrender: "The mission of this Allied force was fulfilled at 0300, local time, May 7th, 1945."†

Eisenhower's postwar career included a return to become U.S. Army chief of staff, succeeding Marshall, followed by the presidency of Columbia University. Shortly, however, he found himself in uniform again, doing his own five-star military reprise, called back to cold war duty in Europe, again as much political as military in its crucial demands, in the role of NATO commander. It was there that he found himself during the MacArthur crisis. Along the way he had been courted by both parties regarding possible interests in the presidency. On more than one occasion, Harry Truman himself had as much as guaranteed Eisenhower the 1948

*Churchill, *The Second World War*, 28.
†Chandler, ed., *The Papers of Dwight D. Eisenhower*, 2696.

Democratic nomination, which he declined. Now, back in civilian life, he was persuaded by influential Republicans to join the 1952 primary race, where he rode to eventual victory in a nomination battle over conservative traditional elements of the party supporting Senator Robert Taft. Victory in general elections in both 1952 and 1956 came easily during his service as an extremely popular two-term president. Afterward, his last days were spent in happy retirement with Mamie; his son, John; daughter-in-law, Barbara; and his four young grandchildren in Gettysburg.

As importantly—in ways, I hope, the summary comments above have at least partially revealed—this account of parallel careers also turns out to be a history of two temperaments, both eventually manifesting themselves in radically contending visions of the world and what sort of leadership would be required in the new American century. For this, MacArthur, slightly older, exercised a calculated belief in styling himself a man of previous ages in many senses of the term. He mixed the classic—aquiline, Roman, imperial—with the romantic—flamboyant, dandyish, theatrical. From the outset he showed a fondness for costume, the outlandish getup, the studied insouciance of the uniformed actor. A 1914 photograph from Mexico shows him with battered campaign hat, corncob pipe, OD (olive drab) shirt and tie, cardigan sweater, and captain's bars pinned on sideways. World War I photos reveal the almost effeminate swank of crushed caps, short jackets, swagger sticks, fine boots, and turtle-neck sweaters. In one photo, so tricked out, he sits in all his glory on a piece of headquarters château furniture much resembling a throne. In another, featuring a full-length raccoon coat and hand-knitted long scarf, were he not obviously military, he would look for all the world like somebody on the way to the Yale-Harvard game with flapper and hip flask. In a much-told anecdote of which the subject himself was decidedly not fond, on the occasion of one of his weird solo forays into the line he seems to have been so preposterously costumed that he was briefly arrested by trench soldiers on suspicion of being a German spy. During his chief of staff era, his deskwork attire featured a kimono and jeweled cigarette holder. The World War II and Korea years brought on the signature, mature, "late" style, with its very plainness calling attention to the embellishments, the decorative departures from regulation: the suntans or working dress of open-collared khakis; the crushed, fifty-mission cap, khaki, too, with the weathered embroidery and scrambled eggs on the visor; the aviator sunglasses; the increasingly outsized corncob pipe.

At the same time, there was much of a secret life. For a man who so fully built his image, character, and persona on myriad forms of calculated, elaborate, outward display, strutting, posturing, and pontificating upon the stage of history, MacArthur notoriously practiced equally elaborate, even bizarre, habits of private concealment. To put this directly, he had enough ghosts in the attic and/or skeletons in the closet to defeat the wiliest psychobiographer. Of his father, he seems always to have held the vision of the boy colonel rising above even the clouds to gain immortal fame at the battle of Lookout Mountain. Of his stage-managing mother, Pinky, the Tidewater aristocrat and Confederate die-hard, one should say that even by nineteenth-century standards she was domineering. She spent four years in the Hotel Thayer watching over MacArthur on the Plains at West Point and then the rest of her days flattering, wheedling, and manipulating whenever an opportunity presented itself to advance her son's career. At West Point MacArthur was legendary for his intense determination and ambition to finish at the top of his class, coupled with an ability to withstand hazing, even to passing out from pain in one case, and then, at his mother's urging, refusing during an investigation to name his tormentors. Something has already been said of his World War I glory hounding, the manifestation of an almost pathological bravery. To this could be added his protégé relationship with Pershing; his rancor at not being approved for the Medal of Honor; but also his sexual rivalry with his mentor/patron, Black Jack, the legendary swordsman, for MacArthur's first wife, the heiress Louise Brooks.

Meanwhile, between the wars, there was also the Filipino-Chinese mistress, concealed from his disapproving mother, with whom he continued to lodge. Eventually came marriage to Jean Fairchild and late-life fatherhood of a son, Arthur, to both of whom he seems to have been utterly devoted and who returned the devotion in equal measure. Yet the weird MacArthur vanities continued. His family blended with his military staff into something resembling an imperial household in which he formally held court. His avidity for being properly photographed became an obsession; his hunger for lavishly approving press publicity was insatiable. At one point, he tried to bribe a key subordinate, a three-star general named Robert Eichelberger, by telling him that if he achieved success in an impending campaign, he would allow Eichelberger's name to be included in major headquarters news releases. As to MacArthur's behavior amid his courtiers, Eichelberger may have had the last word. Throughout the war, in exchanges of letters with his wife, the two of them had their own pet name for the great commander. MacArthur was always "Madame Sarah."

Eisenhower, born in 1890, seems to us now much more a part of the new century, what we might call the age of the executive or management professional, mastering military decision making in all its requisite dimensions—in areas ranging everywhere from grand battlefield strategy to supply, personnel, administration, logistics—and combining it with a leadership style emphasizing delegated authority, cooperative effort, and meticulous coordination. Even the Eisenhower family seemed to present itself as an ensemble: the trim, stylish, flirtatious, Mamie; Ike, handsomely but plainly turned out, completely at home in his duty uniform; John, a wartime West Point cadet and newly commissioned lieutenant; or back in Abilene, the Eisenhower boys, assembled on the porch for regular reunions with their spry, aged mother. The only fashion statement for which Ike was credited, the Eisenhower jacket, was the abstract or epitome of the man, a combination of swank British battle dress with olive-drab American practicality.

The fact was that with Eisenhower, what you saw was what you got. During World War II numerous pictures of him appeared with a cigarette in his hand, held the way serious smokers hold them, barely aware they have one between the fingers, ready for the next quick drag. He smoked three packs a day, the bad habit of the ex-athlete. And he was one, a big man: Mamie called him a "bruiser" the first time she laid eyes on him. A permanently injured ex-football player, he was troubled throughout the war by a bad knee. He was a golfer because he was a keen athlete. He played a skilled game of bridge, and he was a faithful letter writer. He had an inordinate fondness for pulp westerns, prompting a sniffy comment from Dean Acheson that a man favoring the novels of

Zane Grey probably should not qualify as a first-class political thinker into whose hands the destiny of America should be delivered. He knew himself to be a person of uncommon ambition; he also understood he had come equipped with a terrible temper. His life was spent husbanding one and controlling the other. It all came with the package.

Of a secret life, one might adduce his much-talked-about relationship with his World War II British driver and staff aide, Kay Summersby. Yet here even an alleged dalliance comes off as steeped in ordinariness. Notorious passages in a late-life memoir by Summersby are sometimes cited as proof of Eisenhower's inability to consummate the relationship. One would submit that many average men know why. It was not because Eisenhower was unmanned or unmanly, when things came to the test; it was because he was uxorious, so long a husband and a parent that loyalty and habit—or maybe just common willpower—simply overrode sexual desire. Eisenhower's version of a secret life, if he had one, actually came later, once he became a Republican candidate and two-term president, as a kind of accretion or dividend of his celebrity and social status, the benefit of his friendship with a group of wealthy industrialists and corporate managers he called The Gang. From this came corporate board positions, investment opportunities, vacation trips, and memberships at expensive clubs; yet as with everything else, Eisenhower seemed to wear the trappings of late-life privilege and wealth comfortably and in consonance with native honesty and sound personal values.

All images of Eisenhower, through the war years and afterward, show a man who is all business in the largest sense—the business of disinterested, loyal, selfless leadership. The most revealing of his troop photos are surely those taken on the eve of D-Day with the 101st Airborne Division, about to jump into France at a predicted rate of perhaps 70 percent casualties. He looks them right in the eye, and they look right back. In the same spirit of that moment was the note, as Paul Fussell points out, that he kept in his wallet for years, a draft of a letter taking full blame for the failure of the D-Day assault on Europe. There, Fussell says, against a monstrous spectacle of inhumanity and human disarray, was a genuine light, gleaming amidst the darkness.*

*See Paul Fussell, *Wartime* (New York: Oxford University Press, 1989), 296–97.

One might point to certain dark marks on the later record, including a shameful failure, as noted earlier, while on a speechmaking tour during his first presidential candidacy, to respond to Senator Joseph McCarthy's attacks on George Marshall. Later, also mentioned in a previous chapter, he showed a serious cluelessness about the civil rights issues at stake in Little Rock. In the common venality department he certainly accepted many a favor from wealthy and influential friends. Yet even there, one finally remembers how many years Eisenhower and his family had spent in the military wilderness. Mamie's memorable assertion remained true even though her husband had now become president. In an army career of thirty-five years, she calculated, they had moved thirty-five times. The White House, she said, was the first place they could call home.

Most important, as suggested earlier, of two such lives and temperaments also finally came, in a moment that could not have been more crucial to the nation's history, two views of what American democracy was really about. This is true even down to their writings. MacArthur's quaintly entitled *Reminiscences,* for instance, offers anything but an informal reflection on a life and career. The style might be best described as relentlessly oratorical, with a quality of long-winded soliloquizing. Even personal stories have the quality of the well-rehearsed anecdote, the kind of yarn a practiced spellbinder tells over and over again to a captive audience. There are his youthful adventures, feats of derring-do and hair's-breadth escapes in Mexico, the Philippines, World War I. On a secret mission to Veracruz he and local accomplices steal a train, dispatching two villains, as MacArthur does his own *Message to Garcia.* From the Philippines, having drilled two more bandits, he is told by an admiring sergeant "the loo-tenant's future life will be velvet."* World War I exploits come so breathlessly upon themselves that they begin to be detailed as if they happened to someone else. On less-worthy later episodes, including controversial decisions and failures of judgment, the effect of the memoir is that of practiced testimony in a distinctly sanitized official MacArthur version. No responsible commander of the military district of Washington could have ignored the threat of violent subversion posed by the Bonus Marchers. No field commander's alert procedures in

*Douglas MacArthur, *Reminiscences* (New York: McGraw-Hill, 1964), 29.

the Philippines in the hours after Pearl Harbor could have been more fully justified on the basis of information available. Ditto the response to the surprise Chinese attacks across the Yalu. Say what the petty politicians will, MacArthur was the man on the scene, impervious to the criticism of mere mortals, personally taking charge and making history come out according to plan.

In contrast, Eisenhower's postwar writings meticulously divide the professional and the personal. In *Crusade in Europe,* the historical account of his experiences as Allied commander in chief, he is totally effaced, even down to diction and syntax. It makes high command in Europe against the Nazis sound like a big after-action report. A similar staff-study opaqueness—an absence of opinions, personalities, critical judgments—pervades *The White House Years.* Later, he would assume a more personal voice in such volumes as *At Ease: Stories I Tell to Friends* and *In Review: Photographs I've Kept.* Here we find a more human, if guarded, persona with an honesty that shines through.

As noted, the lives and careers of MacArthur and Eisenhower had been deeply intertwined, professionally and personally; moreover, they seem to have understood from rather an early point in their relationship the terms of power, ambition, command style, and political personality that would eventually require them to pit themselves against each other on the grand stage of midcentury history. It is alleged that MacArthur, once Eisenhower had found his destiny, became fond of referring to him as "the best clerk who ever worked for me." Equally telling, but apocryphal, is Eisenhower's alleged counteranecdote, in response to someone who asked him if he was acquainted with MacArthur. Yes, he replied. "I studied dramatics for seven years under General MacArthur."

Not in the least apocryphal are the facts that the war simmering along between two potential candidates for the position of commander in chief came to significant potential concretions in American presidential politics as early as 1944. By then, with much of the worst fighting of the Pacific War still to come, MacArthur was already making sounds of unconcealed interest in being called home as a Republican presidential candidate. Similarly in the air were the plans of Democrats, if this occurred, to solicit Ike, as yet undeclared politically, to run as a vice presidential candidate with Roosevelt on their ticket. Both men must have known

Roosevelt was unlikely to live long enough to serve out another four-year term.

The difference in their views of the presidency could be seen even here. MacArthur, from the 1944 election onward, made no pretense of cloaking his ambitions in anything other than his sense of himself as the savior of the Republic, the government in exile waiting to be called back. To put this directly, deep down inside, MacArthur was a totalitarian personality whose political genius he assumed to be perfectly consonant with that of the American people. He could not have been more wrong, eventually. But even by 1936 it had flowered into a bizarre obtuseness, manifest in a bitter disagreement with Eisenhower while the two were serving in the Philippines, founded on MacArthur's utterly misbegotten but obsessive conviction that Roosevelt was going to lose to Landon in an upset. More astute, however, and dating from the same era, was his awareness that Eisenhower was the man to watch. And here was the chief feature of Eisenhower that harried MacArthur to distraction: that a man of burning ambition like himself could nonetheless project, emanate, even exude normalcy. In this regard, another telling exchange, recounted in rancor by Eisenhower, came ten years later as part of a visit between the two in Tokyo, where MacArthur had staged a full-dress dinner for his former subordinate, now the hero of victory in Europe. They repaired to privacy, where they talked into the night. Eisenhower protested his utter lack of interest in running for president as a view he had consistently held. MacArthur is alleged to have responded, "That's right, Ike. You go on like that and you'll get it for sure!" Eisenhower was infuriated.*

By 1948, one imagines, it was MacArthur's turn to be infuriated, with Ike, as former U.S. Army chief of staff and president of Columbia University, now back as NATO commander and still playing hard to get. MacArthur somehow understood that Eisenhower had found the right combination, keeping himself in play. While all the jockeying went on eventually pitting Truman against Dewey, the imperial MacArthur was stuck where his imperial opinion of himself would do some good—as proconsul in defeated imperial Japan. The attitude seemed to be, "Now that we've got him there, let's keep him there."

*Perrett, *Eisenhower*, 368.

The ensuing victory/disaster scenario in Korea and MacArthur's relief from duty for insubordination became intimately connected with the nervous foregrounding of the 1952 election. McCarthy was still in full cry. A meat-grinder war was still going on in the vicinity of the 38th parallel. MacArthur, back in civilian dress, now persisted in bandying about a "secret plan" to end the war, offering crazily, as Eisenhower became increasingly viable as a Republican challenger, to share it with his younger rival. It involved bombing the Yalu bridges, dropping atomic bombs in Manchuria, and sowing a radioactive dead zone. There was also the complete willingness to take on the Russians as well and get it over with. The Russians by then possessed not only the A-bomb but the H-bomb as well. And Americans somehow knew, had known, that they didn't want a MacArthur making those kinds of decisions. Still, right up to the convention, MacArthur, and the Republican far right, for whom he was the darling, continued the bizarre machinations. To muddle the Eisenhower-Taft contest to the last, MacArthur was installed as the convention's keynote speaker. A plan was also floated to run him as a vice presidential candidate on the presumption that Taft was not a well man and was quite likely to die in office. The exact crossing of arcs in the MacArthur fall and the Eisenhower ascendancy showed itself at the convention itself. The speech provided the moment. It might have been a matter of triumphant stagecraft, performance, lofty and stirring oratory—all the things MacArthur was supposed to be a genius at. It turned out to be so utterly unmemorable that a text is nearly impossible to be found. "Meandering," "bombastic," "tedious and overlong": these are just some of the adjectives to be found in historical accounts. To be sure, nobody remembers much of what Eisenhower really said either. The photographs were enough—Ike and Mamie; and then, with the Nixons, in older and younger images of twinned uxoriousness; a family affair, and a happy prospect of what peace and security in post–World War II American democracy were going to be about.

After growing up in the late 1950s and early 1960s, I find among my most vivid memories of service as lieutenant in the army in Vietnam those of young West Pointers I knew with their competing parodies of MacArthur's farewell speech at the academy. One such performer was the straightest arrow in the army; another was possibly the most insubordinate officer I ever met. It didn't matter. They all seemed to have competing imitations of the old man—it was like some kind of bizarre ring-knocker indoor sport.

In the early 1950s my guess is he didn't seem nearly so funny. A measure of that, I believe, remains that nobody I ever knew in the military or anywhere else ever thought of doing an Eisenhower impression. He was just himself, in that odd way, uniquely himself, a man complete and inimitable.

At the same time, on the basis of this final comparison, it remains important to say what this essay is not. It is not some explicit twenty-first-century American political psychodrama with contending plots and Machiavellian involutions. Nor does it detail some Manichean struggle between the forces of darkness and the forces of light, fighting it out for the political soul of America. Rather, it sets itself forth as a cultural interpretation of what two men embodied and represented: two contending conceptions of leadership and of the directions in which some unifying post–World War II president would have to take the country. It certainly cannot claim a subtitle ("How Dwight Eisenhower Saved America from Douglas MacArthur") implying a direct, active, agency. Such an idea, a cause-and-effect relationship, is just not there. And such a title would be true only to the degree that it described a final net effect. MacArthur, for all his glamour and charisma, always projected an edge of malevolence, or at the very least malevolent power-hunger, vaunting ambition that struck people wrongly—in a word, scared us. In his astonishing conviction of his own greatness, we could not decide what disturbed us more, his personal vanity or his public megalomania. Or perhaps he just reminded us too closely of the fascist totalitarianism that had just been defeated. We admired but feared MacArthur. We liked Ike, and we trusted him—as it turns out, with good reason. We may say that he embodied that quality of selfless devotion to supreme leadership that this country produces when we are at our best: a steady hand, a gift for conciliation, a capacity to inspire public and international trust. As to outcomes, eight years of peace and general prosperity don't look so bad either. A simple sentence beginning Stephen Ambrose's definitive two-volume biography says it all. "Dwight D. Eisenhower was a great and good man."* As everyone knows, with leaders in history, greatness is not necessarily combined with goodness. In Eisenhower, at the crucial time, Americans found one person in whom the two qualities were met. We are the more fortunate for it.

* Stephen Ambrose, *Eisenhower: Soldier and President* (New York: Simon and Schuster, 1990), 11.

7
"Is This All?"

In hindsight of fifty years and more it seems that any person of basic mental competency in post-1945 America should have noticed that the country had a woman problem—a crisis of culture rooted in traditional conceptions of gender and sexual identity that had been irreversibly challenged and disrupted by the experiences of American men and women during the war years and the post–World War I and Depression eras that had preceded them. Equally incredible, in retrospect, is how long it seemed to take the culture to identify the crisis, let alone admit to it. The groundbreaking feminist Betty Friedan had it exactly right: for years postwar Americans, male and female alike, simply tried to live with "the problem that has no name."

The basic facts of the matter were contained in a single word, perhaps the most politically sacred in the national lexicon. The word was *independence.* Many women—as workers, wage earners, and taxpayers; domestic coequals, breadwinners, and heads of household; voters, educators, community leaders, and social and political organizers—had come tangibly to know something of independence in ways traditionally restricted to the lives and activities of men. Socially, intellectually, vocationally, politically, and sexually, over extended periods in their lives, they had experienced what it was like to do things on their own in the world—in significant cases, markedly in the absence of men or, as often, with men identified as male counterparts or adjuncts in ways that women had previously been identified in their relations to men.

Culturally and historically, such openings of possibility seemed the fulfillment of a great national promise, albeit one long deferred. From the earliest days of the Republic, American women had found themselves born for liberty, only to have prospects of independent advancement repeatedly short-circuited into forms of cultural compromise. Revolutionary feminism had elided into the antebellum cults of religious spiritualism and domestic sentimentality; late-nineteenth- and early-twentieth-century attempts at reform had issued into token triumphs followed by one balked contract after another concerning eventual full social, political, and legal equality. This time it seemed as if depression and world war had built the material connections whereby women could finally bridge the realms of the domestic and familial with means of access into full socioeconomic and political participation. Then, suddenly, everything seemed to go in reverse. Men came back to reassume male employments and male roles of domestic and civil authority; women who awaited them were simply expected to relinquish gains in personal agency and social authority and resume their traditional roles as wives, mothers, helpmates, daughters, girlfriends.

As if overnight, memories of women's self-sufficiency were all anyone had left to show for it, with even their retrospective images for the most part strategically feminized. Whatever women had done and whoever they had proved themselves to be in newly independent wartime roles got swept back up in a nostalgic haze of WACs, WAAFs, WAVEs, SPARs, nurses, big-band singers, civil defense volunteers, USO entertainers, pin-ups, and poster girls. Among war workers even Rosie the Riveter got a makeover, as the camaraderie evidenced in photo and newsreel depictions of teamwork on the factory floor—often going so far as to depict racial sisterhood—or the startling mixture of sexualities captured in the insouciant brawn of a Norman Rockwell arc-welder on the cover of the *Saturday Evening Post* gave way in memory to the ideal bedenimed and bekerchiefed beauty in the classic "We Can Do It" poster. From the tempered, late-wartime nostalgia of *Since You Went Away* to the considered ambiguities of *The Best Years of Our Lives,* even the most complex and ambitious of reunion movies, for all their laudable attempts to incorporate hard-won new attitudes of social and sexual candor, affirmed the traditional domestic possibilities of cultural return, with images of lovers, husbands and wives, parents and children, and communities reunited. The multiple anticipations and projections of postwar relationship in both films—the former with Claudette Colbert, Jennifer Jones, and Shirley Temple (by then herself a military wife) opposite a male panoply including Joseph Cotten, Robert Walker, and Keenan Wynn; the latter with Myrna Loy, Virginia Mayo, and Cathy O'Donnell playing against Fredric March, Dana Andrews, and Harold Russell (a double-amputee veteran, wounded in a grenade accident)—became a measure of what nearly had been grasped. It was not to be. Prewar and postwar versions of classic Hollywood pairings could similarly be seen as making the point, at times even down to their titles. The 1942 feminist heroine in the Hepburn-Tracy vehicle *Woman of the Year* earned the title through combining romantic attraction with the dramatic plausibility of Hepburn's portrayal as an independent, award-winning journalist; when she returned to service in the 1952 *Pat and Mike,* basically in a rewriting of the earlier role, it seemed to be as a tedious mixture of harridan and androgyne. Of similar impact was the strange, genetic recombination of the Cary Grant–Irene Dunne match of the prewar classic *My Favorite Wife,* with a plot centered on the female mate's return from her desert island adventures with a loinclothed Randolph Scott, into *I Was a Male War Bride,* where Dunne, recast as a WAC lieutenant stationed in England, plays largely against a gag-occasion for laughing at Grant as a former Free-French officer in military drag. Such retrograde images, as will be seen, would yield shortly to the even more egregious manipulations of TV, advertising, and mass-media culture still on the horizon. After the great war of the democracies, profound questions of democracy regarding gender and sexual roles left behind genuine wartime challenge and revision to become once again more food for conventional entertainment and consumer pleasure than serious cultural contemplation.

From a closer, personal perspective the problem was there to see, I now realize, for any male growing up in post-1945 America who wanted to look. Further, it wasn't just historical; it was also present and newly generational. The fact was that people's mothers and aunts, female family friends and community acquaintances, and in turn one's sisters, cousins, schoolmates, and other female contemporaries, were just mad as hell about something—and that something involved the conditions of assumed general powerlessness or at least subordination to which post-1945 American women had been returned after the advances of Depression-era and wartime empowerment. American women had found out what they could do in the world if they had to or needed to; now it was time to do many of these things if they wanted to.

Ensuing feminist accounts of the "woman thing" so described—Betty Friedan's groundbreaking *The Feminine Mystique* and related texts—gave the problem a basic structure as cultural narrative. The very conditions of unprecedented domestic peace and plenitude in post-1945 America supplied the groundwork for an enormous retrograde socioeconomic swindle perpetrated against women by men for the customary attendant motives of profit and power. Having coped with prewar hardship and deprivation, and cultivated wartime skills common to all Americans of rigorous independence and hardened self-sufficiency—in many cases as heads of households or in new workplace and public-service occupations—women were now forced to acquiesce in a great material and spiritual conspiracy of the male-dominated culture to return them to prewar gender roles and codes of sexual authority.

This was further complicated, according to many accounts, by a complex postwar crisis of male identity. As returning veterans, enormous numbers of American males, to put it directly, remained soldier boys. The military experience, even in extreme conditions of fear, violence, loneliness, discomfort, thirst, and hunger, had in many cases proved anything but a portal to adult manhood. Here, as with other extended forms of war work, military and civilian, in conditions of sexual pressure and social separation they had become victims of a kind of arrested adolescence resulting in serious problems of the most profound developmental sort. This was true for combatant and noncombatant alike. In the first case, a survival mentality emphasized vigilance and self-protective isolation, a comitatus notion of loyalties, and emotional withdrawal and psychological and verbal reticence, except around other veterans, about the experiences of combat. In broader institutional experiences of military service or war work, emotional development was hindered by male sexual segregation, regimentation, and the fostering of the kinds of corporate or team identity frequently associated with high school or college, sports, barracks and dormitory living, and mass-eating. In the sexual dimension a suspended immaturity took predictable forms. Pining for the girl left behind frequently eventuated in quick wartime couplings and other furtive gratifications; idealized memories and images produced by hasty marriages were strained by months and years of separation; in the alternative, there were resorts to pinup culture, prostitute gratification, masturbatory secrecy. "There is nothing like a dame," sang the lusty voices of the sailor chorus in *South Pacific*—in a scene where one of their own appears in Polynesian full-coconut drag while the nurse-heroine dances about in sailor uniform. The scene could not be more suggestive. Behind the slangy maleness of veteranship, many returning men remained lost boys in need of nurture, care, and companionable understanding after a kind of extended, adventurous, imperiled youth, of being brought up to speed sexually and emotionally in terms of relationships and of familial and social responsibilities, the adult world of family, work, and culture. Many men came home traumatized, socially arrested, emotionally underdeveloped, in need of some bizarre hybridization of the girl they left behind and the woman who brought them up. For countless others, domestic life came to be always a second-best excitement compared with wartime duty—and not just in combat, actually experienced by a fairly small percentage of those in the army, navy, and air corps, along with a larger fraction of marines. Even if one had been a supply sergeant in Italy, a cook in Louisiana, or a common sailor in the Pacific shoveling coal into a ship's boiler, there would always be a sense of the vast enterprise, the grand movements, the sweep of the thing, of just being part of it.

Against the backdrop of peace and prosperity, in an array of adjustments extending from the sexual and familial spheres to the vocational and political, such factors played into a kind of composite cultural blackmail resulting in the postwar women's phenomenon of "the forfeited self," as Friedan called it: of women's mandatory acquiescence and complicity in an enormous abrogation of cultural power newly within their grasp. Meanwhile, the prize of their acquiescence and the price of their complicity materialized in both the cultural symbolism and the domestic reality of "The Happy Housewife Heroine" syndrome enshrined in postwar popular media—newspapers, magazines, movies, TV, and, above all, advertising—and was reified in the actual experience of countless women unable to resist the allure of the new, attractive, and luxurious commodifications of identity offered as improvements in their lives. Within the "mystique of feminine fulfillment" the reward of wartime service became a new and improved institutional concept of one of the last ideas on many women's minds: "Occupation: Housewife."

Still, the question remained. After decades and, in fact, even centuries of advance in the voting booth, the workplace, the academy, literature, and the arts, all unbelievably accelerated by the experiences of wartime, "Why did women go home again," Friedan asked, newly to find their lives and identities in crisis?

Friedan's identification of the newly evolving structures and agencies of postwar women's oppression cast a wide net. Frequently, the voices of retrograde tradition and authority were those purporting to be participants in the "discussion": "women's magazines, sociologists, educators, and psychoanalysts," as well as a woman's "husband, her friends and neighbors; perhaps her minister, priest, or rabbi; or her child's kindergarten teacher; or the well-meaning social worker at the guidance clinic; or her own innocent little children."* In the commercial arena came the "The Sexual Sell"—the collaboration of the entertainment, marketing, and advertising industries into commitment of vast sectors of the economy into the lucrative production of beauty products, fashionable clothing, home designs, domestic appliances, furniture and household conveniences, cleaning goods. In the domain of popular psychology proliferated a mass of "Sex Directed Educators," with their emphasis on a concept of sexualized female identity emphasizing—and legitimated by—the ultimate goals of marital and familial happiness.

Friedan's feminist account of the great post-1945 crisis in American women's roles and identities, filtered through successive waves of interpretation according to new narratives of class, gender, and race, would eventually come under fire for its own intellectual bias in favor of women at advanced levels of education, affluence, and social and political awareness—mainly white, suburban, middle-class. For all women, Friedan genuinely got the nomenclature right and the widespread mood of the times that provoked it. Further, then or now, no one has ever improved on her phrasing of the question underlying it: "Is this all?"

*Betty Friedan, *The Feminist Mystique* (New York: Norton, 1963), 338–39.

"Is this all?" Thus was expressed the shared understanding that some opening to a genuinely heroic age of modern American women's opportunity and achievement had come and gone. The evidence of that loss, further, was corroborated nearly anywhere one cared to look in the culture. In image and in fact, the sheer material plenitude and pleasure offered by postwar American domestic culture put women up against the greatest soft machine ever assembled in history for sexual oppression. The myth of feminine fulfillment truly became ratified as reality in a world where reality itself came to consist of materially produced and commodified popular culture images and representations.

Across the cultural spectrum, the prewar phenomenon of the newly liberated twentieth-century American woman, ranging from venerable icons such as Eleanor Roosevelt and Secretary of Labor Frances Perkins to adventurous younger figures such as Martha Gellhorn and Margaret Bourke-White, seemed to go the way of Amelia Earhart. More than metaphorical as well, it might be argued, was the nearly complete erasure after 1945 of corresponding popular-culture images of strong, problematic, independent, career-oriented women presented in theater and film by a host of actresses, including Rosalind Russell, Katharine Hepburn, Bette Davis, Joan Crawford, Tallulah Bankhead, Barbara Stanwyck, Irene Dunne, Ann Sheridan, and others—many of whom found their own Hollywood careers short-circuited in the process. Wartime movie stalwarts persisted as mature figures of self-sustenance, perseverance, faithfulness, and durability: Myrna Loy, Celeste Holm, June Allyson, Joan Fontaine. Wise ingénues growing up into analogous "mature" roles included Judy Garland, Deanna Durbin, and Shirley Temple. Even pinups and poster queens such as Rita Hayworth and Betty Grable somehow combined sensuality with an air of notable self-possession.

Postwar successors frequently devolved into sexual stereotype. The pneumatic blonde bombshell—Marilyn Monroe, Jane Mansfield, Mamie Van Doren—found her dark counterpart in the smoldering, cantilevered temptress—Jane Russell, Susan Hayward, Lana Turner, Dorothy Malone. Somewhere in between, the astonishingly beautiful, unattainable Grace Kelly or Elizabeth Taylor played off against the coy, hoydenish, eternally virginal Debbie Reynolds or Doris Day.

As Hollywood went wide-screen and Technicolor on one hand—

wallowing in overheated melodrama and garish epic—or turned, on the other, to monochrome, mass-production genre—cowboy, war, sci-fi, detective, noir thriller—women's roles themselves underwent a parallel reductiveness of casting, the feature-film goddess playing against the B-movie caricature. To compound the irony, within the new economy of postwar roles and images, postwar women were required to accept casting alongside male icons whose careers and images seemed to carry over easily from prewar and wartime celebrity. A maturity factor actually worked for James Stewart, Spencer Tracy, Humphrey Bogart, Clark Gable, Gary Cooper, Cary Grant, John Wayne, Henry Fonda, and Robert Taylor, or somewhat newer figures such as Kirk Douglas, Charlton Heston, and Burt Lancaster. Younger actors, such as Marlon Brando and James Dean, got to be brooding and dangerous, and others such as Rock Hudson and Tony Curtis were unleashed at full sex appeal. A scattering of women might be seen entrusted with playing complex roles: Anne Baxter and Bette Davis in *All about Eve* or Shirley Booth in *Come Back, Little Sheba.* But even the best of these are now likely remembered in relationship to a classic male performance: Vivien Leigh in *A Streetcar Named Desire* or Eva Marie Saint in *On the Waterfront,* both playing against Brando; Natalie Wood in *Rebel without a Cause,* with James Dean, and in *Splendor in the Grass,* with Warren Beatty. As often, even the most visible and talented of actresses found themselves as interchangeable accessories for male leads basically playing to image. Cary Grant costars included Grace Kelly, Doris Day, Deborah Kerr, Audrey Hepburn, Jayne Mansfield, Eva Marie Saint, Ingrid Bergman, Loretta Young, Myrna Loy, Shirley Temple, and Sophia Loren. Rock Hudson's ranged among Jane Wyman, Elizabeth Taylor, Dorothy Malone, Doris Day, Jennifer Jones, Anne Baxter, and Natalie Wood. In retrospect, one finds a certain amusement in the spectacle of Robert Taylor prancing about in *Ivanhoe* with Joan Fontaine as the fair heroine, Rowena, cast against the far younger more vibrant Elizabeth Taylor as Rebecca, sultry daughter of the Jew, Isaac of York; or of Charlton Heston in *The Ten Commandments,* with a superannuated Anne Baxter vamping it up as Nefertiti while a gleaming Yvonne De Carlo waits as the new Eve of the desert oasis. At the time, such combinations seemed standard.

More important as a direct cultural influence, because of an advent so sudden, invasive, and widespread as a day-to-day presence in people's lives, was the new, wildfire medium of television. Beginning with broadcast times in early morning and the late afternoon and evening, and then quickly expanding to fill the daytime and the hours of the night, it made available to the average American a nonstop surfeit of news, information, entertainment, dramatic series, sitcom, cultural event, sport, interview, documentary, and advertisement. Yet all the while, inside the home, there it sat. In the living room, the family room, the "recreation" room, or quickly just the "TV room," small-screen, black-and-white, it became a new eye on the world where life got small enough to fit inside a piece of furniture. A domestic version of what the ancients called *theatrum mundi,* the drama of earthly life, it too became a gendered medium from the outset. At the top it featured male entrepreneurs of celebrity who got big in ways that even Hollywood could seldom match: big-name show hosts including experienced vaudevillians such as Milton Berle, Sid Caesar, Jackie Gleason, Jimmy Durante, Red Skelton, Bob Hope, and Groucho Marx; recycled crooners such as Arthur Godfrey, Bing Crosby, Dean Martin, and Perry Como; or newly self-manufactured masters of the medium such as Ed Sullivan, Dave Garroway, Steve Allen, and Jack Paar. Serial heroes included Roy Rogers, Hopalong Cassidy, Superman, and the Lone Ranger, Sergeant Joe Friday in *Dragnet* and Marshall Matt Dillon in *Gunsmoke.* Family sitcom dads migrated in from middling screen careers, including William Bendix, Ozzie Nelson, and Robert Young. There was the quick rise of the magisterial male network news anchor: Edward R. Murrow, Douglas Edwards, John Cameron Swayze, Walter Cronkite, and Chet Huntley and David Brinkley. The voice of culture was represented by the English expatriate, Alistair Cooke of *Omnibus,* presented Sunday afternoons by Alcoa; voice-over immortals of TV sports broadcasting emerged—Red Barber, Mel Allen, Lindsey Nelson—fostering in turn the rise of the celebrity athlete, the championship boxer, the home-run hitter, the four-minute miler, the all-American quarterback.

Given its place in the home, TV correspondingly became a medium where women got small, placed almost overnight in domestic roles and situations or in programming emphasizing domestic attributes and values. In serials, sitcoms, soap operas, and game shows, women appeared on television as wives, mothers, daughters, girlfriends. In a rare hostess role, with the emphasis on the gendered noun, Faye Emerson enjoyed brief celebrity as the quondam "First Lady of Television," albeit noted mainly for her low-cut gowns and marriages to presidential son Elliott Roosevelt and bandleader Skitch Henderson. More durable as a pioneering figure of daytime broadcasting was wartime icon Kate Smith of "God Bless America" fame, with her stout figure, plain features, friendly voice and manner, always opening her late-afternoon variety show with her trademark theme song, "When the Moon Comes over the Mountain," and always concluding with the sentence, "Thanks for listenin'." More glamorous, but comfortingly familiar, was former big-band singer Dinah Shore, always signing off with her trademark musical advertising message, "See the USA, in your Chevrolet, America's the greatest land of all, mmm-wah." But mainly on TV, women's place became *The Life of Riley, The Honeymooners, I Love Lucy, Father Knows Best, Leave It to Beaver, Queen for a Day, As the World Turns, Romper Room, Ding Dong School.* On sitcoms the female lead got to choose between playing the long-suffering wife or the manic harridan; on quiz shows women contestants became mainly objects of ridicule where they dissolved under the pressure of gag situations or were rendered dithering and speechless by male raillery. For the younger set there were kid fantasies like Princess Summer Fall Winter Spring; Sky King's faithful niece, Penny; or the increasingly full-figured Annette Funicello, flowering into voluptuous womanhood before astonished Mousketeers' eyes.

Even on the most sedate—or least caricatured—of family shows, Margaret Anderson or June Cleaver were steady and maternal, tolerant of male foible, frequently bringing up dad along with the kids, but always part of a larger world of superior male knowledge and control. To be sure, there was the odd, generally brief exception: the sharp-witted Eve Arden in the title role of *Our Miss Brooks* or Anne Jeffreys doing smart ensemble work with Robert Sterling and Leo G. Carroll in *Topper.* Nearly all of the memorable shows involving domestic relationships, however, even down to their titles, came across in forms of male iteration: *I Love Lucy, I Married Joan, The Life of Riley, My Little Margie, Leave It to Beaver.* The single TV female superstar of the era, Lucille Ball, had started out in the late 1930s in movies as something of a blonde sex symbol with a certain versatility as a "comedienne," as such women were called in those days. (Ironically, it would take color TV for audiences to reimagine her in the trademark image of her later career as a blazing redhead.) On TV she became a screwball on steroids, abetted by the comic-book Latin maleness of her Puerto Rican bandleader husband. What one remembers now is the sheer loudness of the show, the chaotic plots and pratfalls, the mugging, the incessant yelling. A domestic index of the character's bizarre status as a cultural presence was Lucy's TV pregnancy; the birth of her first child, worked into on-air programming as a humanizing celebrity touch. It did not help that the actress herself was in her early forties. But, ironically, it was the caricatured image that made the real thing seem phony. Lucy was just too loud, too wacked-out, too chaotic to imagine as having procreative sex. The whole thing was tantamount to imagining Fred and Ethel in bed or, at most, barely as sexual as somebody's aunt or next-door neighbor being pregnant with the latest kid.

As crucial a popular-culture influence, because now so little remembered, remains post-1945 advertising—even as that industry was busy inventing its own golden age reifications and commodifications of image, appetite, and wish fulfillment in movies, radio, and television, but also in popular print, photography, and art and illustration via newspapers and the great mass-circulation magazines. As to constructions of gender and sexuality, what one observes now is its utter, astonishing consistency and homogeneity in its representations of women, its bombardment of the media with trim, attractive, happy, sexual, and domestic female images. On television and in store displays; in newspapers and mass-circulation magazines such as *Time, Life, Look, Collier's,* the *Saturday Evening Post, Reader's Digest, Ladies' Home Journal,* and *Good Housekeeping;* in advertisements for food, clothing, automobiles, appliances, jewelry, cosmetics, soaps and detergents, and cleaning supplies; in face and feature, figure and dress, social role and self-presentation—one comes to the shocking realization that they are nearly all one single woman, the same woman. She is, basically, that woman, whether she is with a Chevrolet, a Hotpoint, or a Hoover; the Listerine, the Lux, the Midol, or the Crisco. She is the woman in the "We Can Do It" poster with her hair down, but barely. She is pretty in an aesthetic sense, rather than beautiful, regular-featured with an illustrator's ideals of nose, mouth, eyes, teeth, hair. She is, of course, flawlessly white, further unmarred by anything of the unusual or exotic. Her aspect is a natural look, fair complexion, frequently dark hair, in color displays usually dark brown or chestnut. In contrast to movies, there is almost never a suggestion of platinum blonde or jet black. She is usually wearing a dress—most frequently the kind of dress that used to be called a frock or an afternoon dress. (Interestingly, the staple of mature women's wear that nearly everyone remembers from the era, the housedress, is nowhere to be seen.) If the dress is for evening or party wear, a sheath, form-fitting, contoured, stylish. The emphasis is on a tight, curved figure, always with a trim waist. A skirt may be hip hugging or full. Even with the late 1940s and early 1950s New Look, trim, pretty uniformity is the order of things, with the "soft" or feminine geometric and cantilevered.

The most notable feature of affective sexuality one finds in a retrospective survey of visual and verbal elements of golden-age print advertising is a strange disconnect of women's faces and heads from their bodies. Given this, one comes with something of a jolt to the startling frequency of what now seem oddly prurient ads for lingerie, undergarments, intimate apparel, nightwear, dressing gowns, foundation garments, girdles, and brassieres. And in context of the tensions and constrained energies of the era, these may seem sexually very, very powerful, with a tremendous erotic charge. On the one hand, as Gail Collins has noted, "I dreamed I . . . in my Maidenform bra" becomes one of the great protofeminist teases of the era, with its suggestions of daring ellipsis and sociosexual fantasy.* On the other hand, one may look at the vast majority of the undergarment ads and find that they are really not sexy at all but rather are a combination of prurience and primness. They are not sexually inviting so much as they are desexualizing and fortifying, distancing, forbidding, and insulating. As sexual fantasy here, nothing is breaking out or even breaking through. For male viewers, as with cars, houses, appliances, or anything else with modern design features, these are women with a carapace, curves, tailfins, something with a shiny finish you have to work to buy, get, keep, maintain. For women themselves the figures represent desire not in any sense

*Gail Collins, *America's Women* (New York: Morrow, 2003), 397–98.

of actual possibility so much as their acceptance of the fact of complete disconnect between such images and their daily lives.

Indeed across a range of popular representations frequently played in multiple media, even what were considered adventurous or advanced portrayals of women in the era turn out to register the same kind of queer desexualization. The female protagonist in James Jones's novel *From Here to Eternity,* for instance, Karen Holmes, the sexually voracious U.S. Army officer's wife, engaging in a tempestuous affair with her husband's company first sergeant, conceals under her cold exterior an endless passion, albeit neutered by a hysterectomy required after her husband infected her with gonorrhea. The star prostitute of a Honolulu brothel, Alma, is a once-demure small-town schoolteacher from Kansas, a sexual entrepreneur trying to set herself up financially for life. In the movie, a notable postwar black-and-white, the repressed, deeply passionate Karen Holmes is played with tremendous dramatic conviction by the regal, immaculate, blonde Deborah Kerr. In an Academy Award–winning performance, Alma was played by the ingénue Donna Reed, who would eventually go on to a rare female lead role in a family sitcom actually entitled *The Donna Reed Show.* But the memory of both is contained in static images: Karen/Deborah Kerr lies horizontal in the celebrated full-length sexual clinch in the surf with Lancaster, both of them wearing bathing suits; Alma/Donna Reed, stands as the flower in the five-star fancy house, all the sleaze transferred to the madam, the whore with the heart of gold distinguished by her "difference" from the other girls, intelligence, sensibility, carriage. As much to the point, one now sees, is how easily both roles could slide into burlesque. On TV, in a *Your Show of Shows* comedy sketch, "From Here to Absurdity," both figures could be played by the protean, notably unsexy Imogene Coca—slinking around the brothel as her lover-boy Prewitt keeps horning in with his bugle; then, in the great forbidden tryst by the ocean, getting her overheated clinch with Warden repeatedly broken up by people throwing buckets of water on them.

A more straightforward allegory was the classic, wide-screen, Technicolor musical *White Christmas*—itself something of a remake of a wartime favorite, *Holiday Inn.* Again, the plot involves parallel sexual pairings, two male World War II army-vet performers playing against two girl singers in a nightclub sister act. Bing Crosby plays the smooth professional bachelor with a roving eye, a quick innuendo, and a way with a romantic ballad. Rosemary Clooney plays his female counterpart, sensible, mature, vaguely maternal, albeit sexually insulated and inviolate, just old enough and experienced in the ways of men to know that they are basically all rats in one way or another. Danny Kaye plays the fumbling adolescent second banana, and Vera Ellen is the bubble-headed, icy, perfect virgin, the homecoming queen incarnate. The plot involves the saving of a ski resort for the beloved general who saw the boys through the war; the story ends with the surprise holiday reunion banquet at the inn, with Christmas snow falling all around. The veterans, in their tight Eisenhower jackets, have been called away from their own wives and kids on Christmas Eve to one final formation. Serenading the "old man" as they once did in the snows of Europe in the last, dreadful winter of the war, up from the dinner tables around the room they come, up from their cocktails, food, and families. It is an attempt to contain the male memories of combat and comradeship as if in amber. But as if to predict the future, here a TV connection is already written in, with the benefit reunion secretly arranged to be broadcast nationally on an Ed Sullivan–style variety show. The finale points beyond to a future everyone already knows. The soldier boys will have married the singing sisters; they will already have headed for the suburbs, where they can be next-door neighbors and star in their own sitcom.

"Is this all?" Across the cultural spectrum the question of postwar women's identities posed by Friedan and others as arising out of postwar women's experiences became deferred to the arena of popular-culture image in some endless media remake of a standardized cultural comeliness. Even Betty Crocker got younger and prettier, albeit still looking like someone's mother or favorite aunt—showing the way to better pies, cakes, biscuits, and casseroles; she remained several cuts above Aunt Jemima but was hardly a cultural pinnacle. As much to the point was Betty Hutton, screwball comedienne, blonde bombshell, wartime stalwart, back for the Ethel Merman stage role in the Hollywood *Annie Get Your Gun;* or Betty Furness, trim-figured, brainy, well turned out, distinctly thwarted, an actress of substantial gifts reduced to a talking accessory in a world of gleaming household appliances, stoves, refrigerators, washers and dryers.

To be sure, actual women were no more Betty Friedan, Betty Crocker, Betty Hutton, Betty Furness, or her chic advertising counterpart Bess Myerson—a former Miss America, at once promoted and inhibited by her Jewish origins—than they were Lucy Ricardo, Alice Kramden, Harriet Nelson, Margaret Anderson, or June Cleaver. Nor could they find much identification in strange, period, celebrity exotics—Dagmar; Carmen Miranda; or Dorothy Shay, "the Park Avenue Hillbilly." One could write volumes on bizarre evasions and substitutions of race; in movies Hattie McDowell and Ethel Waters played off against the glamorous Lena Horne or tragic Dorothy Dandridge; or the casting of resolutely white ingénues such as Jeanne Crane and Susan Kohner in dramas of racial passing such as *Pinky* and *Imitation of Life.* In music the raw sexual appeal of Billie Holiday had to be recast into the variety show acceptability of cool blues and jazz personalities such as Sarah Vaughn and Ella Fitzgerald or domesticated, in the high-culture Marian Anderson mold, into the newly ascendant opera star Leontyne Price. On TV Amos 'n Andy caricatures persisted in Sapphire and Mama. In the vast new world of advertising, save for the immortal Aunt Jemima (and her occasional cohort Uncle Ben), barely a single black human being, female or male, could be found.

Thus in every corner of popular representation, continued the hazing of post-1945 American womanhood, as one might call it: passed through its own industrial-strength reshapings as part of the apparatus of the great post–World War II American production machine. And the end product was truly something to behold: the desirable woman of movies, TV, and advertising was most often sleek, fashionable, completely turned out, unreal, untouchable. Even when alluringly beautiful, she remained stylish, remote, encased in some strange soft armor, devoid of desirability. And of course so much for sex lives. Kinsey, for all the controversial candor of *Sexual Behavior in the Human Male,* took three more years to produce a second volume proving that woman had them as well. Even swimsuits seemed a case in point. The two-piece wound up largely gone the way of the knockout girl-next-door Chili Williams. The bikini became reserved for the French and peek-a-boo magazines. The new look became full-length, girlish, and/or maternal. With wired bra, corset or girdle-style stomach, and abdominal support, it made any woman impregnable, or, if one may turn the figure, endowed with a uniform happy attractiveness, pre- or postimpregnation.

Meanwhile, back in the alembic of experience that constituted the hard facts of the post-1945 crisis of women's roles and identities in actual women's lives, most white, middle-class females of sexual age could look forward to winding up somewhere between Honeybee Gillis or Ethel Mertz. Many of them actually did start out as baby makers in postwar campus Victory Villages, fertility acres trying to get along with returned soldier-student-husbands on the GI Bill. They lived as wives and mothers in new apartments or cracker-box houses with harried young junior executive men with briefcases. They settled into marriage routines where mom and dad got thick and querulous, and the kids got wise and lippy and adolescent. But they also continued to try finding their own lives, such as they were, everywhere in between: in high school and college, on the farm or in the store, the office, and the factory; doing secretarial and bookkeeping work, nursing, teaching, waiting on tables or working behind the counters, selling things and interacting with customers or holding down a typewriter, a cash register, an adding machine. For many women, single and married, young, adolescent, middle-aged, and old, amidst a culture blazoning images of some seamless ideal of feminine fulfillment, the world of home and the world of work in fact became dismally inseparable.

By the mid-1950s, for postwar women reaching maturity, image and ideal began to feed into strange evolutionary parody. In the public eye the most popular woman of the era was Mamie Eisenhower, a superannuated belle with her thin, girlish bangs, fresh and pin-curled from the beauty parlor. For the somewhat younger set there was Pat Nixon, with her armored sexuality, rigid posture, frozen smile, a rictus of unease and pain. By the end of the decade, they were replaced by Jacqueline Kennedy, with her youth, culture, haute couture, her social-register background, and her single-working-girl "career" as a photographer. Yet her image was as grotesquely unreal in its glossy cosmopolitanism as theirs had been in its enforced domesticity. If anything, she came off as even less sexualized, a thin, long-legged, flat-breasted clothes horse, the proto-X-Ray. Only later would one know of the completely bogus glamour of her marital and maternal relationship with her husband, the afternoon dalliances with prostitutes in the White House swimming pool, the all too visible enjoyment of Marilyn Monroe in a flesh-colored sheath, fresh from a stint in the presidential seraglio, singing "Happy Birthday, Mr. President." Meanwhile, TV images would continue to prove less than helpful. While the new feminism struggled for expression, Marshal Dillon would find vague quasi-marital and maternal comfort with Miss Kitty, and airhead Laura Petrie would match pratfalls with Dick Van Dyke. An acerbic, frowzy, middle-aged housewife from the nether hells of American marriage, Phyllis Diller, would become the queen of talk-show comedy. America's retro dingbat would eventually become crowned as Edith Bunker.

Even these reflections do not go near the hard facts, within anecdotal memory and demographic record, of how nearly impossible it was for American women in the middle of the twentieth century to lead independent, fulfilling, and complete lives resembling in any respect those of their male counterparts. For decades after the war they were simply thwarted in their educational, occupational, intellectual, and cultural aspirations and opportunities, and even when achieving certain prospects of self-realization, then frequently forced to a choice between a single existence or marriage and motherhood. Women of the wartime generation continued to live in a culture distinguished by the extreme rarity of female figures in the professions, business, management, law, finance, accounting, advertising and public relations, medicine, politics, higher education, and religion. Likewise with their daughters. Most men of my own generation, eventually making the passage through high school, college, graduate or professional education, some business or public career, will remember from their formative years very few women in any major male cohort, with some fields simply forbidden. Well into my own young adulthood, I knew one woman who was a physician, one who was a lawyer but did not practice, and one who was an English professor at the local college. There was one well-known congresswoman, Claire Booth Luce; one well-known senator, Margaret Chase Smith; one famous U.N. ambassador, Eleanor Roosevelt. Until the appointment of Oveta Culp Hobby, wartime commander of the Women's Army Corps, to the newly created position of secretary of health, education, and welfare, the U.S. presidential cabinet had not included a woman member since Frances Perkins, Roosevelt's secretary of labor.

In the common world of work, women were required to reconcile themselves to secondary roles in every respect of definition: secondary careers, that is, in their relation to primary ones as wives and mothers and also careers in roles invariably secondary to those of primary male figures. There were gendered pairings everywhere: doctors and nurses; professors and primary and secondary teachers, the latter almost never becoming principals or superintendents; accountants and bookkeepers; ministers and choir directors, organists, ministers of music or Christian education, church secretaries. The parallels could be extended indefinitely, with the legal secretary the adjunct to the lawyer and judge, the receptionist/stenographer-typist/personal secretary as an adjunct to the businessman and executive manager.

Oddly, perhaps the most vital sphere of women's postwar achievement in actual life remained in precincts commonly considered the most benighted: the world of farm, factory, small business, in what were considered heartland forms of manufacturing, light industry, assembly line, plant production, independent business—but as importantly, as noted by Sara M. Evans, what would come to be called the service industries.* There, then as now, plenty of work got done not so much as men's work or women's work but as work done by men or women together. In vast regions of the country women were co-owners and operators of businesses, factories, or farming operations, sharing serious operational responsibility and making major decisions about capital commitment. Meanwhile, they practiced cultural education, involvement, and organization in the largest sense. In an updating of the nineteenth-century age of the lyceum, the church or reading circle, the philanthropic and reform society, in the new suburbs, towns and small cities, rural counties and school districts, study clubs, church, library, and PTA groups, cultural and arts organizations, and ladies' auxiliaries, American women channeled new experiences of community into new forms of cultural education and political empowerment. Their descendants, we remain the cultural legatees and beneficiaries as fully as we are the inheritors of post-1945 peace and prosperity in any political, economic, or military sense. Activities that look quaint or humorously odd now were in fact crucial cultural pursuits, resulting in an

*Sara M. Evans, *Born for Liberty* (New York: Free Press, 1989) 229–41.

unprecedented fund of serious cultural education and awareness: a coffee club, a car pool, a bridge group; a library circle; a ladies' auxiliary; organizing a dance recital, a raffle, a bake sale, a school carnival, a field trip, a potluck supper at the firehouse or bingo night at the church or community hall; an hour's program listening to a local minister who had been to South America on a mission trip; a high school exchange student from Europe; an academic from the local college reviewing a couple of current books; band and choir concerts in church, community, high school, college, mixed American musical traditions with popular classics from abroad, frequently complex in performance and well executed.

People took art lessons, dance lessons, music lessons, learned to master new crafts and hobbies, and became active members of literary and drama guilds, lecture audiences, and library discussion groups. In rural backwaters, small towns, and urban centers of America could be charted the cultural work of women who knew a lot more than their husbands and children about current events, issues, social problems, international affairs, often by listening to the radio or watching TV; or, when they read, by reading Dr. Spock and Daphne du Maurier and everything else they could get their hands on from shelves filling up with Book-of-the-Month Club and Literary Guild specials. Far beyond the nineteenth-century Angel in the House, the Domestic Goddess, chastening, purifying, refining, cleansing husband and progeny of the daily taints and aggressions of the sordid world; and beyond twentieth-century updatings into the thwarted female artist or passionate intellectual from somewhere out in the provinces, a Carol Kennicott in Gopher Prairie or a Constance McKenzie in Peyton Place; the post-1945 American women who brought up younger family members and rode herd on households did so morally and socially empowered by the media culture that intellectual and social critics were frequently prompt to disparage and dismiss. In the lives of a younger generation, women assumed in fact a new, socially complex and culturally conscious developmental role. And by this, I do not mean the overzealous domestic nurture warned about by Betty Friedan, and certainly not the crude caricature of "Mom-ism" decried by Philip Wylie and seized on by adversaries of Spock. Far from a retreat, here was an advance truly beyond separate spheres: in the actual ways of the world, a movement into something more like overlapping or converging spheres, a realm comprising new orders of relationship, in the home and in the worlds of education, work, and culture.

Closest to home, personal memories on the point remain vivid and compelling. Nobody ever called my mother a "Happy Housewife Heroine" for resolutely choosing after widowhood in her mid-forties to accept and honor four and a half decades more of commitment to an unmarried life and the fulfillments of family and community service; or my Aunt Marion, who weathered out her abandonment, along with two kids, by a drunken, philandering bankrupt of a husband through going back to college and graduate school and becoming a pioneering specialist in reading education. The "forfeited self" would have been as alien a concept to them as it would have for Miss Miller, the stern, precise, demanding fourth-grade teacher and full-time caretaker of her invalid parents who taught me decisively how to put myself in the place of other people less well-fortuned in the world; or Mrs. Klinefelter, Mrs. Schwartz, Mrs. Leinhart, or the Taylor sisters, all of whom as wives and mothers somehow managed seasonal and part-time jobs while operating the showroom or sales, service, and repair departments at their husbands' businesses. Nobody ever called any of these women dames or dingbats, either. Maybe they weren't June Cleaver or Margaret Anderson, but they were plenty smart and strong; just how on the dumb and dingy scale—compared with, say, Ricky Ricardo and Fred Mertz; Ralph Kramden and Ed Norton; Ozzie, David, and Rick Nelson—Lucy and Ethel, Alice and Peg, and Harriet now look like Nobel Prize material. And this is what many of us truly remember of real women, in the post-1945 model, endowed with a sense of their own dignity and integrity, of ethical and, in the profoundest sense, cultural authority.

The forfeited choice, in retrospect, for someone growing up after 1945, where it frequently did apply, and continues to apply, ironically, would be with the women of the immediate postwar generation—women who, in the face of radical new openings and opportunities that suddenly were there in a way that they simply hadn't been there a decade or less earlier, somehow weren't sufficiently encouraged to believe they had choices. The two smartest women in my high-school class both had careers as parents and educators in the public schools. I might add that this was also, vocationally, the fate of two of the smartest men. But there were several others of us, male, encouraged from the outset to go to the state university or to selective liberal arts colleges, who wound up getting doctorates in various academic fields, probably because we had good high-school and college mentoring and support systems. Women, it is accurate to say, had nothing of the kind. By educational and cultural default they became channeled to the nursing schools, the business institutes, the teacher-training programs, the lesser liberal arts colleges. Males of my postsecondary cohort similarly found a direct pipeline to graduate and professional education, becoming physicians, lawyers, or business, financial, and management professionals; in contrast, as late as the early to mid 1960s, I cannot think of a woman I knew during my whole four years of college who got a graduate degree other than nursing or education. It would be left to our children to experience the normalcy of women's education in graduate and professional programs, law, medicine, business, finance, management, accounting, and in the laboratory sciences.

We used to have an old joke in my family about women with Ann Sheridan hair and Ann Sheridan shoulders. It has taken me years to realize how much of the world really did rest on Ann Sheridan shoulders. By now the gender joke may be as hoary as the old Charles Atlas bodybuilder ad in the comic books, about the guy who wins his girlfriend's respect by no longer getting sand kicked in his face at the beach. We live in a world now where men and women are people strong enough to carry global burdens. In the process, as with old myths, old jokes get strangely reified. A bodybuilder is governor of California. A woman with Anne Sheridan shoulders came close to getting the Democratic Party's nomination for president. Three women have served as U.S. secretary of state. (Meanwhile, it should be noted, other jurisdictions as diverse as Israel, India, Pakistan, Great Britain, and Germany seem to have done just fine with female chief executives.) Present statistics show that women students now make up half of medical, law, business and accounting, and other graduate and professional programs. In the general populations of colleges and universities they are frequently a majority. In the armed forces women fly combat aircraft and command naval vessels; and on the ground they serve in combat-support units. More than a hundred combat fatalities in the Iraq War have been women. In the worlds of business and commerce, management, banking and finance, there is still the glass ceiling. Similarly, although there has been progress in the local and state branches of the judiciary, we are back to one Supreme Court justice. In politics women are mayors, governors, state legislators, congressional representatives, and U.S. senators. At the same time a more general social conservatism dictates a new soft fascism of women's roles: a sort of *kinder, kirche, kuche* and Oprah. Ironically, this is paralleled by the most serious retrograde challenge to women's identities produced in the last several decades of American cultural development, the rise of Christian fundamentalism. In politics and in the popular media American religion seems controversialized most frequently over gay and lesbian concerns—the more likely crisis, when one looks at it, rests with more general unease over the ordination of women in the pulpit and participation in church governance. As if business, politics, and law were not enough, women must find the answer to the latest challenge in the house of the Almighty. The Father knows best. The old forfeited choice must now be deferred in the hope of eternity. Women know better. Heaven can wait.

8
Name Your Poison

Until early in 2008 I had a friend with whom I had once shared a good bit of common experience. He was exactly my age; we were both Vietnam War combat veterans; big smokers and drinkers, we had both enjoyed the bar and music scene when we were younger; we had both married and become late-life fathers, with daughters exactly the same age. On crucial "lifestyle" points as they used to be called, however, our patterns diverged. I quit smoking in 1979, scared to death by throat polyps. I quit drinking in 1984. My friend went on with both, ostensibly functioning and full of life. When I think of him, he reminds me of a picture from a weekend party or a beach trip, all of us with big smiles on our faces, a cigarette in one hand and a go-cup or a beer can in the other. He died this spring of lung cancer, the first lifelong smoker I personally knew from my generation who paid for the habit with the disease they said we would get if we didn't eventually quit.

Somebody with a cigarette and a mixed drink or a beer, along with a bunch of other people smoking and drinking, having some friendly fun somewhere in America: once upon a time, not too long ago, the average person, if not of some strict social or religious background, even if not personally a smoker or drinker, would have barely blinked at such a scene, which in fact looked pretty much like a magazine ad or a TV commercial. In terms of material wealth, post–World War II America is now rightly remembered as a golden age of consumer bounty, with favored mass-production items ranging from houses, cars, appliances, and fashions to sporting goods, yard and garden equipment, books and musical recordings, and sundry other kinds of modern enjoyments and conveniences. Although appearing increasingly remote by twenty-first-century standards, comparable images persist for many people alive at the time of the glamour and appeal of two everyday consumer products, cigarettes and booze, once likewise almost universally accepted as part of happy living and widely advertised and promoted in all media as among the foremost civilized rewards of American prosperity. For anyone who chose to enjoy them, smokes and drinks just seemed to be part and fabric of the good life after the good war. Questions about the risks of tobacco use or alcohol consumption were regarded as obscurely academic or, when ventured in public conversations, the work of health nuts and blinkered moralists. The great American romances with smoking and drinking reigned supreme in post-1945 image and fact. "Got a light?" "Wanta drink?" Among the two most familiar wartime utterances, these were easy icebreakers, sometimes for a quick pickup but as often an opening to human connection and momentary respite, however brief and fleeting, from a world of terror and menace or maybe just regimentation and sheer boredom. In the world of postwar domestic culture they translated themselves anew through movies, popular music, radio and TV, and lavish newspaper and magazine advertising into irresistible invitations, openings into the happy enjoyment of the postwar consumer good life.

"LSMFT. Lucky Strike Means Fine Tobacco." "I'd Walk a Mile for a Camel." "Call for Philip Mor-ray-ass." Everybody knew the advertising slogans and could name the big brands—Lucky Strike, Camel, Philip Morris, Chesterfield, Old Gold. Everybody knew who smoked what—family members, neighbors, social acquaintances, movie stars, and TV personalities. Cigarette brand loyalties in those days were like marriages, designed as a lifetime relationship, lasting as long as there was a product and a faithful legion of consumers still alive and sufficiently undiseased or uninjured to keep puffing away. All were straight tobacco, with filter tips only gradually a postwar innovation. There were no longer any ads with doctors in white coats claiming a certain brand was good for the throat or an aid to digestion. But any idea of "low tar and nicotine" at the time probably had more to do with advertising novelty than medicine.

The American cigarette industry had gone to war. (In one case Lucky

Strike "Green" even floated the rather silly advertising claim by the manufacturer that it had changed the pack color patriotically because of dye shortages.) There it had done heavy service as a single small pleasure left in life, sometimes the last pleasure in life many people would ever remember. In movies it was offered to a spy about to be executed or a combatant trying to get his nerves settled; it was requested by a wounded or dying comrade; it signaled some small break for human normalcy. "Hey buddy, gimme a smoke." "Anybody got a smoke?" "God, what I'd give for a smoke." "If you've got 'em, smoke 'em." "The smoking lamp is now lit."

When cigarettes came marching home with millions of men and women who had gotten into the habit of enjoying them during the war, and maybe the Depression before that, they were firmly entrenched as personal and social enjoyments. In the years after World War II, one saw the cigarette—right up there with the car, the Technicolor movie, the three-bedroom house, and the television set—as the quintessential American product, universally desired and accepted and in the world, indoors or out, in private or in public, at home or in the workplace, maybe still mostly for men but increasingly for women as well. (Nor, ironically, has much changed in that, save for Americans and the small fraction of other nationalities for whom smoking has become a serious health issue. Indeed, for vast numbers of humans on the planet—as still being acknowledged by the poor, the ignorant, and the addicted at home, as well as most of the populations of what used to be called the Third World—the product, still in large volume American, remains one of life's true small, instant, everyday pleasures.)

Then and now the item was a true work of national genius. Small, cheap, uniform, easily mass-manufacturable, packageable, and transportable in infinite numbers, the cigarette was the essence of the American product: a delivery system for the strangely satisfying and invigorating, not to mention drivingly addictive, smoke from tobacco, an American crop that itself had conquered the world. As with oil, railroads, iron, coal, and steel, it was the basis of any number of well-known great American fortunes, legitimized by the princely glamour of wealth itself and often by much-publicized philanthropy. But this was the wonder of the particular production, so low-tech that it now seems almost no-tech: basically a small, thin tube, open on both ends, made out of dried, cured, finely flaked tobacco rolled in very thin, combustible paper. Sold twenty to a pack, for years they stood in price at somewhere around a penny apiece. The pack fit comfortably into a shirt or jacket pocket. Stubby, compact, easy to handle with the fingers, the cigarette was easy to fire up, quick to suck down and finish (before king size), with ignition possible at either end, depending on one's routine (before filters). The whole point, of course, was stimulating an instant narcotic reaction, but nearly as important to the pleasure was a whole body of ritual: removing the cigarette from the pack; transferring it to the smoking hand; examining, tapping, and tamping it; placing it on the lip; getting lit up; taking the first puffs, followed by a deep, satisfying, hearty, first inhale, and then smoking it down to the butt. The business was timed precisely for the work break or the short passage of social activity, the discussion of a problem, the sharing of an anecdote or a joke. The ritual end came with stubbing it out, in an ashtray or on some nearby object, maybe putting it out on the ground with your foot—with an ex-GI, sailor, or marine always field-stripping it first.

By the twentieth century, traditional grades and categories of smokers had largely been erased through the ubiquitousness of the cigarette, as opposed to the cigar or the pipe, now gauged as a natural evolution of a core product in relation to matters of time and efficiency. Wartime especially made a quick smoke a good smoke. It might be the last smoke. The cigar had a history as the smoke of plutocrats, industrialists, high livers, the emblem of a male establishment ranging from Boss Tweed and J. Pierpont Morgan to Mark Twain. In the twentieth century it made its last bid as a cheap smoke ("What this country needs is a good ten-cent cigar") but became increasingly associated with ward-heeling politicians, labor bosses, car salesmen, plumbers, and Mafiosi. The original "smoke-filled room" was surely filled with cigar smoke. How strange now to live in the world of the Cigar Aficionado—hedge fund managers, investment bankers, stock analysts, lawyers, celebrities: Michael Jordan, James Gandolfini, Arnold Schwarzenegger (with his smoking tent behind the California governor's mansion), everybody waiting for Fidel Castro to die so they can legally get their hands on Christos again. In wartime Churchill brandished the cigar as upper-class British signature. In the tradition of Ulysses S. Grant and William Tecumseh Sherman,

Americans posed as cigar-chomping combatants: Curtis Lemay, World War II Pacific commander of Twentieth Air Force, or Walton W. Bulldog Walker, leader of the Eighth Army in Korea.

Pipes: the wartime image most frequently remembered, no doubt, is that of MacArthur's corncob affectation. Postwar, they came to be associated mainly with people in tweeds, academics and others thought wise and deliberate. Along with them came paraphernalia and ritual, pipe tools and pipe cleaners, tamping, scraping, making sucking sounds, no drool. It was all hopelessly inefficient and dated. Even the advent of the Hugh Hefner–style pipe-smoking swinger and all the sweet and puky new 1960s European blends could not arrest the plummet.

Nothing beat the cigarette—a smoke, a quick one to be instantly enjoyed, savored, in just a handful of minutes, five at most, or extended into a break of ten or fifteen; a couple for those more needful, practiced in sucking them down. Anger, nerves, unhappiness, or simple habit were reason enough for settling down, getting lost in the act of smoking. In the workplace large numbers of people could actually smoke more or less continually unless they were doing tasks requiring both hands or special concentration; and then sometimes they did it with a cigarette in the mouth. Anybody doing desk work or on a job site could usually keep one going. In fact, at work or elsewhere, very few places were sacrosanct, such as churches and public schools. Post-1945 was a world where nearly everybody seemed to smoke cigarettes nearly everywhere: in homes, bars, restaurants, hotels, offices, seminar rooms, and hospitals, in cars and even on airplanes. In virtually any kind of social space where people gathered and met, building hallways and lobbies, auditoriums, sports venues, people smoked cigarettes, and lived amidst the paraphernalia of smoking: lighters, ashtrays, paper matchbooks. And nearly as ubiquitous as cigarettes and their social detritus, it seemed, was advertising for cigarettes, slogans: in newspapers, magazines, and movie trailers, on radio, TV, billboards, and novelty displays like the one in Times Square where smoke billowed out of the hole in the sign. (The Marlboro Man, in fact a chance evolution of advertising for a product conceived of as a woman's cigarette, was still to come; as would be current heartwarming public service spots from the same company, Philip Morris—renamed Altria—on quitting strategies or how to talk to teenagers.)

The later postwar evolutions of cigarettes and cigarette advertising—the stratagems of the tobacco growers, processors, manufacturers, marketers, and corporate managers always to make the product somehow new and improved, more satisfying and (as major public health alarms began to sound) less harmful—are well known and need not be recited at much length here. (It may be worth mentioning, though, that tobacco alarms dated from the early 1600s, when the nascent industry had to survive an antismoking campaign promulgated by King James I, himself having authored the memorably entitled *A Counter-Blaste against Tobacco.* Later writings of Anglo European travelers similarly registered uniform disgust at American tobacco chewing and spitting.) The American cigarette became generally filter-tipped. Menthol was introduced into extremely popular brands such as Kool, Salem, and Newport. New "low-tar" or "low-nicotine" offerings included Kent, Parliament, and Lark. As more and more people began to quit, even traditional big sellers such as Marlboro and Camel had to find new life in the "lite" market. Today you may still see the odd diehard, usually in their sixties or seventies, puffing on a full-powered Camel, Winston, or Marlboro, or visit a house that looks like a smoking museum. The people who hang on are also the ones most likely to remember the old names, a smoke, a butt, a coffin nail, words from a lost world.

Adding, of course, to the problem at midcentury was how common and cheap cigarettes were. My earliest memories as a smoker are of a quarter in the vending machine. Just about the same as a gallon of gas. In North Carolina people would come to the fraternity house and give away free samples. They were nearly free, for that matter, nineteen cents a pack, at the grocery store, even cheaper if you bought by the carton, and even cheaper than that at the Army PX. As late as 1969 in Vietnam, we were still getting a four-pack in C-rations. *Cheap* and *common* were the right words for adult and/or parental warnings as well, utterly empty threats. I had a chain-smoking father and a mother who hated it but smoked socially because so many other people did. On movies and TV nearly everybody smoked well into the 1970s.

And drank. Oddly, although focused on a completely different product, connected with a completely different economics and set of cultural politics and practices, the postwar romance of booze carries a midcentury history of almost uncanny parallels, one may now see, to that of the socially acceptable use of tobacco. A smoke was a smoke, and a drink was a drink. Cigarettes went with booze and vice versa. If anything, although less widespread as a demographic practice, in image and fact the social use of alcohol was likely the more tolerated of the two as a personal and social enjoyment. And thus it had been, largely, from the earliest days of the culture. We may imagine dour teetotalers from the colonial past jostling with James I and his antitobacco indignation, but in fact such forebears prove extremely scarce, even among early groups thought to be piously or self-denyingly abstemious. Nearly everybody—Anglican, Puritan, Catholic, Huguenot, German Pietist, Jew—came out of some tradition of social appreciation of alcoholic beverages as part of God's gifts of nature. Colonial era beer, cider, wine, distilled liquors, rum, and whiskey were palliatives to undrinkable, disease-bearing water supplies. Early American drinking turns out to be a history of prodigious intake, with per capita consumption estimated at its height to be a staggering eight and a half gallons of pure alcohol per year. Particularly in the early nineteenth century, we seemed close to becoming a nation of uncontrolled drinkers. Seasons followed of embrace and rejection. Despite serious pre– and post–Civil War bouts of temperance campaigning, domestic drinkers entertained themselves throughout the nineteenth century in the Anglo American tavern and club tradition, partaking of largely grain-based beverages such as beer, ale, and whiskeys. From the Caribbean came rum, and from Europe came gin and assorted aqua vitae spirits. Apart from cosmopolitan cultural elites, a wine tradition never really took root.

The nation's one serious legal experiment with Prohibition in the early twentieth century, as is well known, failed wretchedly. Jazz Age hedonists and celebrity bootleggers became positive cultural heroes; attempts at enforcement produced some of the most lawless years in our history. Meanwhile, cocktail society carried on. Novels and movies featured drinking sophisticates. The Algonquin Round Table found fame as a gang of well-oiled wags and scapegraces. The heroic drinking of literary idols F. Scott Fitzgerald, Ernest Hemingway, and William Faulkner became enshrined in legend. "Name your poison." In popular representations this insouciant line was uttered by a host or a barkeep. Americans' love-hate relationship with drinking continued, oscillating between prohibition and defiant indulgence.

The war broke everything loose, at home and abroad. Aside from the most committed teetotalers, nearly everybody who went through it anywhere seems to have welcomed the warm, quick, happy release of booze. In the various regions of the European theater, soldiers drank everything they could get their hands on—beer, ale, whiskey. In England the preference was for traditional distilled spirits, scotch and gin. In North Africa, Italy, France, and Germany there was wine all over the place. Like their soldier forebears from World War I, finding quickly acquired tastes for "plonk" *(vin blanc)* or "rot" *(vin rouge),* they filled up their canteens with the stuff. Ditto brandy and cognac, calvados, grappa, or just the local rotgut, whatever did the job. In the Pacific, combatants had to content themselves with improvised "jungle juice" or "steam" or the rare captured enemy cache of beer and sake. No matter where they served, many of the war generation came home as serious drinkers.

After the war, drinking became part of the great social romance of the victory years. After work it was time to have a beer or get home for the cocktail hour. Beer got domesticated as never before, with the home tavern created in the den or the family room. The American brew became an ingredient of the happy home, a means of both personal relaxation and unpretentious, warm, hearty middle-class entertainment. Famous national brands became wedded to their tag lines: Pabst Blue Ribbon ("What'll You Have?"), Miller High Life ("The Champagne of Bottled Beers"), Budweiser ("The King of Beers"), Schlitz ("The Beer That Made Milwaukee Famous"). All the local brews went with their towns as well. Baltimore had National Bohemian; Philadelphia, Piel's; New York, Knickerbocker; Providence, Narragansett; Cincinnati, Hudepohl; Reading, Schaeffer. The big beer towns, St. Louis, Chicago, Milwaukee, had brands off the scale, the national ones, of course, but also Blatz, Hamm's, Carling, Falstaff. Here was a world where nobody ever heard of Bud Lite or Miller Light, where Michelob, Heineken, Lowenbrau, Dos Equis would have been considered pretentious stuff. Solid, satisfying, American-made beer was everywhere in TV ads. On TV shows it was the drink of choice for Jackie Gleason in *The Honeymooners* or

William Bendix in *The Life of Riley*. But it might just as easily (had drinking ever been depicted) have shown up as a hospitality option in the houses of Nelson, Anderson, and Cleaver.

The "hard stuff," as liquor was sometimes called, usually began with whiskey. For most people "whiskey" meant rye—what would now be called blended—in famous brands like Canadian Club or Seagrams 7. It was commonly served mixed with "soft drinks"—hence the new etymology—such as ginger ale or 7-up, or served in bar standards such as the old-fashioned or whiskey sour. Scotch was a learned affectation from the British Isles; bourbon was an American counterpart to Scotch, migrating northward and westward from its southern origins. Rum had become a staple in the Caribbean and South American theaters of World War II, with the Andrews Sisters famously "drinking rum and Coca-Cola." Gin, again mainly associated with the English, became widely popular in such easy concoctions as the gin and tonic and Tom Collins. Vodka, from wartime conferences and banquets, remained Russian in its associations, only gradually becoming popular as an alternative to gin. Nearly nothing was known on the common scene, generally speaking however, of the various aqua vitae, brandies, cognacs, or cordials. These would have to wait until the mid to late 1950s, with a new, thriving liqueur industry.

The domestication of hard-liquor drinking in America proved in many ways a harder sell than beer, although even the wartime White House had done its bit in the legitimizing of the cocktail. The signature FDR drink was the martini, a ritual observance and the product of his personal pride in mixology. (Even so, for a picnic at Hyde Park he served hot dogs with beer to the king and queen of England.) Harry and Bess Truman were likewise known to enjoy the occasional old-fashioned.

Long an observance of the wealthy and upper middle class, such drinking eventually percolated out from the cities and old executive commuter towns into the suburbs and provinces. In a few short years, cocktails were the affluent society's entertainment equivalent of a cottage industry. And, at least initially, the operative euphemism was *cocktail*—the cocktail party, the cocktail hour, cocktails before dinner. People went to cocktail lounges; hosts and hostesses bought cocktail glasses, cocktail napkins, cocktail snacks. Female guests wore cocktail dresses. Once the practice got going, the language got simplified—stopping by for a drink, taking somebody out for a drink, having people over for drinks. From the late 1940s and early 1950s onward, this is what having a drink meant—the domestication of liquor, with beer a lively option. (It would still take decades for wine to join the picture.) The point was doing what alcohol had always done, which was to get people anaesthetized to the world in a relatively fast but still socially acceptable fashion.

And *fashionable* was a good word for the drinking world as depicted in popular-culture myth and image. Through images percolating down from high society, the nightclub or supper club was the domain of the glamour girl and the amiable boozehound and lover-boy—a Dean Martin, Cary Grant, Rock Hudson, Tony Randall, or Gig Young. Through images percolating up from blue-collar life, beer claimed the territory of the ball park, the corner bar, the TV room, the outdoor patio. Beer was somebody's father's or uncle's drink, the regular-guy drink.

As noted above, for reasons still not clear, wine as a freestanding drink option remained completely out of the picture. Actually, paralleling the European practice, when it came, it came with food. Even with a meal, save for the real bon vivant, connoisseur, gourmand, it seemed to remain a British and French affectation, or from movies something having to do with a bunch of sloppy, undershirted, quarreling Italians or beret-wearing, chain-smoking Frenchmen. There remained no American wine industry to speak of until well into the late decades of the century. Even by the 1960s and 1970s somebody's idea of wine was likely to remain Mateus, Lancers, or Blue Nun. (This should probably not be much of a surprise in a country where a lot of Protestant Christians still drink grape juice at communion—washing down morsels of cubed Wonder Bread. To this day, even most Episcopal and Catholic churches go with sweet, kosher, Mogen David.)

In a commonplace that will strike many people today as bizarre and possibly shocking, it was an age in which images of the big drinker could be considered funny, with comedians such as Red Skelton and Dick Van Dyke making hay on a schtick going back to Buster Keaton. Ernest, the harmless, amusing town drunk, had his own key to the Mayberry lockup on *The Andy Griffith Show.* In tuxedo, Dean Martin and Jackie

Gleason played the boozehound as hero, the singer-host-entertainer with a cigarette, a drink, and a snootful, along with jokes about getting waked up in the yard by the sprinklers. The tamest show on American television, Lawrence Welk, opened with a theme song entitled "Bubbles in the Wine."

As to clinically excessive drinking, modern American alcoholism, although it had been invented in the 1930s by AA founder Bill Wilson, was notably put on social hold. The occasional movie appeared about the problem—*The Lost Weekend,* for instance, or later, in the 1960s, with riveting performances by Jack Lemmon and Lee Remick, *Days of Wine and Roses.* Not surprisingly, given the midcentury romance with booze, alcoholism itself went undefined in the official Diagnostic Statistical Manual of the American Psychological Association until the 1960s, however; indeed, it was not really spoken about in social terms until the 1980s and 1990s, and even then it remained a culture of confidentiality and secrecy, something like masons or radical socialists. It is of note that in the twenty-first century, George Bush, the hard-drinking fraternity and cocktail-party rich kid who was once the quintessential product of postwar drinking culture has been America's first alcoholic president probably since Grant, albeit without a mention of the word. A newer culture of therapy and recovery now gets mixed in with born again religion and reactionary politics. Anybody who gets in trouble now goes into rehab.

It is significant that the word *rehab* is now most frequently associated with some form of "drug" culture. With so many narcotic fashions cycling through the national consciousness, cigarettes and booze have moved out of the national spotlight. Cigarette advertising, not permitted on TV, is relatively scarce in other media. Smoking itself has declined radically. In public image, the same sort of fractured alcohol memory remains. Beer ads are ubiquitous on TV, and now there is a proliferation of liquor ads as well. Wine is promoted as increasingly the beverage of civilized drinkers. Meanwhile beer and liquor binge drinking is epidemic on college and university campuses.

Still, there are plenty of places in the world where American smokes and drinks can still recognize themselves. Cigarette companies, now mostly international conglomerates, make up for plummeting domestic use with industrial-strength marketing and distribution throughout the undeveloped world, exporting disease and misery as an "adult" product. At home and abroad booze has assimilated itself into world practice, the Western traditions of Europe conjoined with the hard-drinking protocols of Asia. At home, essentially camouflaged below the drug culture as relatively harmless, it remains the drug of choice for the vast majority of American addicts.

As a survivor of both forms of American romance, I feel impelled to enlarge on the general human stakes of all this: of sanctimonious American multinationals, divested of their domestic tobacco and alcohol divisions going out to addict and poison people with lousy lives just looking for a moment with life's little pleasure. At home, one may still read news items about exemptions being made in tobacco regulation for menthol brands, still being marketed lucratively to African Americans. American liquor around the globe remains the gold standard. Constantly revivifying wine and beer cultures at home create a newest class of problem drinkers. My friend who died of lung cancer went to his grave believing that anybody who drank only beer, albeit at a clip of a six-pack or so every day of adult life, could not possibly have been an alcoholic.

At some point indignation also shades into private memory related to what now seem the old familiar ambiences of cigarettes and booze a lot of us grew up with at midcentury, many of them not without a kind of nostalgic glow that still seems something of a piece with the times—the facts notwithstanding then or now of the ease in those days with which the culture made it possible to become an addicted smoker or a problem drinker. In my life the manliness of smoking was impressed on me in college, the army, an early university career of the bohemian intellectual life. Drinking was from the earliest experiences I can remember of it totally a romance. My alcoholism was there waiting to happen, personally programmed in my genes—with uncles on both sides: my mother's favorite brother, a glamour-boy, handsome, charming, plastered every night before dinner; the other, my father's ne'er-do-well younger sibling, a hopeless toot-drinker, trailing a lifetime of getting soused, getting fired, and moving the family off to some strange new town where the cycle would happen again; but also culturally in a style of living in the world that I took to as a late 1950s and early 1960s kid the way I saw people just a few years younger seem born to be world-class potheads. We are all ourselves, but we are all persons of a very particular time and place. Cigarettes and booze came too easily to me, as they did to many people who associated them with the good life after the good war and are still paying for it.

9
Mastering the Curriculum

Many Americans from the mid-1950s will remember a song by Sam Cooke entitled "Wonderful World." Like other popular classics of the time, it is about a high school kid trying to get a girl. He's not big on book-learning, he confesses to her; but if the two of them can make it together in love, school problems and everything else will take care of themselves. "Don't know much about history," it begins,

> Don't know much biology.
> Don't know much about a science book.
> Don't know much about the French I took.

An ensuing verse continues the "Don't know much about _____" theme, rhyming on various educational subjects—geography and trigonometry; "al-ge-bra" and "what a slide rule-is-for." What the singer does know, of course, is that he loves a girl and that if she were to love him as well, it would be a wonderful world. Further, he pledges, if trying to be an "A" student will help, that too can become proof of his devotion.

The times abounded in songs about teenagers in love. What distinguishes "Wonderful World" is the concrete memorability of the curricular metaphor. Beyond such popular analogues as Chuck Berry's "School Days" and the Coasters' "Charlie Brown," it is the quintessential song about the American teenager as high school kid, detailing the elements of common educational experience for those aspiring to middle-class happiness and success during the era. The standard class schedule is largely there: history, biology, French, trigonometry, algebra. So are some basic stage properties: a science book and—in a reference that now seems touchingly quaint—a slide rule. English seems to be taken for granted, although the clever rhyming and argument suggest a precocious adolescent mastery. Although humorously expressed, there is also the basic idea of social aspiration, on some level an acceptance of the role played by public education in undergirding the good life in America. For an average American teenager, the curriculum, the song seems to say, is part of life, and part of life is mastering the curriculum.

The adolescent is enshrined as American teenager, and the American high school is a model for inculcation of the values of postwar culture. It is an image of cultural connection that has never really quite left us. In movies one traces a short but illustrative pedigree back through *High School Musical* I and II to *Mean Girls, Napoleon Dynamite, Ferris Bueller's Day Off, American Pie, Clueless, The Breakfast Club, Sixteen Candles,* and *Fast Times at Ridgemont High.* On TV, a bare listing of the most recent progeny of the form would include *Degrassi, Hannah Montana, Josh and Drake,* and *Beverly Hills 90210. Chasing Zoe* becomes subsumed in the real-life teen pregnancy of its star, Jamie Lynne Spears—with the scandal eclipsed by daily headlines about the egregious self-destructiveness of her sister, Britney, once the reigning queen of adolescent sexuality. In film and on TV the newest iterations become notes toward a *High School Confidential* for the twenty-first century. Meanwhile the Hollywood genre reaches back through *Hairspray, Grease,* and *American Graffiti* to *Blackboard Jungle* and *Rebel without a Cause,* and on the small screen to *Happy Days* and *Welcome Back, Kotter.*

Mastering the curriculum in the sense of teenage and/or young-adult preparation for citizenship and socioeconomic participation actually goes back at least through John Dewey to the *McGuffey Readers* and beyond. The current regimen of teacher accountability, statutory graduation exams, and measurement of learning outcomes similarly comes trailing a long history of post–World War II anxieties and admonitions: endless arguments over curriculum, classroom goals and objectives, teacher training standards, and student competencies. In a dismal continuity flowing back from the 1990s through the 1970s, tag phrases like "cultural literacy" and "the closing of the American mind" become post-1960s laments over the loss of some golden age of postwar educational efficacy and integrity. Meanwhile, such artifacts as the course schedule outlined in "Wonderful World" must increasingly be seen as not unlike the gatherings from a Babylonian or Egyptian tomb—or stage properties in a bad replay of *Happy Days*. We have come a long way to No Child Left Behind; and before that, Reagan-era crisis rhetoric over illiteracy, innumeracy, lack of shared knowledge, lack of shared skills and essential linguistic, literary, historical, mathematical, and scientific competencies. "Facts and skills are inseparable," warned E. D. Hirsch. Allan Bloom lamented the association of cultural relativism as philosophy of education with the breakdown of necessary protocols of social, political, and cultural authority. William Bennett became a one-man publishing industry with a series of books about the relationship between "hard" knowledge and civic virtue in a democracy. Sometimes the blame was laid on "educationists." As often, the finger pointed at liberal multiculturalists, relativists, anything-goes pluralists. It was they, the story went—finessing the subtexts of population growth, expanded educational access, racial integration, working-class poverty, and urban decline, not to mention the exponential growth of knowledge and the runaway development of information technologies whereby it might be conveyed—who had allowed the dismantling of an ethically grounded and politically well-functioning educational system from a wiser and simpler time.

Yearnings for a wiser, simpler time are a continual temptation and nearly as often an easy path to folly. This is particularly true if the curricular reflections are those of persons such as myself, who, in retrospect, might be considered, for better or worse, people who got to be who they are, accomplished much of what they think they have accomplished, came to be who they are in the world as typical beneficiaries of that educational system—who went through that system in the decade or so just after World War II, in the dreary formulation of the era, as "good" or even "model" students. That phrasing alone should remind us that educational nostalgia is as relative as nostalgia of any other kind. No matter how the song goes, school days, one must remember, were never "good old golden rule days"; nor were reading and writing and 'rithmetic or anything else ever all that well taught to the tune of a hickory stick. For all this, mastering the conventional public-education curriculum after World War II, like so many things about the era, still seems to stand as a kind of national benchmark of accomplishment—the means whereby many young people, confronted with a relatively structured, manageable body of learning, succeeded in the acquisition of basic skills and cultural competencies, standard achievements in literacy, math and basic science, history, social studies, art, music, and literature. To put this another way, the fact of the matter remains that, for the great post–World War II American middle class, one of the chief tangible products of postwar peace and prosperity was education. As the GI Bill opened educational vistas for returning veterans, connecting their frequently incomplete experiences from before the war and during the preceding depression with the idea of a better life, so came the resulting primacy placed by the World War II generation on education for their children. Along with the belief of a victorious people that they had won the war with determination and bravery, to be sure, but also with production and good old-fashioned know-how came a new sense of aspiration and confidence in building a public educational system that must really have seemed the glory of the culture. Public schools implemented standard curricula, combining abstract knowledge with no-nonsense tracking according to individual gifts and social priorities. Students were sectioned into preparations including academic, general, secretarial and bookkeeping, industrial arts, home economics, and agriculture. To be sure, the sectioning came at a price, frequently in the most egregious separations according to race, class, and gender, and particularly in segregated systems—de jure and de facto—an especially cruel neglect of African Americans, Native Americans, and other racial and ethnic minorities. Yet for those who benefited, the payoff came frequently in idealism and confidence—a sense that one had been truly prepared both for productive citizenship and a sense of general, happy relatedness to the world of general knowledge and culture.

The term *teenager* is alleged to have had its first widespread use in 1945. In the context of the educational developments described above, it is thus hard to underestimate connections of this idea of a whole new social category with corresponding evolutions in the particular institution of what was called in those days high school—within a standard, legally mandated twelve-grade educational system, that is, grades seven through twelve, as opposed to grade school, grades one through six, in some places also called elementary school or grammar school. In advanced jurisdictions, perhaps, there might also be an intervening stage, with a separate curriculum and facilities, called junior high—eventually, in a variety of shifting formats, also becoming known as middle school—comprising grades six through eight, seven through nine, etc. But during the golden age of the teenager in post-1945 American culture, the focus of teenage life and experience in America became, in one form or another, the institution called high school. Indeed, the era was also, one might claim, the golden age of the American high school, and during the era everyone seemed to know what the basic curriculum needed to be.

Mastering the curriculum: with an approving nod to Sam Cooke, during the years in question, the lyrics of his song constitute one of those sets of clichés that earn their existence as clichés mainly by being true in the first place. That was high school—a young-adult life stage and a curriculum, a personal rite of passage and a participation in the institutional chronology of a culture, culminating a process most people had started initially around age six and had continued for six more years of what are still called the primary grades. Before what we now know as preschool and kindergarten became widely instituted, there was just elementary school; and elementary school did exactly what the name said, delivering instruction in elementary curricular subjects: basic skills such as reading, writing, and arithmetic; introductions to science and social studies; some acquaintance with art, music, and physical education. In turn, high school—what we would now call secondary education—in those days meant more or less what that phrase said: instruction, beginning in the seventh year for most students, in what would now be considered advanced subjects, albeit initially perhaps in a transitional mode: English, history, social studies; but also a foreign language, in many cases Latin; math, in the form of intermediate work geared for movement into advanced topics such as algebra and plane geometry; general science, with various units again anticipating hard science categories—sections on plant, animal, and human biology; rudimentary physics and astronomy; chemistry; earth science, geography, geology. There would be more music and art; perhaps general home economics for girls and shop courses for boys; and, for the first time, extensive programs of extracurricular, often as institutionally entrenched as any academic subject—athletics, music, drama, speech, special-interest clubs.

For anyone who went through that system, Cooke's song, if the figure may be permitted, rings any number of bells, all of which say "high school." This is to say that the particular lyrics are definitely talking about what very large numbers of Americans alive today still remember as high school—an experience that, if today sounding rather formidable and unfamiliar for many teenagers, let alone in a song from a black kid from the segregated South, was actually fairly common. "History," for instance, stood right there in the middle, coming on year after year as World, English, and American. Ditto literature. The "science book," depending on the year, would actually have been biology, chemistry, or physics. "French," in the late 1940s and early 1950s, for general foreign language instruction in the schools, was frequently the modern tongue of choice, only gradually being displaced by Spanish. (For obvious reasons, just after World War II, German was out, although Latin frequently remained for advanced students.) In math the "trigonometry" and "algebra" mentioned in the song were curricular staples, along with plane and solid geometry. Students on the "academic" or precollege track definitely learned how to use a slide rule. Others were consigned to typewriters and other office machines, wood and metal manufacturing tools, and farm equipment.

All that could vary, of course, according to locality, depending on social demographics and employment needs. Still, the fact remains that whether in the toughest inner-city educational hellhole or in the most undisturbed pastoral backwater, some small-town, consolidated school district or suburban jointure, there obtained for the most part a regular and rigorous curriculum such as that described above. To be sure, most frequently it remained a white, middle-class phenomenon, but even in the literature of segregated or neglected urban systems of the era, it seems to operate if only as a struggling parody. Science was general, biology, chemistry, and physics; math was algebra, plane geometry, trigonometry, and solid and analytic geometry; world history, English history, and American history were paralleled by World lit., British lit., and American lit. with English instruction punctuated by book reports, oral presentations, and term papers. Foreign languages involved mainly vocabulary and grammar instruction rising to rudimentary translation. Current events came under the guise of "social studies," "civics," or "problems of democracy" courses; young-adult development was handled under the heading of "health," with the latter being usually the precinct of underemployed coaches and physical education teachers.

If you look at histories of American education from the late 1940s through the early 1960s, that was it—and not just in showplace elite schools, private or public, but in cities, small towns, district and county systems strung out across America. What would be called the basic academic or "core" curriculum was visible at Choate or Exeter, Germantown Friends or Woodbury Forest, and at powerhouse urban genius factories such as Herbert Lehmann in the Bronx or in the great affluent suburbs, New Trier, Scarsdale, and Shaker Heights. But in virtually every other jurisdiction spread out across America, some model of it could also be found as a classic curriculum in every sense. As old as the classic design of the Middle Ages—the trivium of grammar, logic, and rhetoric, with the quadrivium of mathematics, geometry, astronomy, and music—in turn passed through the advanced English, French, German systems of secondary schooling, it had eventually broken out into a college or university track, a general track, a collection of vocational or technical tracks. But it was still the curriculum, and its cultural centrality cannot be overstated back in a world such as that just after World War II, where public education formed the core of developmental experience for young people and a primary focus of community activity and involvement for their parents and grandparents. In the shaping of Young Americans, the school was right up there with the church and government. A teacher stood right up there alongside the doctor, the lawyer, the banker, the mayor, and the minister, with a principal or classroom teacher of venerable standing, nearly always male, still possibly referred to with the honorific "Professor." And even as high school teaching after the war became an occupation increasingly female, as had been elementary school work from nearly the beginning, the social respect factor still ranked extremely high on the community scale. Teachers and their families were firmly white-collar. Teachers made a decent living; many of them had survived, thusly, during the Great Depression, where it was somehow figured out that the public schools were tremendously important in getting the country out of the hole. They kept their jobs when nearly nobody else could be sure they would still have one tomorrow. Students continued, insofar as their own family situations made it possible, to go to traditional public schools.

The war intervened—albeit, as is frequently forgotten, for Americans, rather briefly in comparative terms, as opposed to other combatant nations. After slightly under four years, for war veteran and war baby alike, mastering the curriculum became the great peacetime pursuit, the portal to success and happiness in post-1945 America. It is frequently emphasized that the returning common soldiers, sailors, and airmen availed themselves widely of their benefits under the GI Bill by seeking as never before the opportunities of postsecondary education—that is, the experience of college and university—traditionally reserved for the more privileged classes. In fact, especially in the lower military ranks, there remained a fairly strong percentage of people who, because of Depression-era or wartime exigencies, had not completed high school and whose belief in the future lay in at least a better chance for their children. These people, too, came home with a new respect for education and an enthusiasm for letting their children avail themselves of the social opportunities provided by secondary education, as well as the broadening activities of music, art, athletics, and various other extracurricular activities. Nearly every postwar high school kid participated in some kind of sport, plus maybe dramatics, band, chorus, the newspaper, or the yearbook. People went to dances, after-the-game hops, teen formals, and proms. Travel might come with a senior trip to some local metropolis or even New York or Washington, D.C.—in those days a signature cultural event, where classmates worked on moneymaking projects over several years so that everyone got to go.

Graduation would be a speech by some civic worthy or political figure, a minister doing an invocation and benediction, struggling efforts by the class salutatorian and valedictorian (frequently on assigned topics of moral or educational uplift), the band playing the alma mater, the chorus singing something inspirational, the diploma walk across the stage, and the cap-and-gown class picture. The curriculum having been honored, the new citizens could go forth—sometimes to big-name colleges and universities, often to state schools and teachers' colleges, one- or two-year secretarial and business colleges, mostly to jobs in business, industry, agriculture, manufacturing, repair and service, agriculture.

More than half a century later, at every step along the line, the whole system now seems to have gotten complicated beyond belief in every realm from demographics and infrastructure to financing and governance. Transformations in curriculum and pedagogy undreamed by mid-twentieth-century progressives have been coupled with vast social adaptations, citizen initiatives, government mandates beginning with integration and forced busing and then returning to neighborhood schools, magnet schools, charter schools, school choice, privatization. State and national requirements for testing and evaluation continually revise pedagogies and teacher certification standards. The latest school kids in the family come home with nearly indecipherable assignments involving math concepts and reading and writing models markedly strange and even counterintuitive to elders who once took the subjects in "straight" delivery, and to all appearances distinguished mainly by the fact that they are teachable. Computerized instruction jostles with distance learning. Assignment posting and teacher-student exchange take place on interactive Web sites. Education departments and colleges constantly rejigger their own configurations of discipline, course offerings, concentrations, educational delivery systems. "Methods" courses attempt to replenish themselves with new infusions of content from constantly evolving academic majors. Social appreciations, values, and interpretations expand with the new evolutions of the culture, while core curriculum designs struggle to observe the primacy of hard-content knowledge and basic skills.

As noted above, particularly for the educational beneficiaries of post–World War II American peace and plenitude—including the generation of the war but also now most notably the generation of their children currently passing into late-life adulthood—there seems considerable befuddlement, if not downright consternation, at constant attempts, largely unsuccessful, to re-envision for today's and tomorrow's younger citizens what now seem yesterday's basic literacy, math skills, general knowledge of science, history, languages, literature, the arts. The old curriculum, as one might call it, just seems like something that someone, somewhere, somehow, could still figure out how to teach: the ability to write a good sentence, a paragraph, a short piece of informational or argumentative prose; understanding basic computations needed for paying bills, making a financial agreement, taking on a mortgage or car, credit-card and other loan payments, filing income tax; in a broader sense, reading about agriculture research in the newspaper and knowing something about photosynthesis without being bludgeoned with the krebs cycle; knowing something about atomic structure without getting lost somewhere in deep space between general gravitation and quantum mechanics; having enough observational or analytical training to know how to read, to observe, to listen; how to conceptualize a basic operation of nature or of work.

Whatever it was we used to call high school is of course now further bookended by a host of other complex institutional forms. At the front end there is early childhood education, followed by the traditional primary grades in one guise or another, and then middle school. As important, on the other side, is the virtually uniform cultural imperative of mandatory higher education in one form or another. In this, especially, we have come a long way from the mid-twentieth-century idea that a high school degree meant something as far as vocation and citizenship were concerned. To be sure, in most places a certain number of graduates would have gone on to liberal arts colleges or universities, perhaps graduate and professional schools. A handful might have vaulted into the upper reaches, the Ivy League, or one of the great national public universities. Those who wanted to teach would have met the entrance requirements for state teachers' colleges, many of them now regional universities. Others would have found advanced training at vocational schools and secretarial or business colleges, as they were called in those days. In some places there might have been a local junior or community college, frequently a two-year extension branch of a larger institution. But a substantial number of graduates in most places would simply have been finished as far as formal education was concerned. Ahead of them would lie a life in some kind of trade—plumbing, carpentry, electronics, farm or factory work; the military or a government job; maybe something salaried in a service industry or small business, construction, maintenance, truck driving, route sales and delivery, automotive, appliance, or equipment repair. Marriage and family would likely come early, frequently spurring zeal for promotion and ambition to move up into foreman or supervisor status, or perhaps independent business ownership. For the vast majority of such people, the American high school provided the basis of an expectation that people would find good jobs and stay with them until their working lives were done and they could retire.

After the post–World War II higher-education explosion, with relentless complaints about the simultaneous building up and dumbing down of the American curriculum, and in an age of No Child Left Behind with new strictures about basic skills and hard-knowledge content extending from earliest preschool to college and university curricula, the historical message of the Sam Cooke song seems to have come full circle. "Don't know much about _____" becomes the general story of our lives. (Ironically, in the discipline of popular-culture studies, during an era when no one allegedly reads anymore, it continues to be a registered trademark for an ever-expanding line of books, by Kenneth C. Davis, beginning with *Don't Know Much about History,* and then the Civil War, Geography, the Bible, and Mythology, before lately spinning off almost exponentially into myriad new topics.) It becomes an elegy for the golden age of the American high school kid and for a system of general education that somehow, we now believe, sent people out into young adulthood with the fundamental kinds of knowledge required to operate as a full participant in the life of the world. But nostalgia on any account will not do. People can fault movies and TV; sex, drugs, and rock 'n' roll; the Vietnam War and the 1960s counterculture; educational overbuilding and the general dumbing down of standards; the decline of local economies and the meltdown of inner cities; racial poverty and forced integration and busing; the breakdown of family discipline; and the political battles of left and right over evolution and religion in the schools; teacher certification and tenure requirements; the pressures of a fashionable multiculturalism and political correctness; a general culture of ethical relativism and instant tabloid scandal, full of consumers with a virtually nonexistent attention span, where people learn most of the things they know from cell phones, the Internet, text messaging, MySpace and YouTube. The list could go on indefinitely. The fact is that after a half century of educational crisis bookended by mass integration on one side and mass immigration on the other, every change that has happened was a change that had to happen, and any hopes or possibilities of control over the changes that continue to happen will increasingly have to be focused ahead on the future directions of change. There will simply be no going back. In ways undreamed with each passing year, reconfigurations of knowledge will require ongoing reconfigurations of the very structures of educational understanding. Reconfigurations of demography will require constant reconfigurations of infrastructure, delivery systems, buildings, classrooms, course content, school hours, and distributions of local, state, and national authority. Reconfigurations of technology will require reconfigurations of curriculum and instruction, standards of teacher competency and effectiveness, and measures of what are now called educational outcomes. The newest jargon from educationists, bouncing from crisis to crisis with the latest piecemeal bright idea in teacher training or computer technology, will not do it; nor will the newest stopgap mandates from educational manager-bureaucrats mired in a chronic reactive mode where *actual* reconceptualization simply lies off the scale of imaginative reach. To be sure, neither will waxing nostalgic over old 1950s songs; watching reruns of David and Ricky, Wally and the Beaver; reprising ideas of homogeneous schools and standard curricula that will never be again; going back to home-schooling Web sites starting off with facsimile reproductions of *McGuffey's Readers,* or if that won't satisfy from the standpoint of traditional values, the *New England Primer.* In America today, "School Days" is not the title of a song by Chuck Berry, somewhere back with Sam Cooke's "Wonderful World," the Coasters' "Smoking in the Boys' Room," or maybe Marty Robbins's "A White Sport Coat and a Pink Carnation." In fact, most people with a knowledge of current popular culture would associate the phrase with a Spike Lee movie about social tensions at a black college. The picture has changed because the frame has changed. They stopped making slide rules in America in 1996. Along with the song "Wonderful World," whence the archaic phrasing derives, gone as well is the graduation picture, the varsity letter jacket, the cheerleading sweater, the script of the senior play, and the honor roll announcement in the local newspaper. For those who remember or imagine a world of relationship between education and community, the song now remains mainly piquant—perhaps, increasingly like many of us, just another cultural curiosity. At the same time, it still strangely resonates down the generations. Where a curriculum bespeaks the idea of a common knowledge, a common education is clearly valued. Where a common education is valued, people seem to find ways of working together toward a goal of community. Ask any teacher.

10
The Fifty-fives

Nobody who remembers anything about American cars will ever forget the fifty-fives. In 1955 cars were American, and they were made in Detroit. People looked forward to a new model year in cars—the fifty-twos, the fifty-threes, the fifty-fours, etc.—the way they looked forward to baseball spring training or a new season of TV shows. "Fifty-five" was roundly acknowledged as a great model year. In the realm of cars, moreover, people didn't just mean to look; with disposable income on hand, generous trade-in terms for used models, installment-loan plans relatively manageable on the average paycheck, and style, horsepower, and mobility on their minds, they also meant to think seriously about buying. The personal automobile was central to the great postwar consumer revolution, of which in many ways it became the material sign and index—the jewel in the crown, so to speak, occupying the great midrange of buying activity between individual family homes on one hand and major appliances such as televisions, stoves and refrigerators, washers and dryers, and the like on the other. Through the development of the great interstate and superhighway systems and their material adjuncts such as the motel, the auto service center, the convenience store, the chain restaurant, and the shopping mall—and to the quick, almost overnight exclusion of travel by the long-distance passenger bus and passenger train, in favor of the passenger airplane—it also wrought a transportation revolution in relation to other forms of mass travel and conveyance that still distinguishes the American system from those of all other advanced countries. (Furthermore, in the dependence of that system on the availability of relatively cheap refined petroleum, the car culture of fifty years ago may now be seen as weirdly continuing to dictate American geopolitical policy more than any other cultural factor. That, however, is a discussion for my latter pages.)

The Fifty-fives. In a marketplace once dominated by familiar models from well-known American manufacturers, there will never be an array of cars to match them. At the basic level the flagship offerings would have included the fifty-five Chevy, the fifty-five Ford, and the fifty-five Plymouth—that is, the standard, entry-level, popular brand offered by each of the big-three automakers—General Motors, Ford, and Chrysler. In turn, each basic trademark beckoned the consumer to consider associated company brands on a generally ascending scale of expense and prestige. Chevy was paired on the next stage up with Pontiac, the latter considered sporty and deluxe. Buick was more luxurious and established. Cadillac was the prestige brand; in ads it was called simply "the car of cars." Ford responded with Mercury as a middle brand and Lincoln, something of a Buick and a Cadillac. Technically a Lincoln product, the Continental Mark II was devised as rare and prestigious even beyond Cadillac. Chrysler had a branding scale reflecting its somewhat catch-all assimilation of companies, moving from Plymouth through Dodge, DeSoto, and then Chrysler itself, again with a prestige brand, the Imperial, albeit like the Lincoln Continental, still technically a Chrysler.

Other brands were going extinct even as a few hung on to a diminishing postwar market share. Henry J. Kaiser, the great steelmaker and Victory Ship manufacturer of the war years, had run the postwar automotive course with cars of innovative reputation (but poor sales) such as the Kaiser, Fraser, and Henry J. The heroic wartime production record of the Willys Motor Company would tail off into much-constricted military contracts and small-scale manufacture of the domestic jeep. Studebaker and Packard, two highly respected brands, and major contributors to the war effort, would hang on in a short-lived alliance. A handful of Nash offerings, the Ambassador, Hudson, Rambler, Hornet, and Metropolitan, would survive for a while longer, reinvented as American Motors.

Within the brands, as with the broader array of corporate offerings, enticing and attractive gradations were set out as portals to continually ascending upward mobility. Ford offered a three-tiered model range and nomenclature: Mainline, Customline, Fairlane. (Sedan styles, coupe and family-size, were cleverly called the "Tudor" and the "Fordor.") Chevrolet matched up with the One-Fifty, Two-Ten, and Bel Air. Plymouth had the Plaza, Savoy, and Belvedere, while also generally trying to set itself off across the board according to size and affordable luxury as "biggest in price field." Up and across various other lines, Mercury offered Custom, Monterey, and Montclair; Buick the Special, Century, and Roadmaster; Studebaker the Champion, Commander, and President; "Rocket" Oldsmobile the 88, Super 88, and 98; Nash the Wasp, Hornet, Hudson, and Ambassador. Even the classy Packard, with its flagship Patrician, offered an entry-level model called the Clipper.

Within the various tiers, model configurations, and styles, manufacturers offered choice and novelty almost beyond belief. Station wagons alone came in a dizzying variety: the Plymouth Suburban; the Chevrolet Nomad; the Pontiac Safari; the Ford Ranch Wagon, Country Sedan, and top-of-the-line Country Squire, with optional wood side-paneling. A hot item was the "hardtop convertible"—a sporty two-door sedan with the door post taken out; among luxury brands there was also the much-admired new "four-door hardtop"—the Buick Special Riviera, for instance, and the Olds Deluxe 98.

Amid the bounteous splendors of the automotive scene, one would have come across the occasional truck advertisement. Chevy and Ford dominated the pickup market, with styling packages mimicking the new car designs. Other options included GMC, Dodge, Studebaker, and the Willys jeep.

An area of virtually complete American forfeit during the decade after the war, oddly, was the sports-car market, which Chevrolet had begun to explore with the Corvette and would be joined in 1955 by Ford with the Thunderbird. Still, then and now, these were comparatively big, heavy, muscular American productions. The sports car, as most Americans still understood the term, remained largely British—the Jaguar, MG, or Austin Healy—or included the occasional exotic Porsche or Ferrari. Imports generally at the time stuck mostly in the upper ranges of luxury and prestige but also came with an elitist reputation for finicky, specialized workmanship. Among the wealthy, one might see the odd Jaguar, Citroen, or Mercedes sedan. Trendy niche sophisticates, prescient advocates of small as better, could tootle around in a Fiat, Renault, or Morris Minor.

On the American side, generally as to size, with the exception of the Hudson Hornet and Wasp, as well as the Nash Rambler and Metropolitan—all pointedly marketed as small cars—everything out of Detroit in 1955 was big and heavy. Terms such as *compact* or *economy* were completely foreign to the American automotive vocabulary. Indeed, as noted by David Halberstam, only in one instance did a major manufacturer, GM, even bother to flirt with the idea of small as a concept, briefly speculating on the production of a small, postwar, entry-level car called the Cadet.* When they did the figures, they observed that producing the basic components for a big car, at least according to the cost structures at the time, cost barely more than dealing with anything smaller. Further, they discovered, they would need to sell three hundred thousand of the new model annually just to pay for tool-and-die manufacturing and other production equipment. The moral of the story was clear. Americans should somehow be encouraged to consider themselves happy to be getting a large car in the first case and then encouraged to move on from large to larger and more deluxe. Ten years later the plan was still working. Indeed, five more years would pass before the first compacts—the Ford Falcon, Chevrolet Corvair, Plymouth Valiant, Studebaker Lark, and Nash Rambler—began production. And one might speculate that this only took place because of the sudden appearance and overnight marketing triumph of the wildly popular German Volkswagen.

Whatever the brand, style, or pitch, it would now be hard to deny, whether in popular-culture retrospect or in actual production history, that across the whole panoply of offerings the fifty-fives marked an absolute watershed year for cars in America. American cars had reached a pinnacle of design, image, and appeal, of size and equipment ranging from body panel, frame, door, trunk, hood, grille, glass, and trim to engine and transmission mechanics. The industry itself had likewise reached a great moment of solidity while supporting a whole set of further layers of production and employment. Dealership sales proliferated into vast used-car networks. (No pretentious phrase like "pre-owned" was

*Halberstam, *The Fifties,* 119–20.

required in such days of assumed sturdy reliability. "Used" was just fine.) The enormous automotive service sector supported a whole industrial and commercial apparatus of standardized, factory-produced, repair and replacement parts, mechanics trades, gas, oil, and tire businesses, independent garages, what used to be called gas or service stations. As much a geography as a market, a whole new service network of commerce and business came to focus on the culture of the car—lodging, food, fuel—moving the focus of life in the country itself from cities and town centers to suburbs and high-traffic belt and connector highways.

Thus had the automobile come to stand dead center in the great American showroom as the chrome and metal dividend of post-1945 peace and prosperity—the gift of a whole flagship popular-culture apparatus that had shaped itself out in the decade since the end of the war. The overnight retooling of heavy industry from war production of ships, planes, tanks, jeeps, trucks, armored cars, landing craft, amphibious vehicles—at the time astonishing in its own right as an economic miracle—brought forth a cornucopia of brands, models, choices, buyer opportunities. To be sure, wartime had enforced its terms of scarcity across the whole realm of what we would now call big-ticket consumer items—homes, cars, appliances, luxury goods. But because of massive convergences of subindustries, supply systems, raw materials, the consumer sector hardest hit was surely the car industry. Vehicle manufacturing production lines ran on immense amounts of iron, steel, aluminum, chrome, and glass; and the vehicles themselves ran on equally immense quantities of gasoline and rubber. In response, for three years, basically, the powerhouse American economy just stopped making cars. What prewar models remained on the road were subject to gasoline and tire rationing; when repair parts ran out, many of these simply stopped running for the duration. GM, Ford, and Chrysler made guns, tanks, trucks, and large engines and weaponry for boats and airplanes; Studebaker specialized in trucks; a small company named Willys got the jeep; Packard made high-performance fighter aircraft and PT boat engines.

In the face of massive postwar consumer demand and accumulated spending power, combined with the memory of a car industry at the end of the 1930s that was just starting to become truly modern in every respect—the retooling of American mass-production automotive genius and enterprise was yoked to the operations of a corresponding promotional genius marketing technological advancements gained during the wartime hiatus. New cars blazoned their attractions in relentlessly hopped-up terminologies of design, performance, and mechanical advantage. Plymouth worked an alliterative vein with the "Power-Flo" engine and "Power-Flite" transmission. Ford similarly touted its "Trigger Torque Power." Mercury's big engine was the "Super-Torque V-8." Ambassador's V-8 was the "Jetfire"; Plymouth's was the "Hy-Fire." DeSoto actually offered two: the "Firedome" and the "Fireflite." Pontiac's was the "Strato-Streak," yoked to the "Hydra-Matic" transmission. The Ford equivalent of the latter was, of course, the "Fordomatic."

Everybody tried to come up with some strange little feature suggesting novelty or technological edge. DeSoto had a "Flite Control Gear Selector" mounted on the dash. Packard advertised "Torsion-Level Ride." Chevrolet had its "Glide-Rite Front Suspension." Sometimes a new concept amounted to paint: in the new age of the two-tone car, Dodge Royal Lancer and DeSoto Coronado could be bought as three-tones. Or glass: the otherwise dowdy Nash Ambassador emphasized its novel "Scena-Ramic Windshield."

Some slogans were familiar. "Body by Fisher." "See the USA in your Chevrolet." "Ask the Man Who Owns One." Some proved mercifully less enduring: "Treat Yourself to a Trigger-Torque Test Drive"; or, the fifty-five DeSoto "with the forward look."

Major car-selling points now sound like some mid-1950s allegory of national desire: bigness, comfort, innovation, convenience, affordable luxury. Automatic transmissions were paired with big, smooth, powerful engines. Surplus power was channeled to power steering, power brakes, and power-operated windows and convertible tops. There were vast improvements in fans, heaters, windshield wipers, radios, along with the first car air-conditioning systems. Although it seems obvious now, the secret of design, production, improvement, and consumer desirability was a simple one that bears repeating at least once: it involved anything to make the capable buyer think that he or she was justified in imagining that there was an ideal new American car out there waiting for him or her that year—and that on this basis alone he or she not only justifiably wanted a new model but needed and probably deserved a new model. A new car would simply bring a new satisfaction through some truly life-enhancing convenience or distinction: a swifter transmission, a more powerful engine, improved carburetion, a more efficient stroke or compression ratio. On top of everything else there was the magic of annual styling change. People waited every year, in a cherished early-fall ritual, to see what the new models were going to look like, who was going to trump whom, not just with mechanical innovation but with memorable body design or some new paint, glass, trim, or bumper scheme. The whole idea was most memorably phrased by George Walker, a Ford counterpart to Harley Earl, the legendary guiding spirit of planned obsolescence at GM. "We design a car to make a man unhappy with his 1957 Ford," Walker drawled, "'long about the end of 1958."*

Looking at such cars on Web sites or in picture books today, one loses the impression of how big, heavy, bright, and metallic they were, rolling temples of sheet metal, chrome, glass, upholstery, and rubber. Even the steering wheels were enormous. They promised satisfaction in a big way, and they didn't disappoint. Brand loyalty was off the scale. A General Motors, Ford, or Chrysler car was a good car. They didn't make a bad car. Somewhere amidst each line was a model making an American owner completely confident that he or she was driving the best.

As to the fifty-fives, pride of place will always have to go to the Chevy. The Ford and Chrysler offerings had partially played their new design hand a year earlier. Distinctive and handsome cars, the Fords and Plymouths especially were both identifiable evolutions of the 1954s. The Chevy, in contrast, represented a quantum leap, looking no more like a 1953 or 1954 model than it did a 1948 or a 1949. It looked like a Chevy all right—sharp, simple, and cleanly angled—but it also looked like the future.

Especially the two-door hardtop. It became the signature vehicle of young America. One might argue that it took until the 1960s for Ford to find a way to begin catching up, which it was able to do impressively with the Mustang. Eventually would come the muscle cars, the Camaro, the

*Quoted in Halberstam, *The Fifties,* 127.

Charger, the GTO; and then the great "personal cars" of the 1970s and 1980s—the Monte Carlo, Cutlass, Gran Prix, Riviera. They would all have a closest common ancestor in the fifty-five Chevy hardtop.

The best place to look to get the feel of what it was all like, hardtops and sedans, station wagons and convertibles, may still be in the great popular magazines of the era. As opposed to black-and-white newspaper ads and TV spots, the magazine displays were invariably in full color, with spectacular graphics and lavish design. Color photographs featured fashion shots with attractive, well-dressed models. Or as often, there were cool, precise illustrations, with cars and people rendered in a kind of hyperrealism somehow even more stylish and glamorous than the real thing. A woman with a Ford Country Squire station wagon full of kids looks like Donna Reed. A gas station attendant in his snappy Sinclair uniform looks like Dana Andrews. A bunch of people getting out of a big, handsome, top-of-the-line Chrysler look as if they go to the opera every night.

Such contemporary advertising scenes and others like them—of suburb, small town, city—were themselves already part of a broader national landscape being transformed overnight as a result of the golden age of the postwar American automobile. An entire transportation, housing, and business and commerce infrastructure was being redesigned in the very image of the car to accommodate its signature characteristics of speed, power, reliability, safety, and ease of mobility. By no coincidence, from mid-decade may be dated the limited-access highway, the perimeter loop, the shopping mall, the planned community, the interstate system, fast-food and lodging chains, theme parks, exurbs, edge cities. That story does not need to be retold here, nor does the saga of Detroit's eventual fall from glory through the late-century onslaught of high-quality competition from Europe and Asia, with myriad state-of-the-art operations of foreign competitors in fact dotting the American landscape as the old domestic component and assembly plants of the Midwest fall to silence and rust. The small pictures described above, it might be claimed, speak vividly of such matters to anyone alive at the time on how far things have come from the year of the great Detroit fifty-fives. In the age of the SUV and king-cab pickup, even as this is written now passing into the new era of the crossover and the hybrid, the American station wagon will seem only slightly less familiar than the Conestoga wagon. Ford made its last models in the mid-1970s. The last time most people saw a wood-paneled Country Squire outside of a car show, it was probably being used as a woody in a surfer movie. Likewise, the uniformed filling-station attendant went extinct decades ago; followed shortly by any vestigial charade of "full service" versus "self-service" at the pumps. People running the cash registers where one buys gas will be workers at a minimart, not a service station. Outside of a big repair shop or an interstate service plaza, an employee who knows how to check the oil is a genius. In all this, one realizes that the Sinclair Oil Company, itself part of a breed long gone in the wake of the great petroleum multinationals and conglomerates, had a dinosaur advertising logo for a reason. As for Chrysler, the company still exists (at least, as of this writing)—having survived an ill-suited transatlantic partnership with Daimler-Benz and now hanging on by its fingernails under the ownership of a private equity firm; and it still actually makes the brand, after a fashion. One model, the Sebring, sports a power convertible top that folds smoothly and invisibly into a hidden boot in the back. Unfortunately, the boot also turns out to be the trunk. When the top is down, everything in the trunk has to go into what passes for a backseat. A more recent offering is the 300, a low-slung, blocky, powerful design reminiscent of the muscle cars of yore. The new iteration, heralding its continuity with the great Chrysler tradition of big-engine horsepower, arrived on the scene just in time for the price of gasoline to double. In one version or another of these imaginary exempla, everyone growing up after World War II in America will have his or her own version of a true story about what happened to the American car—about their uncle's big DeSoto, with monster chrome all over the place and the strange transmission lever on the dash; or maybe the Pontiac Safari with the hot plastic seats and all the windows down taking a driver and ten kids home from a blistering day at the lake or the swimming pool. Like these and others, one suspects, even as the great era of the car passes forward from the Hummer to the hybrid, the hydrogen, and beyond, a passing generation will still find a way of going back and talking as if it all began with the fifty-fives.

II
The End of the World

If there was such a thing as the good life after the good war, the end of it came early for my mother, my brother, my sister, and me on a night now more than fifty years ago. To be exact, at 9:05 p.m., Tuesday, March 5, 1957, in the space of a few minutes, my father died of a massive heart attack. He was forty-seven. My mother was forty-six, my brother twenty-one, my sister ten. I was twelve. The physical particulars of the event were vouchsafed to my sister and me, sitting with our father in a small, cozy room, paneled all around with cabinets and bookshelves, that we used for reading and watching TV. It was what people today would call a family room. We called it the den. Holding up a model ship I was in the final stages of assembling, I turned around to face my father, who seemed to be making some sort of odd movement in his high-backed chair just across the room. My sister, on a small couch off to his side, must have noticed as well. For an instant it must have looked to both of us as if he was trying to offer us one of his myriad comedy turns, perhaps the J. Fred Muggs chimpanzee imitation he had recently perfected that my sister and I found unceasingly hilarious. But instead he seemed to be clutching at something up high in his chest, near the throat. He began to snort and convulse in ways, I suddenly realized, I had never seen a human being do—ways, in fact, a human being was not meant to do. He was dying. My sister and I began to cry out. In a matter of seconds he slumped in his chair. My sister kept calling for our mother. As I vaguely remembered being taught in some first-aid class somewhere—gym class, Boy Scouts, swimming lessons, I don't remember which—I tried to pull forward my father's shoulders and pump his chest. I held my sister. I somehow recall mumbling the Lord's Prayer. I don't remember, exactly, when or how my mother appeared at the small flight of stairs leading down into the room, but she did. She was already too late.

The only detail I can summon back from just afterward is the voice of the doctor when he got there maybe fifteen minutes later. Part of a respected team of country GPs, old family friends and social visitors, he was normally—as distinguished from his jovial, somewhat earthy counterpart—a learned and clinical man, with a reserve many people took for coldness. But now he sounded as if his heart was breaking. "Marty, he's gone," he told my mom. Those were his exact words. "Marty, he's gone." As he spoke, I was standing with my mother, slightly to the side and behind, looking beyond them both down into the den, where my father remained in his chair. I could see his right hand on the armrest.

Two things more come back to me from later. I remember my brother, handsome in his college tweeds, coming up the front walk, trying manfully to hold in his sadness, having driven several hours through the night. Oddly, I also have memories from throughout the long hours of darkness of an uncle by marriage—something of a disreputable character, a drinker, weekend musician, and ladies' man—sitting up with me in the big bedroom I had to myself since my brother had gone to college. I had been sent there to try and sleep. Whenever I woke up, shaking and crying out, as I did every so often before daylight, I could make him out across the room, keeping watch over me, always in the same chair. My recollection is that he must not have left me for a minute. It seemed to be his gift of steadfastness to the family this night.

"Coronary occlusion" was the common phrasing in those days for the thing that killed my father—a form of severe, usually fatal heart attack. I don't think it's used much anymore. I find it strange that it took me decades to find out what any kind of heart attack really was. I always thought it was some enormous clot that stopped up one of the body's big blood vessels, a major vein or artery, basically shutting down the circulatory system so that the heart had to give out. Only a few years back did I discover from reading about cardiac "events," as they are now called, that it was a blood vessel in his heart muscle that became totally and suddenly blocked. That shut down his heart muscle, which stopped it from pumping. That in turn stopped the oxygen to his brain.

Explanations fluttered about in the days afterward about how such a thing had happened so suddenly. It turns out that "suddenly" had nothing to do with it. My grandmother contributed information concerning a bout my father had in his late teens with what may have been rheumatic fever. That, plus exertions as a college track and field athlete, may have damaged his heart. Before my mother died, she also told me about tests he had gotten a year or so earlier in Philadelphia from a heart specialist to whom he had been sent. In the days before standard antihypertensives, cholesterol blockers, plaque preventatives and the like, the basic protocol for treatment had been bed rest for six weeks. That was definitely not in the cards for my father, an industrial chemist and company director, charged with overseeing day-to-day business for a big food processing corporation, headquartered in our town with the main plant but also with operations in several states. My guess is that he'd lived for years with runaway hypertension, complicated eventually by atherosclerosis, gradual blockage in the major heart vessels—the kind of thing they would treat today with clot-busters, angioplasty, or, if more serious, coronary bypass. Whatever the organic cause, it was in my father's case routinely exacerbated by coffee, cigarettes, overwork, tension, lack of sleep. During the high-volume harvest seasons, especially—first raspberries, then peaches, then cherries, then tomatoes, finally apples—he worked around the clock. Out on the production lines he served as the management-level supervisor for hordes of "seasonal" employees—everyone from local women to grade the fruit, wash it, and run the peeling and slicing machines, to farmers and plant laborers unloading the trucks and operating the big juicing and saucing apparatus. Meanwhile, at regular intervals, he ran back to the company labs where he and a permanent staff of chemists and technicians worked nonstop on quality control testing and record keeping. Peaking in the hottest months of the year, this work of my father's took place in the days before air-conditioning. The plant, with its noises and lights and smells, was open to the almost stifling night air. Our house had attic fans and screened windows. My brother says he remembers my father not even bothering to come upstairs at night when he got a break.

He'd just come home, lie down on the living room floor or out on the side porch where it was cool, and catch a few hours sleep.

Of the many questions I would like to ask my father if I had a chance, among the first would have to be one about the unrelenting industriousness. What was it with the work deal, I want to know—finding myself at sixty-four as bad as he ever was, I think, if maybe not worse. What makes it impossible for some people to quit doing it all the time and at just one speed—the latter being in my father's case, as one of his eulogists put it, nonstop "high gear." And I don't mean finding an ability to get up one morning and say, no, I don't have to do so-and-so today, period—an idea that for me seems as impossible, I have to admit, as it must have for him—but just something as simple and sensible as saying, no, I don't have to do 110 percent today. Maybe a hundred will do, or maybe just for once ninety or ninety-five. I may know it too, in myself; but I still understand it even less. I tell myself that when I'm not working, I exercise, don't smoke, don't drink, watch my weight, actively try to manage stress. But back there still is the hundred-percent-plus compulsion, the sense of the imperative, the duty, somehow, not to regard anything as good or worthy work save that which brings some end point in exhaustion.

My guess is that the work in my father's case was connected with a certain idea of providing. To be sure—as someone who has engaged such traditional ideas of achievement in my own education and career, not to mention in a lifelong academic study of American myths of self-fulfillment, happiness, and success—I know that my father enjoyed being well-regarded in business and professional circles and as a prominent citizen and community member. Still, I think that providing trumped professional or personal ambition. The Great Depression certainly had something to do with it. His father, a creamery owner, a clever real-estate investor, eventually at odds with German Brethren congregants because he had in his youth rejected selection by lot for the ministry and later discovered the virtues of life insurance, somehow managed to send four children to good private colleges. My father may have noted that my mother's family, old Quaker agricultural gentry, likewise found money for touring cars big enough to handle eight children and college educations for those so inclined.

But my father's was some desperate wish to provide: perhaps because he watched so many other people go down in the Depression; perhaps because he felt somehow responsible in being singled out for good fortune in having a good job with a big, well-run, family-owned food processing company—itself unique in that it paid monthly salaries and relied for more substantial compensation on end-of-year profits. It was a wish in life in which he certainly succeeded. Ironically, after death he succeeded equally, perhaps even better than he could have imagined. What they would now call estate-planning seems to have been a nascent, mostly neglected, pursuit among working business and professional people of America back in those days—as opposed to those of great corporate or inherited wealth. My father somehow had decided to start early with what was called whole-life insurance, combining casualty benefits with long-term cash value. (A family rumor held that my grandfather had first made the discovery, which resulted in his invitation, as noted earlier, to leave the Mennonite Church. God will provide.) He also managed accumulations of company stock, sold and converted to trusts of one sort or another. After he was gone, we never lacked for everyday means. Among my brother, sister, and me, three substantial educations got paid for. My mother, living into her mid-nineties, must have become a mid-twentieth-century actuary's nightmare. At the end, after more than a decade of assisted-living and nursing care, there were still substantial bequests for the grandchildren my father never knew.

Another side of that working, I have now come to see, involved some kind of internalized payoff—personal satisfaction, family or community esteem, I don't know—that only had partly to do with money and security. Work—and I do mean something as crude as the old Protestant-capitalist idea of vocation or calling—really was its own reward for my father, as it has always been in many ways for me. For both of us, one can certainly call this the idea of a work ethic in its fullest sense, culturally very much of its time and place, I now increasingly see, for both of us: his of the generation of the Great Depression and of World War II; mine of the generation who will always see themselves as the legatees and inheritors and stewards of their bravery, sacrifice, and dedication. But at the same time it remains a lot more complicated even than that. Call it working for posterity, working hard at everything—career, family, friends, community, the respect and recognition entailed in the appreciation of the tribe. Or maybe even call it a form of looking for love. Underneath everything was a desperate wish to please.

That wish was certainly one in which my father succeeded abundantly. The eulogies were breathtaking. And the recollections of those who knew him have changed nothing over all the decades. Albeit distinctly of the world and in the world, a man of family, a man of business, a prominent citizen, my father was, in a word, beloved. That, too, is a part of the inheritance. One of the most vivid images of him—something that speaks out, for instance, from photos in the newspaper depicting him on professional or civic occasions—is that of a youngish man somehow knowing he was not going to get old, trying to infuse the moment with an aspect of goodwill. By reputation, he was a man who defused tensions with humor, who got people to work together when they needed to. He was also notable for his sense of active justice, his concern for those he deemed victims of some unfair imposition. He gave people a break when they were in trouble; he treated them fairly afterward in gratitude for keeping his trust. Over the years I have become fond of saying that my father had the bad manners to die while he was still a saint. This actually does seem to have applied in all his relations—to his family and to the world. It has all been very hard to live down.

What may have been underneath, I also wonder. There was an anger that I saw break out against me just once. It was the only time, in fact, I recall he ever struck me; and when he did, he picked me up by the shirt front and hit me hard, slapped me back and forth across the face a couple of times. I had been nagging him about a Sunday afternoon run to the hobby shop, as I recall, something we did occasionally, usually to get another plastic model kit or maybe something for the electric train setup down in the basement; that Sunday, he made it clear, firmly but quietly, that he wanted to sit in his chair and read the paper. I tromped off sullenly upstairs to my room, down at the other end of the house, melodramatically slamming and locking the door behind me. He followed closely, his anger eventually building and building as he talked to me from the other side of the door. When I let him in, he just exploded, let himself go with a violence I think that must have shocked us both. After he was gone, I remember finding pieces of one of the good mechanical pencils he usually carried in a shirt pocket. What reserves of fury were there? What could such anger have been about?

His old friends have told me since about a visible nervous energy, pacing, jingling car keys and coins in his pockets. This seems to have been the other side of public calm, cheer, patience, affability, an astonishing kinetic drive, an inability not to be in motion. I now find it also connected with a consistency of desire for fine appearance. My mother said that when she cleaned out his closet, she found six or seven immaculate blue worsted suits. The constant motion, the personal orderliness: did he have obsessive-compulsive disorder? Was it like mine—the good, big, mean, end-of-the-world, unhinging, all-consuming kind? Did he know those moments of what would be incidental experience for other people as leading to complete debilitation, emotional shutdown? Did he, too, in the days before selective serotonin reuptake inhibitors (SSRIs), have to beat down loony nightmares and catastrophe scenarios, rising like demons out of moments of conflict, or confrontation, or perceived personal failure, and then haunting and wearing down the mind for weeks and months afterward? My mother said that toward the end he had started having a couple of drinks before bed most nights. "Tippling," she called it, in her signature way. That was certainly my form of medication for a long time. Was he an alcoholic—like me—who had managed—unlike me—to hold it in all those years?

Was it sexual energy? I remember the courtship pictures with my mother, from down in Charlottesville, on the Rotunda steps, where she was attending some University of Virginia summer education institute. She is lithe and flapperish in the 1920s summer dress; he is shining and happy in a white flannel suit. By the time of the wedding pictures it is my young father, with all my mother's clan, the old apple aristocrats. Again the theme seems to be diaphanous dresses and wide, lovely summer hats for the women, white trousers and flannels for the men. My mother looks handsome but ill at ease. Over the course of their marriage, things seem never really to have changed. By the time we were school-age, my father and mother, like Ward and June Cleaver, actually had twin beds. My mother could get on her high horse socially, be censorious and disapproving. She developed a martyr habit, strategically giving and withholding emotion. The results were pronounced personal enmities, among friends and family. My father worked the damage-control of diplomacy and good cheer, meanwhile evincing his utter loyalty to my mother in an indefatigable devotion away from work to family rituals. My earliest memories are thus of the kind of family where during the week people could eat midday and evening meals at home together, where weekends were devoted to aunts, uncles, and cousins, visits to the grandparents, church, Sunday school, Sunday dinner, a picnic or getaway supper at a little place up in the mountains.

My other great memory is of the civility of their relationship—a word, I should note, I openly mean to cherish rather than disparage here. A good deal of the time, this came out for both of them in taste—a certain kind of living well, albeit within small-town, middle-class restraints. The family car was a Packard; my father drove a Ford, the basic sedan, to the plants and on the road. My father bought my mother beautiful clothes, things she really looked good in—dressy dresses, suits, tailored jackets and skirts, all handsome things. He was the same way with tasteful jewelry—earrings, pins, necklaces. He wrote loving letters when he was away. I wonder if the affection-filled page was his gift as well. Was it the tangible place where he could convince them that the marriage was full of loving communication?

Or was it his children who became the objects of his love, filled the emptiness in his heart that comes to many marriages when love has sunk into affectionate, but mainly respectful, formality? We all certainly deemed ourselves the recipients of his genuine love. My older brother, for a long time an only child, was sickly until adolescence, one time nearly dying of pneumonia. He became a good teenager, a great student, a musician, an athlete of some accomplishment. In college, on the way to med school, the year my father died he was a junior-year Phi Beta Kappa. As for me, once my brother was off at school, I had gotten to be a companion at sports events, high school and college football games, once even an Army-Navy game in Philadelphia. I was a golf partner, and sometimes a travel buddy on trips to settle my grandfather's estate, with a trip down the turnpike to Philadelphia and maybe supper on the way back at a Howard Johnson's. My sister was his darling, his wonder. Having a daughter created in him an affection and a loyalty, a devotion so great that at her wedding, more than ten years after his death, my grandmother, still alive, imagined how much pleasure her son might have taken in it all. "Wouldn't Willis have been proud?" she said, in that sweet, humorous Pennsylvania Dutch singsong of hers. "Wouldn't Willis have been proud?" And she wouldn't have meant "proud" so much in the conventional sense as "happy to be here" or "glad to be part of this."

There are plenty of other things I want to ask. Underneath the calm, the people pleasing, did he worry a lot? What did it cost him in personal emotional resources to be so attentive to others? I want to know how he felt about his friendships, his possible attractions to other women, his having to live up to a reputation for pure nonstop expertise and energy. What did he think of the great history he had lived through, helped to make, the Depression he had helped to defeat, the wartime victory he had helped to achieve? As a boy who grew up devouring histories of World War II, eventually to become a combat soldier in Vietnam, I want to ask how he felt about being exempted from military service—as a husband and father in his thirties, not to mention his role as an essential war-industry worker. What did he think of himself during the war, and afterward, when so many of his friends and coworkers came home with experiences behind them of Guadalcanal, Ploesti, the Battle of the Bulge?

What did he really think about his achievements and his visible success, including his great reward, about to be realized, in the presidency of the company, with a longtime friend and coworker moving from there to chairman of the board? What did he think of earthly honors and achievements generally? His early religious evolution, I knew, had tailed off, with my grandmother and grandfather becoming cursory churchgoers. The only visit I remember making to a service of the hometown Brethren congregation in which he grew up—with my sister and myself immensely entertained by the German custom of having a small church orchestra—was with a pious cousin. An elder of our family Presbyterian Church, he was prominently listed, to my great satisfaction, in the weekly bulletin. But mainly among religious duties I remember him keeping the books of the church's home for old ladies. He and my mother always sent my sister and me off with family friends to early Sunday school. My sister thinks it was so they could have sex. Did he believe at all in the possibility of life after death? I don't think so. I actually don't think my mother believed it either. Maybe, in retrospect, it was just one of those things a family like ours just didn't talk about. I think maybe we all stopped believing in anything like that the night my father died.

What I have mainly found over the years are fragments and impressions. In my baby book there is a ticket stub from the 1944 Navy–Notre Dame football game in Baltimore. That is where he happened to be the October weekend I was born—in a day of no cell phones or instant messaging, not to mention no males in the delivery room save the doctor, who of course was always male. I remember his booming laugh coming upstairs from the family room when he watched *What's My Line?*—a late-Sunday-night ritual enjoyment of his. It was a quiz show with a startlingly cerebral cast, even for those days: John Daly, Bennett Cerf, Arlene Francis, Dorothy Kilgallen, Martin Gabel, and—my father's particular favorite—a prune-faced, dyspeptic humorist named Fred Allen. My father got speeding tickets regularly. Was it a function of some obsessive compulsion to get somewhere? Of wanting to get home? In any event, he racked up enough citations at one point that I vaguely remember—an impression confirmed by my brother—his losing his driver's permit for a while. Then there are his letters. They may still be somewhere. I don't know. Personally, I think I'd rather just try to remember them from the last time I actually saw them, twenty years ago, when we were cleaning out our mother's house. He was legendary for his letter writing, to my mother when he was traveling, to his parents and siblings and in-laws when he was at home. What everyone seems to agree on, even now, is the sheer abounding affection, the love that poured out of those letters in the most spontaneous, positive kinds of ways.

My father had made a name in the world—or in our world, at least. In the county newspaper, in existence from back before the Civil War, his death got the upper-right-hand corner on the front page. J. W. Beidler, 47, along with his business title. J. W., alternately signed J. Willis: his first name was John, like his father's. The *Willis* was a German inheritance, out of Anglo-Saxon, as opposed to the more customary *William,* descended from the French *Guillaume.* To family and friends he was "Willie," again a usage specific to the region, something like the German *Willi* and on occasion actually pronounced "Villy" by older people I remember: not at all a Willie, I remember happily noting to myself, like the bank robber Willie Sutton; and certainly not a Willie like Arthur Miller's Willie

Loman in *Death of a Salesman*—mister low-man, mister everyman, walking American tragedy of the common man—a reference I remember bitterly resenting once when I heard it in a sermon from our Presbyterian minister, a Princeton-educated theologian with literary pretensions. My mother's name was Martha, in her case properly English Quaker and biblical. Her father took pains, it was said, to give his children names that were hard to convert to informal equivalents. Although not foolproof, especially among the boys—Chester became Chet, for instance, Cameron became Cam—the scheme worked better with the females—Ruth, Martha, Marion, Edna. Undeterred, my father made his own coinage. "Marty" was my dad's name for her, the German diminutive. That was the name our family doctor used the night he died. As far as I can remember, no one ever called her that again.

Mrs. J. W. Beidler. That is who she was and who she stayed. My mother took her marching orders from that night; that's for certain. There were a couple of suitors, quickly vanquished. We may have checked them out. It never occurred to us to pass judgment on any likelihood of their taking our father's place. My mother was married to my brother, my sister, and me.

The outpouring of grief and love for our father has never left me or my brother and sister. In odd times we still talk about it, dazzled by a desire to be known as our father's children—and, in complicated ways, subsequently to have accrued the right to be known as our mother's children as well. In the domain of social or public conduct we have certainly tried to be citizens, coworkers, attentive, open listeners, ready with a nod or a good word. We have probably done best by our genetics of personal temperament. We seem to have inherited from my father's family a kind of worldly south German ease and respect for comfort sown in with a prudential way with land and money. My brother can still tell wonderful stories about how, at family holidays, all the Beidlers would nearly fall out of their chairs laughing at old Pennsylvania Dutch dialect jokes. Like the family Quakers on my mother's side we can also be withdrawn, emotionally reserved, private. On both counts we seem to have always been accorded the special affection of being Willis's and Martha's children. For all that, then and now, well into our sixties and seventies, the entwined amiability and reticence habits persist into efforts to combine civility and good nature with plain-spokenness and fair-dealing. To this day we have never had a serious quarrel between or among us. As with our mother, after the end of the world, it never occurred to us to do anything but carry on.

12
I Was a 1950s Teenage Media Junkie

With apologies to Michael Landon and Steve McQueen—may they both rest in peace—people my age will understand the dumb movie references in the title of this essay. Like many Americans growing up in the post–World War II era, I remain the kind of person who inexplicably relishes knowing that, before there was *Bonanza* or *Little House on the Prairie,* Michael Landon got his start in a movie entitled *I Was a Teenage Werewolf* and that Steve McQueen's breakthrough role was that of a high school kid nobody would believe with his stories of a strange, spreading, all-devouring alien monstrosity in *The Blob.* The odd jumble of dictions is another giveaway. *Media* back then was still the plural of *medium:* when used at all, it was a technical term having to do with the advertising industry and only gradually widened to embrace technologies of mass communication—as in Marshall McLuhan's 1964 *Understanding Media.* A junkie was somebody who did heroin, like the Frank Sinatra card-shark guy in *The Man with the Golden Arm.* To the best of my knowledge, I had never even heard of William Burroughs.

All that notwithstanding, I assert that the titular proposition carries a substantive truth of memory and history from the times. As a young person in post-1945 America, I was probably among the original information freaks. And it wasn't just me, I honestly believe. In a great post–World War II stew of evolutions in twentieth-century information culture of daily newspapers, mass-circulation magazines, and general-interest books; of movies, popular music, radio, and TV; and of mass-market advertising, a lot of us—quite average American young people, by today's standards—became astonishingly knowledgeable on what were called in those days "current events": everything from popular personalities to politics, history, and world affairs. And I do not mean something as somber and formal as "cultural literacy"; rather, I propose to recapture what must have seemed at the time to most people general information: the kinds of things an average person might be expected to know.

Our fund of lore was wide and substantial, with even a certain amount of depth. We knew that Eisenhower had become president, rather easily defeating the Democratic Party candidate, Adlai Stevenson; but we knew that he had done it only after winning a big nomination battle, at least the first time around, with a Republican establishment headed by a stuffy-looking senator from Ohio named Robert Taft; meanwhile, Stevenson had gotten the Democratic nomination after defeating a Kentucky senator named Estes Kefauver, a bespectacled and otherwise dignified figure who oddly chose to campaign wearing a coonskin hat. We knew that the challenge had been strong enough for Kefauver to be made the vice presidential candidate on the Democratic ticket. We also knew that Ike's running mate, a much younger senator from California named Richard Nixon, in order to stay on the Republican ticket, had been forced to go on national TV and explain his personal finances, in a maudlin performance called "the Checkers speech" that even most loyal Republicans found creepy and distasteful. We knew the identities of world leaders including Anthony Eden, Pierre Mendes-France, Konrad Adenauer. We knew about the lives and histories of David Ben-Gurion of Israel, and King Farouk of Egypt, with the latter shortly to be ousted by a young army general named Gamal Abdel Nasser, who in turn would be militarily humiliated by the Israelis along with the English and French in the 1956 Suez War. We knew that the consort of the young English queen Elizabeth, by marriage the duke of Edinburgh, was actually Prince Philip of Greece, and that when Sir Edmund Hilary reached the summit of Mount Everest, he was accompanied by his faithful Sherpa guide, Tenzing Norkay.

We were proud to know that a manly American writer named Ernest Hemingway had won the Nobel Prize in literature for a famous novel called *The Old Man and the Sea* that an average person could actually read and appreciate; that the musical movie star Mario Lanza had a respected career at the Metropolitan Opera, as did the soprano Patrice Munsel—while regularly appearing on variety shows along with Sophie Tucker, "the last of the Red Hot Mamas," or Dorothy Shay, "the Park Avenue Hillbilly." We knew that Red Skelton, for all his clowning as Clem Kadiddlehopper, Freddie the Freeloader, and Heathcliff the cross-eyed seagull, was secretly "literary," allegedly writing a short story every night about a character with red hair; that Charles Van Doren, a big winner on *The Sixty-Four Thousand Dollar Question,* was an English instructor at Columbia University who came from a famous New York intellectual family. We didn't know exactly what that meant, but it somehow made him a very different kind of famous person from Mamie Van Doren. We knew that the movie star Rita Hayworth had married a playboy named Aly Khan, who somehow combined a life of Gran Prix auto racing and high-stakes gambling in Monte Carlo with world eminence as "spiritual leader" of a large sect of the religious group we called "Moslems." We knew that Danny Kaye's costar in *Hans Christian Andersen* was a real-live French ballerina named Jeanmaire; that the role of the baby Moses in *The Ten Commandments* was played by Charlton Heston's own son, Fraser; that Davy Crockett, played by Fess Parker, actually had served in the U.S. Congress before he went down fighting at the Alamo with Jim Bowie. We knew that the voices of all the big Looney Tunes/Merrie Melodies characters—Bugs Bunny, Daffy Duck, Porky Pig, Sylvester the Cat, Elmer Fudd, Tweety Bird, Yosemite Sam—were done by a single manic genius named Mel Blanc; that Patty McCormack, who played the homicidal child in *The Bad Seed,* was really a quite normal young person; that the teenage singer Paul Anka was Canadian by birth; that Fabian's last name was Forte, and that he had been discovered by Dick Clark right in Philadelphia, the home town of *American Bandstand.* We knew that Lana Turner's daughter, Cherry Crane, had stabbed her mother's boyfriend, a second-rate gangster named Johnny Stompanato, in the stomach and killed him; that the actress Laraine Day was married to the baseball manager Leo Durocher; that American worshippers of sundry Protestant denominations had become tremendously excited over a new evangelist named Billy Graham.

We hummed popular tunes we thought amusing: "How much is that doggie in the window?" or "Whenna the moon hits your eye like a bigga-pizza pie, that's amo-ray." We knew the popular jingles. "Mil-ler; High Life; the Champagne of Bottled Beers." "You'll wonder where the yellow went, when you brush your teeth with Pepsodent." "Kel-logg's Sugar Corn Pops (pop, pop); Sugar Pops are tops." We were sufficiently indoctrinated in questions of grammar to know that "Winston tastes good like a cigarette should" was regarded in some circles as playing fast and loose with adverbs and subordinate conjunctions.

A lot of information we got from radio and TV. But we also read a good deal of it in the newspapers, still part of a world where most people felt linked to a particular one they considered their primary information source—local, small city, or county, often from the nearest municipality or population center most closely identified with the region: Harrisburg, Montgomery, Akron, Albuquerque. Many homes received two or more, afternoon and evening. Often a local paper was paired with a city companion. In my small world alone, one saw regularly the *Philadelphia Inquirer,* the *Baltimore Sun,* the *Washington Post,* and the *New York Times.* Whatever the origin or venue, most publishers went all out with the Sunday papers, expanding to big features, style, sports, entertainment, and opinion sections—including, of course, deluxe, freestanding, color comic pages. People talked over Monday-morning coffee about Stalin or Yogi Berra, but they also had words as frequently for the previous day's Li'l Abner or Steve Canyon, Dagwood or Beetle Bailey.

In addition—to a degree now hard to recreate mentally—post-1945 popular print was further distinguished by the eminence of mass-circulation magazines. These could in certain cases be distinguished as having something of a highbrow reputation—the *Atlantic,* the *Saturday Review,* the *New Yorker*—or in others decidedly lowbrow, extending into true crime, sex, scandal, adventure, what we would call today tabloid and gossip. But most of the great magazines enjoying a last, postwar, golden age were resolutely middlebrow, with a certain distinction and pride being attached to the idea. Foremost was the publishing empire of Henry Luce, sometimes known as Time-Life, but more properly Time-Life-Fortune, further opening up a new mass readership in 1953 with *Sports Illustrated.* The term *middlebrow* is almost invariably used now as disparaging. These, it might be argued, struck a halcyon moment of such popular reading where the world's best photojournalism and illustration could be coupled with prose of substantial intellectual craft and insight—albeit with the latter certainly conforming to the "American Century" promotional politics of Luce, Inc. To this day, *Life* remains the nation's twentieth-century photojournalism archive of record. In the last great age of news photography, when indeed reporting current events through the photograph was still considered a professional art, *Life* had the corner on the market and most of the masterpiece work, with such figures as Margaret Bourke White, Eliot Elisofon, and Robert Capa working at home and abroad from the 1930s all the way up through World War II and still commanding the scene well into the 1960s. Simultaneously, Time-Life produced some of the era's most important feature writing, reportage, and historical documentary, sometimes conjoined with literary exclusives. This was a popular publishing era when *Life,* the flagship, could do a feature series titled "The World's Great Religions" or serialize Churchill's *History of the Second World War,* in all cases with lavish illustrations. Printed in a single issue was the full text of Hemingway's *The Old Man and the Sea.* Nearly as important in circulation and influence, *Time* perfected a style of reporting so brisk and innovative as to spawn the literary adjective "Time-ese." *Fortune* remained for decades the publication of record on the prospects and possibilities of the nation as the world economic powerhouse of the century.

Time, Life, and *Fortune,* to be sure, always had their counterparts and worthy competition in popular analogues, all carving out their cultural niche in the politics of the middlebrow—widely popular weekly and monthly productions such as *Look, Collier's,* the *Saturday Evening Post,* and *Reader's Digest.* Substantial women's magazines also carried on what had proven a well-established tradition in America, including *Good Housekeeping, McCall's, Ladies' Home Journal,* and *Redbook,* the latter a source of noteworthy fiction. Men's special-interest offerings included *Sports Afield, Field and Stream, Popular Science,* and *Popular Mechanics,* the latter in the great American vein of "useful knowledge" and "self-improvement." Fund-raising "magazine campaigns" were common in public schools, enlisting students in big annual subscription drives. Young people themselves read *Humpty Dumpty, Jack and Jill, Boy's Life;* meanwhile they cultivated their own secret subculture of comic books—we will never know how many passed from hand to hand: DC, Marvel, Dell, EC; superhero, war, horror, cartoon adventure. *Classic Comics,* condensing and illustrating great literary works, became the schoolroom cribs, the *Cliff Notes* or *Spark Notes* of the era, a staple of who knows how many junior-high book reports, including one of my own, much praised by the teacher, on *The Hunchback of Notre Dame.* For the avant-garde, soon to make its appearance was *Mad* magazine.

Another salient print memory of sons and daughters of the American middle class growing up in the years after World War II is likely to be recurrent memory of looking about one's own "living room" or "family room," or visiting homes of friends and relatives, and finding bookshelves that all seemed to be stocked with identical titles. Here, too, *middlebrow* became a term of distinction for those who saw themselves as the great post-1945 readership inheriting from their wartime and depression predecessors what Janice Radway has called "a passion for books." This was obviously an imagined community—one decidedly not resident on the landscape of rural day-labor or in the teeming blue-collar sections of industrial cities. On the other hand, as soldiers had demonstrated with the popularity of World War II overseas paper editions of popular and literary titles numbering in the hundreds, and as the postwar flourishing and public school and community library circulation lists continued to show, something more than stolid middle-class diligence was at work in the numbers of titles making the best-seller lists and the monthly offerings of the great mail-order book clubs.

That is, for all the much-publicized attractions of the post-1945 nonprint media—the continuing importance of radio; the ever-enlarging allure of movies; the advent of television, with the new popularity of game shows, soap operas, comedy-variety, drama, and sitcoms—Americans remained a nation of readers (consumers of books, specifically) as no other nation in history had ever been or was likely to be. Accordingly, what they read, or at least what they bought as culturally desirable and important popular reading, continues to tell much of the story of the times, with titles pouring off the presses, blazoned in popular reviews, in newspapers, magazines, literary digests, and book-society newsletters. This was the golden age of the subscription book business, of the Book-of-the-Month Club and the Literary Guild, but also of mass-produced standards and contemporary classics in series called Modern Library, Popular Library, Readers' Library, and so forth. To be sure, as noted, the age marked the rise of the modern mass-market paperback (about which more below), but it remained as well the golden age of the popularly available, marketable, and saleable hardback. Perhaps this was the result of a hunger, after wartime regulation, for familiar paper quality, binding, print design, frontispieces, interleaves, and end papers. Perhaps it was an extension of consumerist desire combined with a new ability to pay for nice books to put on home display. To whatever end, people growing up in those days can probably still launch into quick recitation of titles from the shelves. *The Captain from Castille; The Egg and I; Crusade in Europe.*

Paperbacks burgeoned eventually into mass-market and trade editions. Educationally, they started to become a curricular staple. But for decades after the war, it remained the traditional hardbound best-seller lists that could be reckoned a real indicator of what middle-class people were thinking, how they sought to shape their lives, and in particular how they understood the larger values of their culture as it had emerged from the struggle against the World War II Axis totalitarianisms, only to be plunged at home and abroad into a new global struggle against communist world domination.

Best-seller listings in fiction were mainly novels, with the occasional story collection. No category existed for poetry, although some figures sold well—aging popular worthies such as Carl Sandburg and Robert Frost or humorists such as Richard Armour and Ogden Nash. Nonfiction ran to self-help, cookbooks, autobiography or memoir, popular history, inspiration, humor.

The titles best remembered from fiction were likely to be historical and religious novels, romances, escapist fare, love stories, heroic sagas. Some big, new World War II combat novelists emerged, including James Jones, Norman Mailer, Irwin Shaw, Leon Uris, and Herman Wouk. At various levels of audience appeal there was a steady growth of mysteries, with favorites including Ellery Queen and Agatha Christie. Women's writing notoriously featured what would now be called bodice-rippers. Historical romancers included Kathleen Winsor and Daphne du Maurier. At home, a popular favorite, deemed cosmopolitan and witty, was Frances

Parkinson Keyes. These had their male popular counterparts in figures such as James Gould Cozzens and John P. Marquand.

Fiction went on a notable binge with midrange religious entertainments—*The Robe,* followed by *The Big Fisherman, The Silver Chalice,* and others of the sort—a choice of genre reinforced, as seen below, by the proliferation of highly popular movies based on such books. Inspirationalism also figured highly in the drift of nonfiction, with self-help instruction from Dale Carnegie or Norman Vincent Peale (in the latter case mildly mixed with religion) or sometimes emphasizing the charmingly humorous, as in Art Linkletter or the teen spokesman Pat Boone.

What would now be called pulp fiction flourished. Dwight Eisenhower was a renowned reader of Zane Grey. Sex, violence, and adventure were purveyed by figures as various as Grace Metalious, Mickey Spillane, and Frank Yerby—the latter, as was generally undiscovered, an African American. Underground stuff—William Burroughs, Henry Miller, and the like—showed up as paperbacks in the drawer of your parents' nightstand.

The school curriculum still featured *A Midsummer Night's Dream, Julius Caesar, Great Expectations, The Return of the Native.* To cement the popular connections, however, I might adduce yet another of my own golden moments in oral book reporting. Having pulled off my parents' shelf a volume entitled *The Catcher in the Rye,* I summarized faithfully, with emphasis on certain creative profanities I had found particularly eloquent. The teacher muttered something about my "advanced" taste in books as she returned me to my seat.

At the same time, even amidst this great print–common knowledge explosion, for large numbers of Americans, especially younger ones like myself, reading stopped dead one night of the week. Once upon a time in America, Saturday night was movie night. That was what people did. Friday night was for certain things: high school sports or band concerts, TV boxing matches, grocery shopping, card parties or church hall bingo games. But nearly as much as Sunday morning was for church, Saturday night was Saturday Night at the Movies—the phrase itself almost a redundancy that nearly any post-1945 white, middle-class American understood in a very specific way. Eventually it became the title of an early 1960s song by the Drifters, a black group. By then the mood was nostalgia. One can simply say that up until that time it was just what everybody did. To put this in a vivid, if simplistic trope, after 1945 movies suddenly leapt off the screen. It became the age of Technicolor, CinemaScope, VistaVision, Todd-AO, 3-D, Cinerama. The color processing just kept getting more and more vivid, and the screen just kept getting wider and wider.

As important at the time was the respect still paid to what was called the feature film as a great vehicle of literacy and taste. This involved distinct canons of prestige. Saturday night at the movies was for mainstream viewers Saturday night at the Majestic, the Crown, or the Regal, where you saw basically the "A" production that everybody else in American movie towns and cities was seeing that Saturday night—the aforementioned "feature" attraction having gotten there on Wednesday and leaving after Sunday. In such films, from the late 1940s onward, traditional, popular, "big" actors and actresses tried to do serious dramatic performance within increasingly heavy, overblown, garish vehicles. James Stewart, Gary Cooper, Henry Fonda, Gregory Peck, Clark Gable, and John Wayne; Susan Hayward, Maureen O'Hara, Lana Turner, and Elizabeth Taylor—all were required increasingly to navigate bizarre costume shows and wide-screen spectaculars. Productions bulged with opulent sets and casts of thousands, frequently built around whole constellations of big-name players. *The Robe* featured Richard Burton, Jean Simmons, and Victor Mature, attended by Michael Rennie, Dean Jagger, and Richard Boone. *Ivanhoe* starred Robert Taylor and Elizabeth Taylor along with Joan Fontaine and George Sanders. *The Ten Commandments* marshaled popular favorites including Charlton Heston, Yul Brynner, Anne Baxter, Edward G. Robinson, and Yvonne De Carlo, as well as veterans Sir Cedric Hardwicke, Judith Anderson, and Vincent Price.

There were heavy-duty book spinoffs from the big World War II novels, including *From Here to Eternity, The Caine Mutiny, The Young Lions,* and *The Naked and the Dead.* Sentimental melodrama likewise made the screen transition with Lloyd C. Douglas and Morton Thompson weepies such as *Magnificent Obsession* and *Not as a Stranger.*

To be sure, the heavy diet of such serious offerings was leavened by sexual comedy, as well as new genre fare. Doris Day played the perpetual virgin against Rock Hudson, Cary Grant, Tony Randall, and Gig Young. Marilyn Monroe, meanwhile, made Marilyn Monroe movies: *Gentlemen Prefer Blondes, How to Marry a Millionaire, The Seven Year Itch,* and *Some Like It Hot.* Once the formula had been discovered in *Jailhouse Rock,* Elvis made Elvis movies. In a broader franchise, beginning with *Rebel without a Cause* and *Rock around the Clock* and extending to *Beach Blanket Bingo* and *A Summer Place,* the teen movie burgeoned into one of the great genres of the period.

Especially for the young, a major alternative venue of the times was the "B" movie—low-budget fare nearly always shown at the "other" theater in town; the Strand as opposed to the Majestic, or maybe the Village versus the Royal. In a kid version of what used to be called the Saturday afternoon matinee, here the offerings were quick and various, usually with multiple attractions on one bill—cowboy, horror, detective, war. B movies were shown to B-movie audiences in B-movie venues and featured B-movie actors and actresses doing B-movie material: over-the-hill gunslingers and gangsters, ranchers' daughters and gun molls, with their performances in predictable scripts frequently accompanied by leftover installments from serials such as *Flash Gordon* and *The Three Mesquiteers.* It was the same with cartoons. At the A place one could expect the latest Looney Tunes/Merrie Melodies. At the B place the cartoon was going to be some kind of old-time off-brand like Felix the Cat.

On all such matters of Hollywood memory, it remains nearly impossible now to explain to people who weren't there what the movies meant to post-1945 Americans by way of a generally assumed knowledge about the world. Each person, no doubt, will have his or her story. At the Majestic, the first A movie of any kind I remember is *Scaramouche,* with Stewart Granger, in 1952—although, as strangely, one of the first movies I remember seeing in our local B theater was an estimable color remake from the same year of the World War I classic *What Price Glory.* For the most part, though, it was standard Majestic fare, from *The Saracen Blade* on. I caught all the big toga and sword-and-sandal spectaculars: biblical ones such as *The Robe, Demetrius and the Gladiators,* and *The Ten Commandments* but also *Alexander the Great,* with a blonde Richard Burton, and *The Egyptian,* with another English actor named Edmund Purdom. In science fiction, listening to insect noises at night, I got bad dreams after

Them; one Saturday night I was put so badly on edge by a double bill, *Attack of the Crab Monsters* and *Not of This Earth,* I got up and left. Of the great 3-Ds, I remember the original *Bwana Devil* and a Guy Madison cavalry one called *The Charge at Feather River.* From the time I got my driver's license until I went to college, on date nights it was always the Majestic, of course, the good theater, in the balcony, where we sat out whatever happened to be playing, committing popular favorites as various as *The Horse Soldiers, The Apartment, El Cid, Blue Hawaii,* and *The Guns of Navarone* simultaneously to the vaults of romance and memory.

An odd reflection that may stand out for people with parallel experience of the big popular movies—and an attendant feature of what might still be called their store of cultural reference—concerns the persistence and plenitude of musicals. On the one hand, it may be that I had something of an unusually receptive predisposition. My father loved Broadway shows, took us to see them in performances by their touring companies, and bought them in long-playing records. On the other hand, no one can dispute that the years following the end of World War II also constituted for general audiences the golden age of the great American Broadway musicals, many of which made it on to the screen. Rodgers and Hammerstein movies alone included *Oklahoma, South Pacific, The King and I, Carousel,* and *State Fair*—with the latter actually produced first, on film, as a Pat Boone–Ann-Margret feature. Other big shows transferring memorably to the screen were *Guys and Dolls, The Pajama Game,* and *Damn Yankees. Peter Pan,* with Mary Martin, scored big on TV. Broadway musical references became common currency. For those touched by the medium in performance, on records or in film, on radio and TV, and in the daily media, Ethel Merman belting out "No Business like Show Business," Janis Paige slinking through "Hernando's Hideaway," and the forlorn Washington Senators trying to lift their spirits with "You Gotta Have Heart" still carry an extraordinary weight of cultural presence.

In popular music of the era generally, popular memory is likely to find a stock of reference in a blend of ubiquitous, middle-of-the-road favorites, love songs and ballads, dance and novelty numbers, their lyrics quoted and melodies hummed and whistled by average people. "How Are Things in Glocca Mora," from *Finian's Rainbow,* mixed with Rosemary Clooney's "Come On-a My House," and "Oh! My Papa," by a younger heartthrob named Eddie Fisher, and movie themes such as "The Ballad of Davy Crockett" and "Do Not Forsake Me, Oh My Darling," from *High Noon.* Meanwhile, original record singles were doing their own thing, as it might most pointedly be termed, turning into platters. The heavy, fragile 78s gave way to the light, portable 45s; the 45 singles were collected into the big-selling 33⅓ album. This, in turn, brought about the fundamental post-1945 revolution in the prewar entertainment and information form that had previously been matched in popularity and influence only by newspapers and movies. That was commercial radio.

It is sometimes assumed of post–World War II media history that the radio era was basically just subsumed overnight into the television era. The change was not nearly that radical or rapid. A measure of this—of how firmly, in fact, radio reorganized its influence, assuming a new format and a new role perhaps even more consequential in the formation of cultural attitudes and values—comes rather in the simplest appeal to living memory. The fact is that today, as surely as people like me remember running out and buying a disc like "Flying Saucer" or "Come Go with Me" because I heard it first on the radio, this old, familiar medium still does for us, as for our children and their children, what it did more than fifty years ago, when it changed its basic identity because it had to: it plays popular hit music of one description or another and does news, traffic, and weather.

At the beginning of the great transition, pop radio was nearly all AM; FM was for cities, connoisseurs, and intellectuals. Out in middle America, for the average young person there was usually one local or regional AM station appealing to the teen and college-age audiences, spinning platters, mixing the music with humorous chatter, popular slang, celebrity gossip, with five minutes out per hour for news and weather. Disc jockeys became "radio personalities" of considerable celebrity for high school– and college-age young people. This was particularly true at night in many markets, with powerful "clear channel" stations broadcasting from population centers over very long distances at night to faithful audiences: on the East Coast, for instance, WLS in Chicago; WABC in New York; WBZ in Boston; WLAC in Nashville; WWWL in Wheeling, West Virginia; and, on a good night, even WWNO in New Orleans. It is certainly one of the things *American Graffiti,* for all its California spin on the more general culture, got right. The search of the Richard Dreyfus character after the real Wolfman Jack is a true pilgrimage to the source, the DJ voice beckoning to young people out of radios in cars—the four-wheeled entertainment centers where they spent increasing amounts of time practicing privacy, mobility, and sociability; heart talk and revelation; even intimacy—as the medium had gathered families after school, work, or supper in the living room around the Philco or Atwater Kent a bare five or ten years earlier.

The latter function, of course, was already being dominated by the great media miracle of the era—the source of a revolution in the possibilities of human entertainment and information, the production of popular knowledge, at the time so breathtakingly unprecedented and explosive that everyone seemed to understand it as such even while it was being experienced. That, of course, was television. TV. Suddenly everybody had a TV in the house or apartment, and every house or apartment was hooked up to some kind of TV antenna. Rich and poor, old and young, urban and rural, educated and uneducated, people tapped into a vast engine of transmission that served simultaneously as a frame of understanding. Overnight, people started getting their basic ideas of the world mainly by watching TV, and I was one of them.

Memories of how TV began for most Americans will probably be located somewhere in the late 1940s to early 1950s. My own family's experience may be taken as something of a typical case. The TV was a Sylvania—sold by the TV dealer down the street. We started with a seventeen-inch, soon replaced by a nineteen-inch, further improved by an illuminated framing feature, alleged to be restful to the eyes, called Halolight. (It was rumored at the time, mostly by people professing worry about "the young," that too much TV watching could hurt your vision.) The TV was in the den—also called the TV room. Network TV, from the beginning, comprised the big three channels—NBC, CBS, and ABC—along with Dumont for a while, and a longer-lived Washington, D.C., independent. Local transmission, in our case out of Baltimore, was introduced by test patterns in late afternoon. First came *Paul's Puppets,* a kids' marionette show sponsored by Hutzler's Department Store, the most stylish one in town. The opening was a grainy black-and-white "art" shot through a kaleidoscope being twisted by hand, accompanied by the opening bars from Tchaikovsky's "Dance of the Sugar Plum Fairy." A better puppet show by far, the one we were all waiting for, was *Howdy Doody,* a national broadcast, with characters everybody knew as well as their own family: Howdy himself, along with Buffalo Bob, Clarabelle, Mister Bluster, Princess Summer Fall Winter Spring, Flubadub—and, of course, the Peanut Gallery. When the great moment came, everybody in the Peanut Gallery, in the "studio audience," as it was called, as well as at home, shouted in unison. "Hey, kids! What time is it!" cried Buffalo Bob. "It's Howdy Doody time!" came the screaming response, while Clarabelle wildly honked his horn. As kid-world competition there was *Kukla, Fran and Ollie,* a much quieter show with a less-satisfactory bunch of hand puppets; and another with a very strange character, a kind of Pee Wee Herman type, a manic vaudevillian with a pronounced lisp named Pinky Lee. There was a regular late-afternoon slot, *The Kate Smith Hour,* always opening with the star singing "When the Moon Comes over the Mountain." It is hard to remember much about this show except that the host was a very big, fleshy woman (probably what we would now call morbidly obese), plain-featured but friendly, with a bright and winning smile. Smith's fame had come through her rendition of "God Bless America" in *This Is the Army,* a patriotic movie produced in 1943, and her wartime Bond Tours and flag-manufacturing promotions. She seemed rather old. The same could be said of the heroes from most of the first television cowboy shows I remember: *Hopalong Cassidy* featured a silver-haired William Boyd from back in the 1930s, along with a horse named Topper and sidekick named Lucky. *The Cisco Kid,* recycled out of the B movies, played off the debonair Duncan Rinaldo, as Cisco, against Leo Carrillo's buffoonish, slovenly Pancho. (No one, to my knowledge, had ever heard of Don Quixote or Sancho Panza.)

The evening news began as a fifteen-minute show, narrated by John Cameron Swayze. Sponsored by the world's most popular cigarette, it was called the *Camel News Caravan.* "Let's go hopscotching around the world for news," Swayze would always say at the beginning. At the end he would close with, "That's the story, folks. I'm glad we could get together." A main rival was Douglas Edwards on CBS, rather more low-key and dignified, without Swayze's populist touch.

My memory is that, in the beginning at least, not much at all came on weekday TV until late afternoon. In the morning, for those with time to linger over their breakfast or coffee, there was Dave Garroway on *The Today Show.* A new morning niche was developed for families with toddlers and preschoolers, in quasi–day care shows such as *Romper Room* and *Ding Dong School.* Mister Rogers was still in the distant future, although there was a good science guy named Don Herbert, who billed himself as *Mr. Wizard.*

Evening TV quickly broke itself out into comfortable, familiar categories. The weekly thirty-minute comedy series enjoyed instant popularity, topped by raucous marital knockabouts such as *I Love Lucy* and *The Honeymooners* but also featuring offerings as diverse as *Mister Peepers, Our Miss Brooks, I Married Joan, The Life of Riley, My Little Margie, Topper,* and *September Bride.* An attempt to transfer the radio favorite *Amos 'n Andy* into a TV version featuring black actors was mercifully short-lived. Newer family shows such as *Ozzie and Harriet, Father Knows Best,* and *Leave It to Beaver* would come to dominate the field.

Cowboys were everywhere. Along with Hopalong Cassidy came well-established movie favorites such as Roy Rogers and Gene Autry. *The Lone Ranger* moved over successfully from radio for a stellar run with Clayton Moore as the masked man and Jay Silverheels as Tonto. The big cop show was *Dragnet,* with Jack Webb as Joe Friday.

Variety Shows were hosted by Arthur Godfrey, Milton Berle, Ed Sullivan, and Sid Caesar. Predictably recurrent guests included singers and movie stars but also odd specialty acts and personalities, ventriloquists and other exotics such as Edgar Bergen, Victor Borge, Señor Wences, Carmen Miranda, and Dagmar. In music there was an extremely popular show, unimaginable in the age of MTV, entitled *Your Hit Parade,* where top-selling records by original artists were sung in dramatic performance by tame, amiable stand-ins with names like Dorothy Collins, Giselle MacKenzie, Russell Arms, and Snooky Lanson.

There was a brief golden age of serious TV drama, with venues including *Playhouse 90, Chrysler Theater,* and the *Hallmark Hall of Fame.* What we would now call PBS-style cultural or educational programming—reserved usually for Sunday afternoon—was highlighted by *Omnibus,* with Alistair Cooke, presented by ALCOA, pronounced "Al-u-min-i-um Corporation of America." Historical information and entertainment were provided in the dramatic reconstructions of great world events on *You Are There,* hosted by Walter Cronkite. The only one of these that I really remember was an installment from the first (1953) season on the death of Socrates. I recall being saddened by his suicide, on the grounds that he was possibly "corrupting the young."

Late night was in its nascent stage, with Steve Allen and then Jack Paar. The only people that ever seemed to talk about them were definitely adults. The late night show most people remembered from the early days out in the provinces was probably the signoff, the flag shot with the national anthem, and then the test pattern.

Daytime TV came along eventually, albeit for most people outside the home remaining for years a strange terra incognita. Soap operas dominated, some coming over from radio, along with live tear-jerkers such as *Queen for a Day* and *This Is Your Life.* Game shows were something of a staple from the beginning, both daytime and evening, including *Truth or Consequences* and, most memorably, Groucho Marx in *You Bet Your Life.* "When the Duck comes down," he was always saying; and the duck actually did come down with some bizarre message in its mouth.

Weekends became something unto themselves. Saturday morning cartoons, initially, for the most part recycled old movie fodder—Felix the Cat, Woody Woodpecker, Tom and Jerry. Disney animation classics were still a tightly held franchise, with no syndication. Looney Tunes remained a top-of-the-line movie-theater specialty. Kids comedy was also consigned to grainy old prewar shorts: *The Little Rascals, The Three Stooges, The Bowery Boys. Covered Wagon Theater* did the same with recycled Roy Rogers and Gene Autry, along with B-movie favorites such as Lash LaRue. Drama shows included *Captain Midnight, Sky King,* and *Highway Patrol,* with Broderick Crawford. *Superman,* with George Reeves as the man of steel, was deemed sufficiently important in its audience appeal to get an evening slot.

Friday and Saturday nights brought the movies to TV. On the *Late Show* or *Weekend Classic,* people saw Errol Flynn in *Elizabeth and Essex,* Richard Widmark in *Halls of Montezuma,* Cornel Wilde and Merle Oberon in *A Song to Remember,* James Cagney in *Yankee Doodle Dandy,* Pat O'Brien in *Knute Rockne, All American,* and Bing Crosby and Barry Fitzgerald in *Going My Way.*

TV sports were initially dominated by boxing and baseball. *Gillette Friday Night Fights* drew a regular audience, as did diamond broadcasts of professional teams. The World Series became an annual TV event. Increasingly, college and professional football began to draw crowds in the fall. The great innovation of the late era would be Olympic coverage, and regular specialty-events programming such as *Wide World of Sports.*

The latter observations may serve as a point of entry to the state of the medium as it now exists, in what may be properly called the last days of TV—at least as it was once known. Networks now hang on by bare knuckles, amid twenty-four-hour news, sports, weather, and myriad specialty and premium channels. In sports alone nearly any cable plan features venues in double figures. Specialized entertainment programming exists in a complementary array. The two frequently converge in multimedia promotions. *Sports Illustrated* has for decades published a *Playboy*-style annual swimsuit issue. It is now the subject of one of the most eagerly awaited sports specials on cable. Enhanced viewing includes new digital, home-theater, and flat-screen technologies undreamed of a few years back by the most eager devotee of the medium. Meanwhile, the real future moves progressively offscreen to new, instant, on-demand sites from the nearest computer to the personal cell phone. In the age of MTV, TIVO, iPod, iPhone, or YouTube, what a strange, primitive thing it all seems to have been to us fifty years ago.

This is particularly true for those of us who remember TV as a suddenly emergent way of looking at the world, at once a content and a frame of reference, a new medium of cultural figuration where image and idea came together as shared knowledge, culture, collective literacy. The recitation above, at once partaking of memory and history, will no doubt strike many readers as personal, individual, eccentric, even idiosyncratic. Yet many Americans who were alive at the time will still recognize in it, I would propose, the sense of a collective past. In the TV era they were there at the great moment of transition, one surpassed in its impact on knowledge, information, and community only at the end of one century and the beginning of the next, with consequences we are still trying to sort out.

One could fill a book with mere references to the books spawned by developments in mass-media information and entertainment during the era I have described—beginning with Marshall McLuhan and Roland Barthes and extending into work of successors as diverse as Jean Baudrillard or Sven Birkerts. From the perspective of someone standing at the particular intersection described between popular-culture memory and history in America, the matter remains fairly simple. Newspapers, magazines, mass-market books, movies, popular music, and radio were the popular media, the means of popular-culture production, that shaped the knowledge and information world of most Americans in the first half of the twentieth century. Television changed everything. This is simply true. People began reading less, going to movies less, and relying on radio less for information and entertainment, and increasingly turned to TV. By the season, the month, the day or the week, by the hour or even the minute, real time, as it is called, changed forever in America. Post-1945 America became a world where people stopped telling the day and hour by the radio—not to mention the daily newspaper, sometimes morning and afternoon; the weekly magazine; the monthly book-club section and annual best-seller list; the latest A- and B-movie releases available for viewing at local theaters; the current musical hit parade. In all these respects there simply arose profound differences in the regulation of life, as the term is used by social historians—involving traditionally the seasons, the cycle of religious festivals, the observances of the calendar, the rhythms of the day. A new information and entertainment technology brought a profound shift toward the organization of life and a completely new way of looking at memory and history in the era. Once the medium became dominant, from the early 1950s onward, it was as if the world ran on television time. The rhythms of life divided into early morning television, daytime television, after-school television, evening television, and late-night television. (The concept of prime time was still on the horizon.) American families gathered nightly for supper, the news, family TV; for the kids it was time for bed; for the parents it was the late news and then maybe bedtime; for those who didn't have to get up or were willing to sacrifice sleep there was the late show. The fall was the new TV season, springtime for the sponsors, a time to try out new programs and a new season of the old favorites.

The rhythms of domestic life merged family TV rituals with the media history of the tribe. My most distinct memory of late Sunday nights is that of my father, with his big laugh, howling over Fred Allen as a panelist on *What's My Line?* I've always been proud that it was something of a witty show he watched, with a notably cerebral cast including Bennett Cerf, Dorothy Kilgallen, Arlene Francis, Martin Gabel, and the host, John Daly. The early variety shows likewise left a cultural imprint: Milton Berle, dressed up like Carmen Miranda; the wild skits and parodies with Sid Caesar, Imogene Coca, Carl Reiner, and Howard Morris on *Your Show of Shows;* Ed Sullivan, solemnly bringing on the popular ventriloquist Señor Wences, whose "Johnny," painted with lipstick on his hand, squealed in a strange falsetto, and "Pedro," a disembodied head in a box, said in his gruff voice, "'s all right." As noted elsewhere, there was the night we all waited to see Elvis on live TV—wondering if Sullivan would make good on the threat not to show him from the hips down.

The Elvis concession—in the various senses of that phrase—proved particularly notable for an important new concentration, as the years went on, concerning the TV regulation of life for young people. Kids shows, for what we would now call preadolescents, preschool, kindergarten, and elementary-school students, were there from the beginning and persisted. Most singular, though, particularly for those who were themselves in the process of going through the developmental stages of youth, was a new focus on junior- and senior-high-school-age people, the life and world of the American teenager: David and Ricky in the Nelson house; Wally, Beaver, Eddie Haskell, and the Cleavers; Betty, Kathy, and Bud Anderson in *Father Knows Best;* and on the *Mickey Mouse Club,* sacred to the memory of every American boy alive during the era, Annette Funicello. Like us, certain shows, and their characters, grew up with television. Further, we were complete suckers for TV inventiveness in what we would now call media synergies. Ricky Nelson became a rock 'n' roll singer, and Annette a beach-blanket movie star, along with Frankie Avalon, late of *American Bandstand.* Ed Byrnes flaunted a pompadour on *77 Sunset Strip,* and perky costar Connie Stevens got a Gold Record for "Kooky, Kooky, Lend Me Your Comb."

The corporate archetype or epitome of this endlessly self-reifying process was surely Walt Disney. From the start, by focusing on the new TV culture of youth, Disney saw that the medium could ultimately offer something for people at any stage of education and development and then continue to spin off into endless—and ageless—new forms of information and entertainment production. *The Mickey Mouse Club* begat *The Wonderful World of Disney; The Wonderful World of Disney* begat Disneyland and Disney World. Through television, Disney, Inc., became a great metonymy of the world as media creation and event. From the cap with ears on it to the corporate trademark, the Mouse has become proprietary in the fullest sense. Or, as Paul Fussell has phrased it, the way of the world since 1945 has been toward Higher Disneyfication.

The image and the reference go far to locate where I personally broke off from the media universe of my youth. Once, when I was a kid, Fantasyland, Frontierland, Natureland, and Tomorrowland, it is not too far-fetched to say, struck me fairly as great subworlds of information, entertainment, and popular knowledge. Then, as theme parks were being invented, I went off to college, a year of graduate school, and a war. Accordingly, while strangely fortuned to have been there from the beginning, once I left home in the early 1960s, I basically stopped watching everything popular for the most part, starting with TV but extending to movies, videos, DVDs, Internet Web sites—a practice I maintain to this day. In college I was studying too hard. Ditto graduate school. Then in the army I was too busy getting ready for combat and later trying not to get killed. Or maybe I locked into preferences formed in early life. A college English major and apostate pre-med—apparently *Dr. Kildare, Ben Casey,* and *Marcus Welby, M.D.* didn't do the trick—who went on to a Ph.D. in the subject and a career in university teaching and writing, I suppose now I was, always have been, and always will be one of those people who prefers to read.

To the best of my knowledge, I did not see a color television or perhaps even a television show in color until I came back from Vietnam in 1970. I did not have a TV or watch TV until somewhere around 1979. It was almost impossible sometimes not to dip back in and out of it, the palpable extension and emanation of a world we never really outgrew. I gave in to the world TV movie premiere, the occasional television event, a news or documentary special, maybe the rerelease of some classic or a remake of something so old that most people did not realize it was a remake. A distinct memory remains of being at somebody's house seeing *The Godfather;* another, more fugitive, is of being somewhere else watching *Fan-*

tasia stoned. I made one small weekly exception in the mid-1970s, when I usually went somewhere that had a TV on Saturday night at ten, as did everyone I knew, to watch the original *Saturday Night Live,* which provided a storehouse of popular culture anecdotes to supply at least a week's worth of classroom illustration. Aside from sports, which I still can't seem to shake, and news, which I usually see while I am at the gym, I still don't watch anything. Not Showtime, not HBO, not even PBS. Not even—save for film versions of classic American texts I enjoy discussing in the classroom with my students—movies on VHS or DVD, including favorites now brought in by my wife and my daughter. For me these mainly sit now, like old Book-of-the-Month-Club or Literary Guild selections from my parents' house, gathering dust on the lower bookshelves. I just don't like the current media generally for longer than a peanut-butter-and-jelly sandwich or a quick naptime in a family-room chair. I hear about things. "Reality" TV sounds like a bizarre concept if I ever heard of one. Come-ons for forensic-investigator shows seem to be everywhere, for whatever reasons nearly always featuring beautiful women who love to cut up smelly corpses. Actually, if anything, I seem to have found my own attention span with a new generation, including my sixteen-year-old daughter, who watches nearly no television at all, preferring DVDs of favorite movies or snippets of *South Park* or *The Daily Show* on MySpace and YouTube.

The true end of it for me, I am pretty sure now, ironically involving one last brush with the Mouse, Inc., came nearly twenty years ago, at the end of the first Iraq war, watching General Norman Schwarzkopf, the architect of desert victory, at Disney World in Orlando (conveniently near Southern Command Headquarters in Tampa) flanked by Snow White in full costume and a small, hirsute, second-line country singer named Lee Greenwood belting out a recycled minor hit, "Proud to Be an American." It was a pop-culture collector's prize, a kind of ultimate American epiphany—what Michael Herr, in his great book about the Vietnam War, *Dispatches,* would have called a "mythopathic moment." Ensuing decades have not improved on the picture, or on the state of current events, as we used to call them, in Orlando or Baghdad. Nor, for that matter, in Music City USA or Washington, D.C., do we seem to have made any notable advances in figuring out what might be wrong with a sound track that keeps mixing "It's a Small World After All" with "The Star-Spangled Banner." Or maybe it is all nothing but a great, giant reality show, as fully preposterous and stupid as Michael Landon in *I Was a Teenage Werewolf* or Steve McQueen in *The Blob.* After all these years, it just seems so much more depressing, albeit, as they used to say, of nonstop importance and excitement.

13
Remembering On the Beach

Before World War II, Hollywood scared people to death with mad scientists and monsters. During World War II the industry specialized in strutting Nazis and villainous Japs. After the war political subversives mixed with space creatures, and vice versa; as important, in what had come to be called the nuclear age, a whole new category of fear film centered on atomic mutants: *Them, Godzilla, Attack of the Crab Monsters, It Came from Beneath the Sea.* More directly, *Invasion U.S.A.* (1952) combined fear of nuclear attack with communist takeover, helping to usher in the new cold war genre of Soviet/U.S. atomic-mass-destruction movies culminating in such boomer classics as *Fail Safe* and *Dr. Strangelove,* both issued in 1964.

Less frequently remembered, perhaps because slightly older—albeit now decidedly more interesting for its emphasis on the human depiction of nuclear aftermath than on the Pentagon-Kremlin mechanics of initiating wars of mutual annihilation—is the film that first got the attention of popular audiences on the subject. That would be *On the Beach* (1959), Stanley Kramer's elegiac representation of the dying remnant of a world in the wake of global atomic warfare. In the golden age of Technicolor and CinemaScope—and to this degree anticipating its better-known successors—it was a black-and-white film of stark, muted, austere genius, featuring career performances from a number of important actors: Gregory Peck, Ava Gardner, a pre-*Psycho* Anthony Perkins, and Fred Astaire, in his first purely dramatic role. In all these respects it became a movie that challenged people who saw it never to look at the world in the same way again.

As was characteristic of the times, the origins of the film lay in a moderately popular, Book-of-the-Month-Club or Reader's Digest Condensed Books sort of book: a novel of the same title by a prolific, but relatively uncelebrated, Anglo Australian writer named Nevil Shute, that had showed up two years earlier and had gained a certain cachet of intellectual discussion. The author, whose full name was Nevil Shute Norway, by birth Anglo Irish, had served as a teenage stretcher-bearer during the 1916 Irish Rising and then been conscripted to brief World War I service in the British Army. After a university education at Oxford, he had trained as an aeronautical engineer and then had again returned to military service during World War II as a Royal Navy Reserve officer working with secret weaponry. In the meantime he wrote substantial amounts of fiction. A postwar emigrant to Australia, today he remains something of a cult figure, though with no single book remembered to most readers save *On the Beach.* At the time, a lot of people seem to have bought it—with sales of a quarter million, it ranked number eight on the 1957 best-seller list for fiction. One wonders how many read it. I certainly did, although it is hard to say just when, looking back on events fifty years ago. Whether I came to the book before or after the film, I'm not sure. I have certainly never forgotten it.

At the same time, even as a post–global conflict, end-of-the-world text, it wasn't unique. Most American public-school students, for instance, would likely have remembered Stephen Vincent Benet's "By the Waters of Babylon," a pre–World War II fable about a postapocalyptic New York City, which seems to have been standard curricular fare during the era. Those of more advanced predilections might also have been aware of a sequence of mid-1950s stories by popular science-fiction writer Walter Miller about a postnuclear landscape, eventually assembled into the 1960 cult novel *A Canticle for Leibowitz.* Like these in many ways, in the fable dimension at least, I can see now that *On the Beach* was not a particularly good novel—workmanlike is the best one can say, at least until toward the end, with a lot of rather stilted dialogue, quasi-scientific exposition, backstory, plot rigging, and typecast major characterizations. The American submarine captain, Dwight Towers, having brought his command south by submerged route from the contaminated Northern Hemisphere, is U.S. Navy by-the-book and relentlessly faithful to a wife two years dead, in sum a rather wooden, if sententious prig. Moira Davidson, the unmarried Australian woman with whom he falls in love, and she with him, is a boozy sexpot, the kind of single girl-about-town Americans would have considered the local whore, in the specific instance also decidedly in the thrall of what would now be understood as alcoholic drinking. Symptomatic of the problem is a sailing race in which the two participate, early in the book, where she manages, in the course of overturning the boat, to ditch the top of her swimming suit, coyly called a bra. The bra is not the problem; the boat is. Shute, it turns out, was himself an avid sailor; the pages devoted to the race are filled with opaque summary of the most useless nautical jargon. Similarly, in the book's final quarter, scenes devoted to the fatalistic passion developed by the cynical Australian scientist John Osborne for grand prix auto racing, Shute the engineer and driving enthusiast emerges, with loving attention and detail devoted to various automobile makes, designs, racing techniques, and protocols. A younger Australian couple, Peter and Mary Holmes, facing death with their infant daughter, Jennifer, are ingénue material in the customary parallel relationship with the more problematic Dwight Towers and Moira Davidson. The aforementioned John Osborne, as in all the analogous books and movies, is the "scientist," explaining things so that laypeople can understand them, within the text and without. At the same time, in spite of all this, one must concede that even fifty years later, the evolutions of the major characters through their intertwined stories and those of the lives of others surrounding them make their fates both individually and commonly affecting. I shall return for more about this later.

The basic outlines of book and movie are relatively congruent. The major characters form the core of a various and interesting group of people assembled in southern Australia, around Melbourne. They are all basically waiting to die as a result of radiation sickness after a global nuclear war two years earlier.

In the book the war has begun, as far as anyone can tell, with a bomb dropped on Naples by the Albanians—a good choice for the times, in the late 1950s the quintessential rogue nation, loony, dark, and secretive, an off-brand communist dictatorship menacing even by Balkan standards.

(Not for nothing in 2008 are ethnic Albanians, after the bloody 1990s mass killings in the former Yugoslavia, the people now prepared to set off the newest round by just declaring Kosovar independence from Serbia.) Then someone unidentified has dropped one on Tel Aviv. The Egyptians, equipped with nuclear weapons and sophisticated long-range bombers by their Russian sponsors, are an obvious choice; and the United States and Great Britain become involved. With Cairo menaced, the Egyptians retaliate by dropping bombs on London and New York. Meanwhile, this plotline has been tied up with a whole other scenario—now a curious blend of the imaginary and prophetic—involving a quite specific conflict between two expansionist Asian powers, Soviet Russia and Communist China. Russia wants the port of Shanghai as a trade outlet for the great production centers west of the Urals, those having progressively grown into Asian space after their World War II relocation. The Chinese want the new industrial areas and the vast lands on which they sit for population expansion. It is the Russians and Chinese who have begun seeding bombs with "cobalt" as a nuclear contaminant producing enormous amounts of lethal radiation. At the same time, it is noted that the British and Americans, along with the Russians, have initiated the great campaigns of bombing for "destruction." None of this was particularly good science, even for the time. Most pertinent for early-twenty-first-century readers is the idea of a "limited" nuclear war, a "tactical" exchange of bombs between lesser nations. As phrased by the scientist, John Osborne, "It wasn't the big countries that set off this thing. It was the little ones, the Irresponsibles."* Thus has come the unfolding of catastrophe, rather like the popular conception of a nuclear chain reaction, that quickly becomes an all-out war of global destruction among all powers, major and minor, with an estimated forty-seven hundred weapons finally exploded worldwide, wiping out all major political and military targets and population centers in the Northern Hemisphere.

Accordingly, thus has occurred basically offstage, for those awaiting the deadly radiation cloud being carried by the rotation of the earth and the patterns of the prevailing winds, what we would call now the nuclear holocaust, had the expression been coined. It hadn't, in fact, barely just

*Nevil Shute, *On the Beach* (New York: Ballantine, 1983), 79.

in evidence at the time referring to the Nazi annihilations of the Jews. Still, as to biblical proportions, Shute does it religiously by the numbers. The setting is seven years in the future. The time covered is the last nine months of people's lives and loves. Armageddon or apocalypse would still have been mainly scriptural, finding popular-culture currency only later in the *Terminator* movies or in popular texts of Christian fundamentalism such as the *Left Behind* series. (In movies, ironically, the former would become most closely associated with the Vietnam War, the latter with the scenario of a racing comet about to make impact with planet Earth.) *Doomsday* would probably have been the operative adjective—linked to a quaint word and idea, fifty years later, known as *Fallout.* To borrow a literary reference, in the present case from a curricular staple widely known in the culture, T. S. Eliot's "The Hollow Men," "This is the way the world ends, not with a bang but with . . ." radiation sickness. It is the disease of nuclear victims, that is, described indelibly by John Hersey, among others, in his postwar classic *Hiroshima.* Its main features are weakness, flulike symptoms, fever, cough, aching joints, nausea, and diarrhea. The latter are the primary processes whereby one dies, as Shute is at pains to emphasize in the deeply moving human final portions of the book: vomiting one's guts up and shitting one's pants off.

A nice geographic touch for the times, in both book and movie, is its setting in Australia, a vivid, interesting place of great appeal to post–World War II Americans. A vigorous young democracy of the land down under, something of a Pacific counterpart or national alter ego, quaintly British and brawlingly American, it had figured highly in the Pacific War against the Japanese. It was the place where MacArthur had gone after the fall of the Philippines, according to media legend, to secure its defenses and to begin rebuilding American land armies. From Australia had been launched early, desperate attacks to reclaim New Guinea, Bougainville, and the Solomons, first for the protection of the Australian continent and then as part of the great troop movement across the Southwest Pacific conjoining with the great navy and marine campaigns of Nimitz to the north. Many Americans who had served in the Pacific, in the marines, army, navy, and air corps, had spent time there. As recorded through Leon Uris's *Battle Cry,* itself greatly popular as both novel and film, it was a place where Americans like the lumberjack-marine Andy

Hookans find both true love and a true home, in the outback with a wise, sturdy Australian girl, the widow of an Australian soldier. Australian soldiers themselves were famous as fighters in far-flung theaters of war and as brave coast watchers on Pacific Islands, secretly reporting Japanese movements. The regions of Oceania themselves had further gained celebrity through James A. Michener's best-selling *Tales of the South Pacific* and the celebrated Rodgers and Hammerstein Broadway musical that had sprung from its pages. Pacific travel generally was enlarged through Hawaii statehood and growth in the vacation industry once air travel became popular and convenient. On a more somber note, Bikini Atoll became the much reported site of American Pacific H-bomb tests, combining exponential aggravation of nuclear fears with notorious developments in the swimsuit industry.

In all this Australia became America's great South Pacific ally, known to schoolroom geography aces as the only island continent and the biggest island in the world. Previously known to Americans through Mark Twain travel books such as *Following the Equator*, in the age of film and TV documentary it became the land of exotic flora and fauna and in global athletics the ground of sturdy, sportsmanlike competition by its jumpers, runners, and tennis players. The groundbreaking British four-minute miler Roger Bannister found his competition in the ascendant Australian challenger John Landy. Sports magazines featured Aussie Davis Cup tennis heroes like Ken Rosewall and Lew Hoad. Meanwhile, in popular science Australia figured as a gateway to the Antarctic regions as part of the highly touted U.N. International Geo-physical Year.

In *On the Beach* Australophilia is the only form of admiration left. Australia becomes the good last place on Earth, a good place for the human species to go down swinging. Throughout the movie, in an ineffable sadness, the band even plays "Waltzing Matilda." The Northern Hemisphere has simply been wiped out. Now a miasmic cloud of radiation moves with the prevailing winds and global climate patterns, steadily down the southern latitudes, bringing with it the deadly radiation sickness to the last places of human habitation, the southern parts of Africa and South America, Australia, and New Zealand. The early symptoms, weakness and nausea, are already the kiss of death. The diarrhea part sets in at the last, with everyone, young and old, especially in the book, trying to die with dignity basically while shitting themselves to death. There, too, in a kind of admiring hymn to Aussie pragmatism, healthy acceptance, bodily candor, the government makes available basically painless death kits: tablets, presumably cyanide with some sleeping ingredient, and a syringe for those—children, pets, and the like—where injection might be preferable to oral administration.

Some small mention is made in the book of missiles, as well as bombers. One suspects that this surely heightened American interest by the time of the movie; after all, 1957 was the year of the Russian *Sputnik,* followed in early 1958 by America's *Vanguard 1.* Space rocket aspirations were quickly translated into a race for missile nuclear-warhead delivery systems. Within years silos were going in across Nebraska and the Ukraine.

Accordingly, it was probably the 1959 movie that nailed most Americans on this one and helped them identify with the all-American cast. Gregory Peck is Dwight Towers, the American submarine skipper, having brought his boat to Australia from a dead Northern Hemisphere, a silent world with hundreds of millions, billions, of silent, decaying corpses, including those of his wife, son, and daughter, he knows, back in suburban Connecticut. Ava Gardner is Moira Davidson, the hard-drinking, sexually promiscuous, independent Aussie woman, off on a final, end-of-the-world toot devoted to racking up as many laurels as possible in both fields before it is over. A younger, parallel couple, the Australian Navy lieutenant Peter Holmes and his wife, Mary, recent parents of their first child, are played by Anthony Perkins and Donna Anderson. The scientist in the book is named John Osborne—in a contemporary literary reference, the name also of the author of *Look Back in Anger,* one of the English playwrights and novelists grouped as "the angry young men." Renamed Julian in the movie, and given a kind of wise savoir faire, he is played by Fred Astaire in a graceful, elegiac performance for which he received an Academy Award as Best Supporting Actor.

In the book and the movie the doomsday scenario is writ large into a last political plot and also into the closer cultural endgame, the web of individual psychological and social accommodations. The Australian Admiralty, assuming command over the U.S. captain and crew, devise a scientific mission for the sub to cruise back to the West Coast of the United

States. In a reprise of World War II adventure movies such as *Destination Tokyo* and *Run Silent, Run Deep,* with a nod perhaps to Disney's *Twenty Thousand Leagues under the Sea,* the destination of their globe-girdling underwater mission is Alaska, to see how fast the cloud is moving south. It is also to resolve the mystery of a single radio signal, mysteriously emanating in strange, indecipherable Morse code, from a coastal station in the U.S. Pacific Northwest, near Seattle. In the movie it is San Diego. That mystery is depressingly resolved when an attached Australian officer goes ashore in a radiation suit and finds the source: an overturned coke bottle—in a bald symbolic reference—wedged between a broken window sash and a transmitting key, rocking on its side when the wind blows and sending out intermittent gibberish. The power supply is a hydroelectric generating station, where the turbines have somehow, against all engineering expectations, held out for two years without servicing. One of the great, conclusive moments in the book and the film comes at the point in the mission when the scientist shuts down the power for the last time. Another involves a common sailor, one of the U.S. Navy crew, a native of San Francisco, who has escaped while the sub has been at periscope depth looking for life in San Francisco Bay. From the sub he can nearly see his house. When we see him last, he is back on the bay in a rowboat, bidding his shipmates farewell. He is trying to fish.

In these respects a possible title for this text, capitalizing on a mixing of the sardonic and nostalgic that frequently makes itself available as a mood in retrospective writing about postwar popular-culture productions of this grim, melodramatic sort, might well have been "How *On the Beach* Scared the Be-Jeezus Out of Us." That would have been amusing, but it would have grossly mischaracterized the somber beauty of the film in the social dimension and the chastening effect it clearly had on thoughtful audiences. It is repeatedly the small, human detail of the cultural endgame that strikes us. It is as if an ensemble such as the doomed chateau party assembled by Jean Renoir in *The Rules of the Game* has done a small tutorial in Kubler-Ross. All the steps are there: denial, anger, bargaining, depression, acceptance.

But there is more than just modeling. Indeed, in retrospect, whether rereading the book or going back to the movie, one is finally struck by the end at how well people die, both as individuals and as people understanding their role in relationships to each other and the world. Most wind up bearing to the end the stamp of personality that used to be called character. Generally, in making their forms of separate peace with doomsday, they all just basically opt to go crazy in their own ways; in the process they find their own personal codes of endurance and acceptance, their small pieces of dignity and integrity. And this is no Hemingway conceit; this is how average, in many ways typical, people learn how to die. Peter Holmes, the young Australian ensign, and his wife, Mary, foolishly plan to replace trees and redesign their garden. As they take their death pills, having made sure their child is dead first, they express quiet gratitude for the time they have found with each other. "I've had a lovely time since we got married," she says. "Thank you for everything, Peter." "I've had a grand time, too," he replies. "Let's end on that." John Osborne restores a vintage Ferrari, stores up a special alcohol-based racing fuel, and competes victoriously in the giddy, murderous, wreck-strewn trials and finals of the last Australian Grand Prix. Moira, calling on influential friends in government, has gotten the trout season set forward for one last year. She and Dwight go together to a celebrated mountain resort with a hotel full of jovial anglers. As with Jake Barnes and Bill Gorton at Burguete in Hemingway's *The Sun Also Rises,* the mood is elegiac and sacramental. It is also the last chance for Dwight and Moira to sleep together. As people do in this book, they do the right thing—each according to their poignant, crazy lights. Dwight, the American skipper, remains faithful to Sharon and the kids, all of them two years dead. By now he talks about them as if they are alive somewhere in Connecticut; he is actually using a fishing rod he has bought to take home as a present for the boy, to make sure it is fieldworthy; he has bought his wife a jeweled bracelet; he has been unable to find a Pogo stick for his daughter; Moira, using as a model a castoff from her childhood he has seen at her house, has had one fabricated. Moira has mysteriously stopped drinking and enrolled in business school courses in typing and stenography. She has also accepted the rules of the game sexually. Rather like Lady Brett Ashley—played, ironically, by Ava Gardner in the Hemingway movie—she seems to feel good at the end not being a bitch.

Meanwhile, especially in the book, one is struck also by how well old people face the end. Osborne's mother relieves him of his fears about final caretaking; his dotty old clubman uncle goes down trying to drink up all the vintage sherry in the club cellars. Moira's father and mother send her on with humorous farewell encouragement to her last happy days with Dwight.

The movie, visually and verbally, affirms the better parts of this. The main changes are in the Moira and Julian roles. Moira in the book is blonde, athletic, in her mid-twenties. In the movie Ava Gardner is in her late-thirties prime, dark, somewhat worn, utterly womanly. The Astaire role makes Julian an aging bachelor, as opposed to the solitary, acerbic John Osborne of the book. Julian is wise, self-aware, not merely cynical. One of his great moments comes on the sub, where he is asked who started the war. "Albert Einstein," he says. He continues: "Everyone had a bomb, an atomic bomb, a counterbomb, countercounter bombs, the devices outgrew us, we couldn't control them. I know. I helped them. God help me." Toward the end, the film largely pares down the focus on a more general cast of characters. One particularly grim final exchange, in abridged version, takes place between Perkins and Anderson as they lie beside each other in bed, knowing that they have killed their baby and will now take their own lives. "I think I'll have that cup of tea," she says. Other changes seem less well imagined. In the movie there is the attempt at a U.S.A. moment, when the sub crew is shown as having taken a vote to head the boat home. In the book, having lost members to everything from Australian shotgun weddings to alcohol, VD, and the first cases of radiation sickness, Towers can barely muster a big enough crew to take the sub out and scuttle it in deep water—a thoroughly proper and official plan required by his military code. Moira is last seen in the film watching from the headland by the sea, waving.

A singular feature of the movie—perhaps making it more palatable to popular Hollywood audiences—is that nearly all the death is left to the imagination. In the book Julian lovingly goes through a whole series of technical, mechanical steps for putting the Ferrari into mothballs. Then he gets in the driver's seat, where he has survived what may now seem all the strangely prophetic Mad Max carnage of the final races, and takes the poison. In the movie Julian is last seen preparing to die by carbon monoxide, running the racer inside a closed garage. In the book Dwight Towers has affirmed his conviction that he is "going back to Mystic," when he and Moira know he and the crew will be taking the boat down forever just offshore. In the movie Moira waves as the silhouette vanishes against the gray sea and sky. In the last scene in the book she sits in her car washing down her death pill with a big slug from a bottle of brandy.

Despite such avoidances there is plenty of sad starkness to go around in helping to recall how bleak the composite impression of the texts must have been at the time. Even now, my memory of *On the Beach* remains sufficiently vivid to outpace the conventions and commonplaces of description born of fifty years of popular-culture overload. An adjective used by people responding to the book and the movie is "depressing." That is true, one supposes, but only in the way students in critical essays use "sarcastic" when they mean "ironic." At the other extreme, it is probably now too easy to develop high-culture literary or cinematic constructions of response. The Hemingway influence may be evident, but this is no time for T. S. Eliot. If there is to be an ultimate wasteland, no one is going to be around to see it. Likewise, *M*A*S*H* is still a long way off as well, with its fashionable, black-humor ditty that "suicide is painless." What one takes away from a reencounter with *On the Beach* is the deeply human element of the text in relation to the times: of people doing their best in learning how to come to terms with themselves and the world in what Philippe Aries has called "the hour of our death."* That is the true impression of memory in all these relations—a profound sadness that it had to turn out this way, that human beings could not have done a better job with the world.

Such feeling—genuinely tragic recognition, it might be termed—is what one recalls now in something of a grand, noble, composite effect. As Fred Astaire/Julian says in the movie, echoing the parallel figure in the book, "The war started when people accepted the idiotic principle that peace could be maintained by arranging to defend themselves with weapons they couldn't possibly use without committing suicide." By comparison, Dwight Towers, the American and something of a moral and intellectual prig, seems not notably perceptive save on matters military and familial, as in the way they do it in the U.S. Navy or the Connecticut suburbs. Still, in the book, reflecting on the natural beauties of shore

*Philippe Aries, *The Hour of Our Death* (New York: Knopf, 1981).

scenes he has seen on underwater mission to already dead regions along the North Australian coast, he can remark, movingly, "Maybe we've been too silly to deserve a world like this" (80). He and Moira likewise achieve remarkable consonance in their deep understanding of how people are going to need to react individually. Apropos of Dwight's advising her to humor Peter and Mary Holmes on their garden plans—"'Don't you go and spoil it for them telling them they're crazy.'"—she reveals that she is already out ahead of him: "'I wouldn't do that,'" she replies. "'None of us really believe it's ever going to happen—not to us,' she said at last. 'Everybody's crazy on that point, one way or another'" (102). For her part, Moira rises late in the book to deal with Dwight himself as something of a childish idiot, actually enabling him in his comfortingly delusional conviction that somehow his wife and children aren't really dead. Both Moira Davidson and John Osborne become Shute's memorable interlocutors. It is hard to say who gets the best lines. Witty and half-loaded, he tells a party crowd early in the film, "I shouldn't drink, you know. I inevitably say something brilliant." And so he does, more than occasionally, even down to his incidental revelation, in a last conversation with his sherry-soaked uncle, that the Australian rabbits will be among the last of local animal life to go. Such ecological insouciance has been preceded in an earlier conversation with Towers in which he observes, "It's not the end of the world at all. . . . It's only the end of us. The world will go on just the same, only we shan't be in it. I dare say it will get along all right without us" (80). Eventually, he seems double-teamed with Moira, bantering with Peter Holmes on how any future race may attempt to reconstruct knowledge of a ruined world. "'What sort of books are they preserving?'" she asks. "'All about how to make the cobalt bomb?'" (106).

This is the way the world ends; there is no denying. But one resists updating the anachronism into equally inaccurate, current reference, as is sometimes now done, calling the book and movie "postapocalyptic." That, too, would be an eviscerating conceit of these lives being played out against a human backdrop of social breakdown, public drunkenness, and general anarchy. People lie in the streets near the entrances of pubs, not particularly hurting anybody. Stores and businesses more or less arbitrarily decide to stay open and then more or less arbitrarily close. Always there remains the queer, close, human focus. Suddenly, average Australians start driving cars and trucks for the last time on gasoline stores everyone seems to have been hoarding, albeit for no particular reason. As noted, nearly everyone, everywhere, makes no end of goofy plans. Moira's father gets ready for the next year's work on the farm, spreading manure, making sure the cattle will get hay. John Osborne's dying mother sends him out to get mothballs for all the clothing left behind. Serious last-minute discussions are held by well-intentioned members of government on how trout populations might be affected by moving up the fishing to intersect with a late seasonal spawning period.

Certainly there is enough apocalypse on the horizon for people around Melbourne to know what it looks like to them—even if probably now recalled in the Australian connections of futuristic, dystopian Mel Gibson fantasy. Planting things back in context, one now can trace out a series more imminent and immanent grounds of cultural fear. The novel was published in 1957; the movie was released in 1959; the world depicted is set in 1963. During these years occurred the 1956 Arab-Israeli War and the 1958 formation of Egypt and Syria into the short-lived United Arab Republic, with distinct Soviet bloc affiliations and massive supplies of Soviet-bloc military equipment. Just earlier, in 1954, a Balkan crisis had been averted by absorption into Italy of the post–World War II free city of Trieste. After 1957 came the new fail-safe anxieties promoted by a nearly overnight changeover from nuclear bomber forces to intercontinental ballistic missile systems. At around the same time came the highly publicized voyage of the USS *Nautilus* under the polar icecap and the ensuing rapid conversion of nuclear subs to nuclear-missile subs. Khrushchev sat at the United Nations pounding on the desk with his shoe and stood bragging from the podium, "We will bury you." People somehow knew he was not talking just about material and economic production. Meanwhile, between 1956 and 1959 Fidel Castro and his forces effected the communist revolution in Cuba. By 1961, Russian missiles would be pointing at the U.S. mainland from barely offshore, prompting a U.S. naval blockade that now seems to have come within an inch of provoking a nuclear war.

In such times of geopolitical and military fear one is not surprised to find that the U.S. Navy refused to cooperate with the movie of *On the Beach* by providing a nuclear sub, with the filmmakers relying instead on a borrowed British diesel and battery boat. For his part Shute had nothing to do with the film. Dwight Towers is stiff, boring, domestic, sanctimonious—Gregory Peck does John Kerry. He is the Eisenhower-era good military man, the man in the conning tower, a towering individual. The only thing that saves the movie is the degree to which Peck could do such characters and stay this edge of likability; that, and the addition—deeply offensive to Shute—that the Peck character has the good sense to sleep with Ava Gardner/Moira Davidson. Both Gardner and Astaire manage in the script to capture the book's sense of the English civility of major characters, mixed with Aussie realism, resilience, earthy vitality. Australia, as a kind of cultural last refuge of human character, also supplies the clincher in the last scene of the movie. Once more, the band plays "Waltzing Matilda." The shot is of the deserted streets of downtown Melbourne, with a banner that reads. "There is still time . . . Brother."

A 2000 remake of the movie featured an actual Australian cast, headlined by Bryan Brown, well known to U.S. audiences as a kind of quintessential down-under type from films such as *Breaker Morant, The Thorn Birds, Cocktail, FX,* and the like. Armand Assante played the U.S. Navy submarine skipper; Moira Davidson was played by Rachel Ward, actually British, but also Bryan Brown's wife. Most people just complained that it was too long. At the time, the contention might have been added that it was irrelevant at the end of the cold war and in the ensuing era of nuclear arms limitation treaties.

After 2001, in the Age of Terror, it all seems much less far-fetched again. Planes have come from nowhere, flown by suicide pilots into the World Trade Towers and the Pentagon, and splattering an aborted mess of people all over a cornfield in central Pennsylvania. The terrorists and their state sponsors tauntingly encourage large-scale nation-state retaliation. Meanwhile, a marketplace in Baghdad, a café in Tel Aviv, a polling station in Islamabad, an underground station in London, a commuter train in Madrid become places for people to die en masse in a world where death can come basically any time, any place, out of nowhere, like mass murder, starvation, ethnic cleansing, epidemic influenza, uncontrolled HIV. In the case of public violence, within and across national and international borders, suicide bombers provide the main delivery systems for now. The fact that they are human delivery systems quite likely may mean little, very soon, in a world of endlessly proliferated and proliferating nuclear weapons. Suicide bombers all over the globe will have nuclear capability. The number of potential atomic explosions around the world will make Shute's bizarre and imposing 1957, 1959, 1963 number look positively miniscule. The temptation to respond with massive nuclear retaliation will become nearly irresistible. One wonders how many bombers it will take to ultimately provoke such multiple and manifold responses by nuclear national powers. A new book may try to tell us the story that the end is near—if any books are left around to read or if anyone is left around, of course, to read them.

14
America the Ecumenical

In 1954, following a national campaign by the powerful Catholic fraternal organization the Knights of Columbus, a congressional resolution decreed that the phrase "one nation indivisible" in the Pledge of Allegiance be amended to incorporate the phrase "under God." A parallel dictate of 1957 authorized American paper money to bear the motto "In God We Trust"—as had the coinage for nearly a hundred years. Both were considered militant ripostes to the threat of godless communism. The U.S. president, Dwight Eisenhower—for most of his life not conventionally religious, having joined a church and begun attending services regularly when he decided to seek the presidency—endorsed these measures soundly. Eisenhower, when quizzed on his own theology, demonstrated by reaching in his pocket and pulling out a dime and reading aloud the motto, "In God We Trust." As to constitutionality, both provisions went without notable challenge in the courts.

From the perspective of the religious wars of the late twentieth century and the early twenty-first, the endless clash of fundamentalisms at home and abroad, one word comes to mind about the possibility of the enactment of any such present scenario so tranquilly and uneventfully yoking politics and belief in American life and culture—be that possibility contemplated by the most committed secularist or militant evangelical. The word is *unimaginable.* From advocates of the classic disestablishmentarian tradition such measures would draw immediate condemnation as a brazen attempt to mingle the discourses of religion and politics; from the standpoint of the religious right they would be considered a hopeless overreach in an era when the courts have repeatedly ruled against prayer in schools, the teaching of religious alternatives to scientific evolution, and the Bible as history and literature. Fifty years ago the whole business was done basically without a peep. Accordingly, the intervening decades measure one of the truly epochal passages the nation has made from the years just after World War II—in this particular case from certain attitudes of consensus, comity, and community prevailing on matters of religion in the years just after the war and, to the current atmospherics of religious controversy, themselves nearly unimaginable five decades earlier, now infusing national life in every dimension of culture.

In the first modern nation-state arising essentially de novo out of the twinned impulses of Renaissance humanism and Reformation Protestantism, with its basic documents of government instituted by linguistic fiat, one of the most notable features of the secular religion of democracy in America has remained its collision at nodes of cyclical conflict with risings and fallings of Christian idealism and popular sectarian enthusiasm. Great Awakenings seem to be written into the American genome. G. K. Chesterton, a popular English novelist and religious writer of the late nineteenth century and the early twentieth, has been famously quoted as describing America as "a nation . . . with the soul of a church." What is less known is the degree to which Chesterton, a Catholic intellectual, was actually describing the susceptibility of a certain kind of generic American Protestantism to forms of cultural theodicy, with a politics frequently seeming but a few short steps from merging a happy reign of religious consensus into a civic totalitarianism of fundamentalist mind control. There is not a great distance, Chesterton seemed to suggest, between a nation of churches and a nation with the fascist soul of a true church. In context the observation seems particularly apt. For a person growing up in America after 1945, one of the great measures of the particular distance the nation has traveled in memory and history will now always be a religious one, measured essentially, if still somewhat unbelievably, by the sense of menace conveyed in Chesterton's strange, prophetic admonition.

This is to say that in retrospect, for many of us, surely one of the foremost features of American domestic culture at midcentury seemed to be the happy, comfortable, positive accommodations of politics and religion with each other as positive cultural energies. Actually, one could claim more than that. In a postwar nation where, in 1955, 60 percent of citizens claimed church membership and 50 percent claimed weekly participation in some kind of religious activity, to borrow from the current language of corporate enterprise, faith and citizenship were believed by most to be enriching synergies. Further, it seemed a natural victory dividend, a social evolution directly in keeping with the principles of liberty put to the test in the war just concluded. The Four Freedoms of World War II, articulated by Franklin D. Roosevelt in his January 1941 State of the Union Speech and immortalized in the great wartime Norman Rockwell illustrations, along with freedom of speech, freedom from want, and freedom from fear, included as the fourth among the most basic of freedoms that of religion. The preservation of freedom to worship, as it was called, was deemed almost universally by Americans as integral to the imperative of defeating Hitler and Mussolini, with their false god of the fascist state, and of the Japanese, with their warrior cult of bushido. Even Stalin, the totalitarian apostle of godless communism, proved no fool when, after the German attack on Russia, he quickly reinstituted the cultural status of the orthodox church.

In immediate post–World War II America, perhaps because so many Americans had journeyed so far from home into the vast regions of the world, gaining new experiences of the almost infinite possibilities of social organization and culture, freedom of religion suggested an openness of attitude and acceptance, a generic concept of religious liberty perhaps in the closest proximity it has ever come to some sense of genuine pluralism, tolerance, coexistence. In short, America seemed culturally on the road to a genuine ecumenicism. Respect was uniform for leaders of mainstream denominations—Protestant, Catholic, Orthodox, Jewish. Christianity gained respect for its response to modern intellectual challenges, with bracing discussions by well-known theologians such as Paul Tillich and Reinhold Niebuhr, who became major public figures. Those same theologians frequently engaged philosophy itself, with Judeo-Christian texts heavily citing Kierkegaard, Sartre, and Camus.

Meanwhile, a more general manifestation of such openness to a tolerant ecumenicism could be found in the happy convergence of respectable, mainstream, middle-class religion with new venues in popular culture entertainment and information. Here, highly regarded popular representatives of religion such as the Reverend Norman Vincent Peale or the Catholic bishop Fulton J. Sheen combined serious theological status with practical, concrete social guidance. Both were what we would now call television preachers in the broadest sense, albeit without the showboating flash or an ounce of today's relentlessly proselytizing venality. But both certainly possessed important practical cultural authority in the broadest sense. Peale, the most generic of Protestants, presided over the Marble Collegiate Church in New York City. He never really had a television show of his own, relying instead on personal appearances and recorded sermons. In the general culture, however, he still had a kind of ubiquitousness that made him something of an early media conglomerate. A popular radio show was paired with the editorship of *Guideposts Magazine,* an overtly religious competitor with *Reader's Digest* for pride of place on toilet tanks all over America. He was also the author of best-selling books, most notably *The Power of Positive Thinking* and *How to Stop Worrying and Start Living,* which combined Dale Carnegie–style motivational coaching with the promise of spiritual peace and wholeness.

Sheen, in vestments, miter, and all the rest, enjoyed a six-year run on New York TV, nationally syndicated, with a show likewise combining commentary on social problems and personal advice with spiritual comforts. He too was the author of widely read books, including *Life Is Worth Living, The Way to Inner Peace,* and dozens of others. As a result, he too, like Peale, managed to make early TV a respectable religious venue of cultural seriousness. As if to seal the intellectual bargain, both, it turns out, made wildly publicized appearances on *What's My Line?*

A third figure, a rabbi named Will Herberg, was thought of as speaking for a socially relevant Judaism in the midst of postwar peace and prosperity—although his promisingly entitled book, *Protestant, Catholic, Jew,* was less a hymn to ecumenicism than the sociological picture of a triad of American faiths, with all three according to Herberg in need of spiritual cleansing in a nation increasingly combining "a pervasive secularism with a mounting religiosity."* Still, the fact remained that virtually any public religious conference, celebration, or event seemed now auto-

*Will Herberg, *Protestant, Catholic, Jew* (Chicago: University of Chicago Press, 1960), 2.

matically to involve a preacher, a priest, and a rabbi—as did a whole new genre, one strangely now recalls, of happily recounted dialect jokes and shaggy dog stories, not infrequently shared by ministers.

At the time, all these seemed quite logical developments arising out of a postwar religious culture in which organized, doctrinal, sectarian religion seemed engaged in plotting its own obsolescence. For many Americans who thought about it as a crucial part of their way of life, it seemed to be making its peace with philosophy, politics, education, and general intellectual culture. Religion worldwide seemed on the verge of being considered the highest expression of a common human spirituality, reading itself out into the great historical traditions of culture in all given times and places. The endorsement of such a view, as in so many other postwar instances, came in any number of popular books and articles, including an epochal Time-Life series entitled—of course—"The World's Major Religions."

At home, the God of mainstream popular religion was probably best thought of as latitudinarian Protestant—Methodist, Reformed, Lutheran, Presbyterian, with an eye and ear to Catholics and Jews. Off to one side of the intellectual communion lay liberal Unitarians, to the other Baptists, Mormons, Jehovah's Witnesses, and Seventh Day Adventists. At the time there were no Muslims, Buddhists, or Hindus to speak of. Popular books, doling out a generic Christian inspirationalism, ranged from blockbuster novels such as Lloyd C. Douglas's *The Robe* and *The Big Fisherman* to Jim Bishop's quasi-journalistic *The Day Christ Died* or Dr. Tom Dooley's propagandistic account of medical missionary service in Indochina, *Deliver Us from Evil.* Women weighed in as well with popular books on religious and spiritualistic themes, including Anne Lindbergh's *Gift from the Sea* and Dale Evans's *Angel Unaware.* Magazines from *Reader's Digest* to the Sunday newspaper supplement featured reflections by famous people on faith and stories of everyday religious courage.

At the movies it was the heyday of the great sword-and-sandals religious spectaculars. Garish, banal, vaguely spiritual and wildly successful at the box office, these included *The Robe*—from the best-selling Lloyd C. Douglas novel described earlier about a centurion converted through witnessing the crucifixion, starring Richard Burton, Jean Simmons, and Victor Mature—and an equally popular sequel, *Demetrius and the Gladiators,* which paired Mature with Susan Hayward. The Big One, of course, was Charlton Heston in *The Ten Commandments,* famous for its astonishing, never-before-attempted special effects—the magic-rod tricks, the burning bush, the visitations of the Egyptian plagues, and the parting of the Red Sea. Lesser spectacles of the era included *Samson and Delilah, David and Bathsheba,* and *The Big Fisherman.* At the turn of the decade came the other scenery-chewing, chariot-driving Heston spectacular, *Ben-Hur,* followed by *King of Kings, The Greatest Story Ever Told,* and *The Bible.* Smaller Christian classics included *A Man Called Peter,* the biography of Peter Marshall, a Scots immigrant who rose to become chaplain of the U.S. Senate, and *Battle Hymn,* with Rock Hudson as a former World War II pilot whose ministerial calling is tested by his recall to air force combat duty in Korea.

Institutionally, the rise of the National Council of Churches was given much media visibility. Similarly, the World Council of Churches, first envisioned in 1937, after 1948 undertook a parallel evolution coincidental with that of the United Nations, with a general secretary and international headquarters in Geneva.

In my own world God had to be a liberal Presbyterian. Eisenhower was one, attending our own Gettysburg Presbyterian church when he was in town. Henry Luce was one, as was Secretary of State John Foster Dulles. So was the ascendant leader of the World Council of Churches, Eugene Carson Blake, moving there from his position as moderator—a great ecumenical word if there ever was one—of U.S. Presbyterians. All in all, it seemed a good time for American religion, or at least it seemed pretty good to me, as a churchgoing small-town kid, particularly as I moved from childhood into my teens. Everybody seemed to be getting along, religiously, and a kind of natural evolution between faith and public culture seemed to continue well into my young adulthood. Ecumenicism was all the rage, somehow encoded, as far as I could see, in the national genome. To this day I still think of myself as a kind of sociological case study. My mother was a birthright Quaker, my father descended of Mennonites. We became Presbyterians, just like the Eisenhowers, although we had been there first. Still, the church had been a social choice: a denomination in the top rung of community prestige—as was often, in those days, dictated by the historical patterns of local religious settlement. Among Gettysburg's founders had been influential Scots. The church still had some of the ruling families: McPherson, McIlhenny, Hewetson. The church was also the place where Lincoln had worshipped on November 19, 1863, on his way up to Cemetery Hill to give the Gettysburg Address. Gettysburg had its own history as a Lutheran college and seminary town as well. Lutheran prestige thus also ran high, with Christ Church for the intellectuals and St. James for the local politicians and merchants. The Episcopalians were, as in most places, country club people, considered somewhat cocktailish, uppity, and nouveaux. Down the various side streets of the town could be found houses of worship for a host of other denominations: Reformed, Brethren, Methodist, Seventh-Day Adventist, Catholic. On Washington Street, part of an old pre–Civil War free black community, was the AME Zion. There was no synagogue. The only visible Jew in town was a shoemaker named Eli Lock, whose wife, it was alleged, would chase you all the way down the street if you had a price disagreement.

The ecumenical history of the country could be traced out in the smaller population centers. All the upper county towns were versions of a protestant microcosm: Lutheran, Reformed, Methodist, Baptist, Brethren. To the south, bordering Maryland, were mainly Catholic towns. Scattered across the rural landscape were two-hundred- and three-hundred-year-old historical specimens, most of them still functioning, of founding Lutheran, Presbyterian, Quaker, or Mennonite congregations. Such evidence of what had been called "Penn's noble experiment" actually persisted into the world of my early years; or, to cite a contemporary colonial-era text, the place seemed a page out of Crèvecoeur's *Letters from an American Farmer,* where the narrator describes his pastoral environ as a religious melting pot, a haven of toleration where "the Americans become as to religion what they are as to country, allied to all."

I could personally recall visits to the Menallen Friends' Meeting, where the old families got together once a year for what they called the Quaker Picnic, or trips farther away to the German Brethren in my father's hometown, where they had a church orchestra. In the summer my sister and I walked to a Lutheran Vacation Bible School; we got sabbaticals at both Lutheran and Presbyterian summer camps up in the mountains, one week each. Youth activities in my own congregation, centering on intellectually serious Sunday school units and weekly evening sessions of something called the Westminster Fellowship, featured advanced discussion of great philosophical questions and points of theology such as Double Predestination. These were tied in with the sermons of an intellectual minister, whose long exegeses and commentaries bristled with big names ranging from Paul Tillich, Dietrich Bonhoeffer, and Reinhold Niebuhr to Harry Emerson Fosdick and, yes, Norman Vincent Peale. A brief leavening highlight of pulpit memory, I recall, came for me during Boy Scout Week one time, on a visit with my scrubbed and uniformed troop to the local Evangelical United Brethren (EUB) church, where a revivalistic preacher, so much the opposite of the Princeton-educated theologian in the Presbyterian pulpit, so arrested and entertained me that I was ready to sign right up. I remember my mother rather sensibly talking me out of it.

Religion for me as I went off to college, to a good college in the South, nominally Presbyterian but mainly focused on hard-driving preprofessional studies, remained mixed with ecumenical theology, albeit at increasing levels of personal discomfort. The more general cultural and philosophical cachet with which religion was invested, the less sense it made to me intellectually or emotionally. It became a structuralist myth system, a social science discipline, a popular-culture commodity. Like most of my generation in academe, especially, I eventually just got rid of it. For me there was no particular anguish. To me the religious question was just irrelevant. There was not one scintilla of evidence to suggest that we were a special order of creation, save for unsubstantiated supernatural claim. Accordingly, it wasn't worth fooling with. It was cultural excess baggage; it just didn't apply. Vietnam clinched it for me. Joseph Heller was right. And even he didn't go far enough. Man was matter, period. Dead was dead, and even "sorry" didn't mean shit.

For a lot of other people my age it was a much longer story. Many, drawn by the interfusion into American religious life during the 1960s of Eastern religion—Hindu, Buddhist, Taoist—found themselves in esoteric, obscurantist spiritualities. For African Americans the rise of Black Islam came first, eventually filtering for many into traditional Islam. More generally, religion became part of what Theodore Roszak called an "easy-do syncretism."* Crazy hybrids popped up like Transcendental Meditation, Hare Krishna, Rastafarianism, and Jesus People. The list continues today with Scientology, the Kabbala.

Amid all this, public religion mounted the predictable reaction, attempting to link Christian spiritualism with patriotic ideology. Figures such as Jerry Falwell and Pat Robertson vied for the title of America's preacher, with the latter eventually mounting a serious, if short-lived, presidential campaign. The Moral Majority arose to take charge again over a culture of political disobedience and sexual libertinism, of anti-establishment bias, rebellious music, and general hedonism, featuring drugs, alcohol, gays and lesbians, and all other manner of apocalyptic abomination.

In the upper ranges of public identity, a prerequisite for political or religious character became a generic, Bible-based, fundamentalist, but resolutely blissful, ecstatic, personalized born-again-ness—once associated largely with primitive rural congregations or inner-city temples of the poor and downtrodden but now extended into affluent nondenominational independent churches. At the center was required some distinct social experience of transcendent, spiritually illuminating, and permanently transforming fundamentalist epiphany. A representative story, well known, is that of the forty-second president, George W. Bush, healed of alcoholic drinking (although the diagnostic adjective is never mentioned) by the intervention of the Reverend Billy Graham. The details of the counseling session remain vague. He says it led him to becoming born again, but he doesn't make much of an issue of going to church. Raised an Episcopalian, with his wife a Methodist, he never says particularly what church. If anything, he is something of a new-age Dwight Eisenhower—as are all aspirants to the position, it now seems, required to style themselves in one way or another. Republican primary candidate Mitt Romney felt obliged to make a speech—analogous, many said, to that made by John F. Kennedy about his Catholicism—proving that Mormonism was a form of fervent Christianity. A popular rival for a time was

*Theodore Roszak, *The Making of a Counter-Culture* (Garden City, NY: Doubleday, 1969), 144.

Mike Huckabee, a former governor of Arkansas and an ordained Baptist minister, whose belief system included a genius for stand-up comedy but a decidedly bonehead grasp of evolution. Then-Democratic candidate Barack Obama, at pains, like his liberal-intellectual rival, Hillary Clinton, to present himself as a sincerely believing Christian, was forced to distance himself from a controversial minister in whose congregation he had spent twenty years. His eventual Republican opponent, John McCain, haunted by his famous televangelist "agents of intolerance line" from an earlier campaign, found his attempts to make up with evangelicals stalled by the continual making and breaking of alliances with right-wing adherents spouting bigoted nonsense about Hitler and the Jews or Islam and Armageddon.

In what might be called the great middle landscape of everyday American life, religion came out of the 1960s tumults of the Vietnam War and the counterculture, followed by the crises of the Watergate 1970s, in a new marriage with spiritual healing. A culture of therapy found itself revivified in fashionable appropriations of the solaces of "a higher power" previously the province mainly of alcohol and drug addicts. Motivational spiritualisms also came back to life. Bookstore shelves overflowed with popular republications of hoary inspirational classics such as Charles Shelton's 1896 best seller *In His Steps*—the source of the phrasing "What Would Jesus Do?" and the marketing inspiration for WWJD bracelets that began appearing on born-again wrists everywhere; Bruce Barton's equally popular 1925 *The Man Nobody Knows,* where Jesus was touted as the first great advertising man. Norman Vincent Peale and Fulton J. Sheen were reinstalled as Dale Carnegies with cassocks. Vaguely spiritual 1960s volumes such as *I'm OK, You're OK* yielded to the naked worldliness of *The Seven Secrets of Highly Successful People.* A higher synthesis was once again reinstated with *The Purpose-Driven Life.*

On the born-again scene, America's hottest popular preacher of late has been a young evangelist in Houston, a freshman-year Oral Roberts dropout who inherited his father's congregation. To prepare for the coming of his media kingdom, he bought the Houston professional basketball coliseum and gave the place a $65 million makeover, including two waterfalls. Meanwhile, in Colorado Springs a major Christian organization sponsored the tenth annual Purity Ball, a kind of born-again debutante party where fathers in white tails read scripted vows to their daughters pledging the protection of their chastity until marriage. Several other groups, it should be noted, offer Web-site advice on revirgination, a kind of sexual time-out and celibate cleansing for young couples who managed to go too far. Of appeal to Christians and Muslims of late are new surgical techniques of hymeneal reconstruction.

But it is not just the right-wing exurbanites and cuckoos. The Episcopal Church, the last bastion of traditional upper-class white supremacy, continues to be riven by quarrels over homosexuality, the role of women priests, and the politics of world communion, with American social conservatives joining forces with black African archbishops. Sex scandals have staggered the American Catholic priesthood; meanwhile, the church in Rome elects to continue a string of conservative, even reactionary, papacies frequently making common cause with radical evangelicals.

Things come and go with blinding speed. A few years back, during the flurry of WWJD logo merchandise, one of the bracelets was worn by a professional golfer named Payne Stewart, young, handsome, successful, with a beautiful wife and family, every day. The bracelet was chosen to go along with his signature stylish golfing pants, called plus fours, cut at the knee, a pair of which he allegedly owned, with matching outfit, for every day of the year. No doubt he was wearing it when his private plane ran out of fuel and went down in the desert Southwest, after flying aimlessly on automatic pilot for hours and hours with everyone on board already dead as the result of a faulty oxygen system. If there is suggestion of allegory, it has all become rather perplexing to me.

One could go on endlessly with a train of bizarre anecdote. Ministerial scandals have now involved celebrity evangelists including Jimmy Swaggart, Jim Bakker, Oral Roberts, and Ted Haggard. The first paid prostitutes to talk dirty to him at an airport motel outside New Orleans—he was the first cousin, after all, of Jerry Lee Lewis. The second evangelist got involved with an innocent, nubile young parishioner; he lost his garishly cosmeticized wife in a divorce; the parishioner became a Playboy playmate; the wife became a gay icon; the reverend got time in jail for stealing money from his religion-entertainment conglomerate. The third sequestered himself in a tower at the nearly bankrupt Tulsa, Oklahoma, university named for him and swore that God was coming to take him unless someone was willing to bail him out financially. The fourth, celebrated for his championing of the American family against the omnipresent threats of homosexuality, got caught with a male prostitute who was supplying him with sex and methadone. Meanwhile, the gigantic churches just keep filling, the big-time megachurch and television preachers keep preaching, and the coffers just keep jingling. It is as if the spiritual hunger just can't run quickly enough to outpace the ministerial cynicism and grotesque misbehavior.

Whatever it is that makes this keep happening, I find, has now been way behind me, maybe as long as fifty years. Actually I think I can date it. During the summer of 1957, after my father's death, my mother, attempting to continue a habit of family trips to the city, had taken us to New York, where we were actually visiting at the time Graham was conducting his first great evangelical crusade—a much-heralded spectacle that went on at Madison Square Garden for sixteen weeks, with one big event in early July at Yankee Stadium and a farewell performance on September 1 in Times Square. No slouch on the national current-events scene—and perhaps, in ways my sister and I could not appreciate, desperate for spiritual uplift in her sudden widowed state—she noted, while consulting the local things-to-do listings, Graham's much-heralded nightly presence at Yankee Stadium. I was one ahead of her. I had found out that the Dodgers were in the middle of a home series in Brooklyn. At the same time, something must have kicked in about the old family spirit. The question in her mind, I am surely convinced, became, "What would Willie have done?" To her everlasting credit, clenching a subway map, she herded me onto the train to Ebbets Field, where the Dodgers, in their last season in Brooklyn, were playing the Braves. I got a Dodgers pennant, which I hung religiously in my room until I went away to college. My mother's choice—albeit one that prevented me from seeing American religious history in the making—remains to me the greatest of ecumenical gestures another person has ever bestowed.

I should add that I finally did get to see Billy Graham, close-up and in person, later on. The occasion was during my military service in 1969, when my armored cavalry regiment was detailed to riot-control duty in the military district of Washington. My platoon was assigned to a gate for special dignitaries. When I saw Graham, he couldn't have been closer. At a side entrance to the U.S. capital, he was getting out of a big, black limousine. He was there to preside spiritually, as America's preacher, at the second inauguration of Richard M. Nixon.

15
It Wasn't All Elvis

In the vast body of post-1945 popular-culture production one is surprised not to find at least one American movie somewhere about the rise of rock 'n' roll entitled *And God Created Elvis,* in the way the French showcased the heart-stopping Bridgette Bardot in *And God Created Woman.* Actually, the one movie that leaps to mind on the musical subject—*Rock around the Clock*—still holds up remarkably as a chronicle of how things actually were in the beginning, featuring on one hand Bill Haley and the Comets as pioneers of white rockabilly and on the other the Platters combining doo-wop with African American blues and gospel—the kind of music in those days called "race." And that was just the way, it was told, in which God actually created Elvis. Further, I would propose, something persists even in current American rock 'n' roll lore of the idea of a great, incarnational narrative in which it all happened—or, in memory at least, may be said to have happened. In television history the legend would center on one nationally electrifying appearance on *The Ed Sullivan Show* (there were actually three, over a period of six months, with the camera positioning in the third notoriously truncating the performance from the waist down). In records it would immortalize a place called Sun Studios in Memphis, where a beautiful walk-in, an Indian-looking kid with a gospel-blues background and a truck-driving job got to make a trial cut of "That's All Right," and boom, suddenly there was "Blue Suede Shoes" and "Heartbreak Hotel." In the movies, although maybe it took a little longer, there was *Love Me Tender,* then *Jailhouse Rock,* and then a whole legendary Hollywood cycle.

An alternate creation narrative cherished by many is the one that might be called the American Hot Wax scenario, spotlighting such popular-culture convergences as the rise of the teenager; the growth, following from the breakdown of school segregation, of an interracial youth culture; the transformation of radio into a largely top-forty musical format; and the emergence of the celebrity disc jockey and the TV bandstand and dance party shows. One reads the runes of early legend, remembering James Dean and Natalie Wood in *Rebel without a Cause;* Ricky Nelson moving from a 1950s family sitcom to the top of the record charts; Brenda Lee from Nashville, Chuck Berry from New Orleans, Frankie Lyman and the Teenagers from the Bronx; Frankie Avalon and Fabian, both from Philadelphia; a first constellation of teen icons; and then Buddy Holly, Richie Valens, and the Big Bopper, going down to eternal memory in an airplane crash on the day the music died.

Popular-culture musicologists frequently go back further to a kind of Old Testament foregrounding steeped in folk, regional, and racial vectors, a convergence of deep-seated, history-laden, profoundly political American cultural narratives: C&W, country and western, white; R&B, rhythm and blues, black. It makes for a kind of nice, acronymic plan of historical cross-reference and intersecting genealogies of class and race. The white, hillbilly tradition is made to summon up Anglo-Saxon and Celtic ballad minstrelsy, along with the keening harmonics of the backwoods church, shape-note singing, sacred harp, and the like. The "Negro" blues legacy in turn becomes that of the work song, the African chant, the whole alternative tradition of black minstrelsy, coupled with its own parallel religious inheritance of spiritual, gospel, shout, and call-and-response. Rockabilly and race: as a roots narrative it also legitimizes the new mythology of an insurgent post-1945 culture of youth, prefiguring its eventual 1960s breakout in early forms of musical and popular culture rebellion. Jerry Lee Lewis, Bo Diddley, James Dean, the Beats, jazz legends such as John Coltrane or Billie Holiday—all become avatars of the Beatles, the Rolling Stones, Bob Dylan, Janis Joplin, Jimi Hendrix, and Jefferson Airplane.

Meanwhile, as anyone who was actually there can tell you without much structural argument or scholarly exertion—anecdotally, experientially, that is, as part of living in the world—it was much, much more complicated than any of that. For a young person growing up in the rock 'n' roll era, that is to say, music was simply the most exciting thing in the world, absolutely the place to be. Furthermore, it was a place right in the middle of the media mainstream—even as Elvis began to make his appearance—already populated by, yes, Bill Haley and the Comets, the Big Bopper, Richie Valens, Buddy Holly and the Crickets but also, simultaneously, for any kid who knew anything, Chuck Berry with "Maybelline," Little Richard with "Tutti Frutti," Jerry Lee Lewis with "A Whole Lotta Shakin' Goin On," not to mention Billy Ward and the Dominoes with "60-Minute Man" or a country guy named Carl Perkins, who did "Blue Suede Shoes." There were soul pioneers such as the Platters and the Coasters and white doo-wop groups as diverse as Danny and the Juniors and the Dell Vikings. On a single playlist one might find the Four Preps with "Twenty-Six Miles," the Teddy Bears with "To Know Him Is to Love Him," the Penguins with "Earth Angel," and the Monotones with "Book of Love." This was decidedly no longer the world of *Your Hit Parade,* with Russell Arms, Dorothy Collins, Snooky Lanson, and Gisele MacKenzie doing homogenized TV covers of Jo Stafford or Frankie Laine. Every week, it seemed, there were new releases, with no single song sounding like any other before it: the Chordettes' "Mister Sandman," the Skyliners' "Since I Don't Have You," and the Big Bopper's "Chantilly Lace" mixed it up with the Coasters' "Yackety-Yack," the Everly Brothers' "Wake Up, Little Susie," the Rays' "Silhouettes on the Shade," and the Flamingos' "I Only Have Eyes for You." Strange imports like "Mondo Cane," "Alley Cat," and "Volare," made the charts along with melodic instrumentals like Hugo Winterhalter's "Canadian Sunset," Bert Kaempfert's "Wonderland by Night," and, as late as 1958, Percy Faith's smarmy "Theme from a Summer Place." There were stealth sex songs for clueless white kids like "The Hokey Pokey" or "Willie and the Hand Jive," and wacked-out novelty records like "Flying Saucers" or "Purple People Eater."

Even when the dangerous, smoldering Elvis himself made his appearance on the scene, first through records and then on TV and in movies, he had a direct, mainline competitor in the ostensibly straight-arrow Pat Boone. Further, through an elaborate style, image, and public-relations contrast between the two, enthusiastically orchestrated by the media, was conducted a serious cultural contest of entire contending legends and personae. At the risk of excessive metaphorical ingenuity, I now remember it somehow as all wrapped up in images of signature footwear, a cultural figure of blue suede shoes on one hand against white bucks on the other. The first hit phrasing, of course, belonged to Elvis, channeled by way of a rockabilly counterpart named Carl Perkins, the kind of preening, garish thing, along with a slicked-back ducktail haircut and a sullen sneer, something that rebellious white kid would wear while acting black. White bucks from the outset, in contrast, were the trademark property of Pat Boone, a nice, well-barbered, morally upright, baritone-voiced boy from Nashville, Tennessee—allegedly descended from the great frontiersman himself—who could take the whitest of middle-of-the-road ballads and the blackest of blues and make it all sound socially acceptable from top to bottom; oddly, as will be seen, it was Boone who most routinely did white covers of black hits.

As noted, one risks elevating an already facile metaphor into an excursus on competing cultural discourses. The idea of the media heartthrob as basic American boy, after all, was as familiar as Huckleberry Finn versus Tom Sawyer, not to mention being marketably renewed in the movies with James Dean or Marlon Brando versus Tab Hunter or Troy Donahue, or on TV with Eddie Haskell and Wally Cleaver. (In a further oddity, it should be noted, by 1956, at the height of the Presley-Boone competition, the former was twenty-one and the latter already twenty-two.) Still, as hard as it may be to grasp now, for anyone who was alive at the time, the essentially Manichean details of the contrasting popular narratives of background and image are well remembered.

For Elvis, at least, it was always all about the whole nine yards—race, class, sexuality, a kind of great American annunciation. The first name alone will always suffice. Elvis. (Although no one knows the etymology of *Elvis* proper—probably just as well—*Alvis* means all-conquering.) Elvis Aron Presley—pronounced "Elvis Ay-Ron," it quickly came to be known—was actually the brother of a stillborn twin, Jesse Garon. The Presleys were Mississippi hill-country people, none of Faulkner's fallen aristocrats but rather poor whites out of Tupelo. Even for the region they were people from nowhere, white trash maybe mixed up with some Indian, with the latter a crucial element of the legend: in the age of the juvenile delinquent, the motorcycle hoodlum, the rebellious Beat, another kind of outlaw boy—wild, backwoods, maybe even half-breed—a figure Presley often played with authority in movies. The story quickly became known everywhere: the kid shows up in a Memphis studio, Sun Records, where he gets discovered by a wildcat record promoter named Sam Phillips; he is blue-collar, hillbilly, poor white; the father is a truck driver who has done time in the penitentiary during the 1930s for forgery; the mother has come of an equally hard life. For all that, the son is something of a momma's boy: an only child, obedient to his father, worshipful of his mother; respecting elders with a "yes ma'am," and "no sir"; brought up Christian in the old-time gospel religion, the primitive church, remaining partial to the old hymns.

Thus the strange, complex, in many ways even self-contradictory legend incarnates itself—from start to finish, in the most literal of ways, just below the hot glamour, Elvis is so thoroughly an American kid of the era, shy, trusting, polite with elders, utterly loyal to family. He doesn't smoke or drink. Everywhere he goes, his family goes with him. The point of his entertainment wealth is to provide for his mother, father, grandmother. Shortly, in the area of citizenship and patriotic duty, he does the unthinkable, becoming the only celebrity remotely of his significance ever to serve a full, standard enlistment as a common soldier in the U.S. armed forces. In photograph after photograph and story after story we see Elvis Presley getting his hair sheared, taking his inoculations like a man, being issued standard khakis and fatigues. He is the most beloved enlisted man in the U.S. Army since Audie Murphy or Alvin York. In the process he accommodates an astonishing career hiatus, drafted at the relatively late age of twenty-three but doing his duty in a tank division in cold war Germany. Along the way he falls in love, with perhaps a faint tinge of scandal, with an officer's daughter he has met who lives, underage, in his household. Still, there remain strong and believable claims of premarital chastity. Eventually Elvis and Priscilla get married and have a daughter, Lisa Marie.

Thus the adolescent rock 'n' roll rebel grows into a young adult. But along the way, he has never been exactly the prince of darkness. It has all been carefully titrated. Even the sneer, the haircut, and the clothing are those of the kind of high-school student most places in America you'd find in the industrial arts or agriculture curriculum, with black leather jacket or—if he is a country boy—maybe the FFA blue corduroy, pompadour hair, upturned collar, pegged pants—a "cat." (In fact, an early nickname, "The Hillbilly Cat," has been applied to distinguish him from "cool cats" who are urban, with their coffeehouses, jazz, poetry, and bongo drums.) Design details from the common scene also include the flashy two-tone clothes, pink and gray, red and black, the colors matching the tones of popular cars: the blue an aqua, the green a lime, the pink a glaring Pepto-Bismol, the red a bright, fire-engine red. They are clothes frequently bought from black peoples' stores but mixed with country-bum stuff, T-shirts, blue jeans, brogans, white socks. You can see Elvis dressed like this in informal shots. The signature hair in those days is called a ducktail or a DA—duck's ass. In its glistening, immaculate, pomade sheen, it is actually light brown, seemingly blackened by the dressing. As to the face, the gorgeous, dark, "bedroom" eyes, as they were called in those days, come together with the cheekbones, the straight nose, the strong jaw line, and the handsome mouth. The smile is a wonderful, sweet, lovable smile, yet still a smile that is always, simultaneously, exactly, just a twitch away from a sneer.

From the outset the Pat Boone competition from the image industry knows its job and the limits of its challenge. Pat Boone is not so much the anti-Elvis as the un-Elvis, something like the way 7-up once styled itself against Coke as the un-cola. Fresh-faced, never in need of a hair trim, perpetually dressed in white bucks, khaki trousers, button-down shirts, V-neck sweaters, or a snappy coat-and-tie outfit, he is what people used to call clean-cut. Most evident somehow is always the blinding, white-toothed, Ipana smile. His reputation for right living derives from growing up as an all-American family boy in Nashville, the home of the Grand Ole Opry, where he had been a student at David Lipscomb College, a church school. In everything from his deliberate embrace of a *Your Hit Parade* singing style—despite his heavy reliance on remakes of decidedly raunchy black tunes—to his choice, in eventual competition with Elvis, of sanitized, in-character movie roles, he radiates white from head to toe.

Everything about him is trustworthy and clean. He is your daughter's ideal date for the junior prom, although decidedly not a teenager. In fact, besides being a year older than the decidedly more "experienced"-seeming Elvis, he has been married since 1953, at age nineteen, to the daughter of country star Red Foley. Not surprisingly, he will become eventually a Christian fundamentalist icon, a hero of the new religious right, a noted political and cultural conservative. In an eerie parallel to the later Elvis, with his darkening passion for gospel, Boone will define his later career, along with his family, as a religious performer.

At the height of things, one now sees, the music that lay beyond the comparison of styles was in fact based on comparable assimilations, albeit played to exceedingly disparate images and ends. In the beginning, Elvis mixed rockabilly with race, with everything in between, from traditional country and western to the Christian hymnal. Early hits after "That's All Right (Mama)" included "Blue Moon of Kentucky," "Baby Let's Play House," "I Don't Care If the Sun Don't Shine," and "Good Rockin' Tonight." In 1956, when he may be properly said to have found his style, he came forth with "Heartbreak Hotel," "Hound Dog," "Don't Be Cruel," "I Got a Woman," and "Love Me Tender," but he also did "white" covers of race favorites such as "Tutti Frutti" and "Shake, Rattle and Roll." He continued in 1957 with "All Shook Up," "Teddy Bear," and "Treat Me Nice" but again added covers of "Long Tall Sally" and "Blueberry Hill." Notable in all the early favorites is the conventional, middle-of-the-road background accompaniment of the Jordanaires, frequently locking him into a sound reminiscent of a 1940s big-band crooner such as Frank Sinatra with the Dorsey orchestra or a singing cowboy such as Roy Rogers with the Sons of the Pioneers. Toward the end of the decade there was a religious collection, with "Peace in the Valley" and "I Believe," as well as the inevitable Christmas album. The rest, as they say, is history.

In somewhat surprising retrospect, it was Pat Boone who made it initially in rock 'n' roll by doing sanitized white covers of largely forbidden and disreputable black music, beginning with the 1955 Fats Domino hit "Ain't That a Shame" and going on to one well-known sexually explicit original after another, including "Tutti Frutti," "Long Tall Sally," "Maybelline," "Boney Maroney," "Good Golly Miss Molly," and "At My Front Door ('Crazy Little Momma')." "Good Golly Miss Molly," goes the first line of the Little Richard original, "sure like to ball." Similarly, "Long Tall Sally" and "Boney Maroney," along with the composite "At My Front Door ('Crazy Little Momma')," are titles that say exactly what they mean. Ironically, it was also Boone who popularized early soul ballads such as "Chains of Love" and "I Almost Lost My Mind." But then, as quickly, just as Elvis was hitting his rock 'n' roll stride, Boone also made a severe cut to the right, redirecting his appeal into the racially and socially hygienic middle-of-the-road mainstream with what now seem signature hits such as "Love Letters in the Sand," "April Love," "Bernadine," and "Don't Forbid Me." Soon the Boone competition seemed less with Elvis and more with Johnny Mathis, a fellow romantic balladeer. "When the Swallows Come Back to Capistrano" mixed with movie themes such as "Thee I Love," from *Friendly Persuasion,* and "This Land Is Mine"—itself a vocal remake of the lush, top-selling Ferrante and Teicher piano hit single—from *Exodus.*

A review of early TV history concerning the two figures reveals a similarly complex, if involuted, pattern of cross-referencing and then diverging image and celebrity. In the early months of 1956, it is now little remembered, it was Elvis who made a first appearance on *The Milton Berle Show* and then on Steve Allen, where he was compelled to do a stupid pet trick, himself duded up in a tuxedo and singing "You Ain't Nothin' but a Hound Dog" to a droopy-eared basset likewise attired. Further hazing was required as part of a country skit where he exchanged backwoods nonsense with Allen, Andy Griffith, and Imogene Coca. The far better *Ed Sullivan Show* appearances, three of them, actually, occurred late in the year. For any person who remembers early TV, the first, it can now be said, may have been one of those that changed music and television forever. I certainly remember it, the sheer nerve-tingling, set-your-hair-on-end excitement, the palpable electricity, an energy that just radiated out from the screen and grabbed your American teenage heart and soul. This was followed by a second, watched with equal thrill and avidity. The one most likely to be remembered now, of course, is the celebrated night of network-imposed camera censorship, with live performance footage restricted to shots from the waist up. Ironically, it was on that same night—having arrived at the pinnacle of pelvic notoriety—that Elvis also received the famous moral imprimatur from the uptight host as "a real decent, fine boy." He went on, speaking directly to Elvis: "We want to say that we've never had a pleasanter experience on our show with a big name than we've had with you."

Pat Boone, in predictable contrast, never got near TV notoriety. He did make a certain history, actually appearing on the first *American Bandstand,* February 15, 1958, along with the host Dick Clark and fellow singers Jerry Lee Lewis and Connie Francis, and a group called the Royal Teens, sporting a current single, "Short Shorts" (or, in the classic New Jersey inflections of the era, "shawt shawts"). But after that it was mostly musical guest spots, variety show performances, and comedy sketches for the pleasing, mediagenic Boone as a fixture on mainstream TV. Along the way he became a teen inspirational and guidance writer, with an advice book, *Twixt Twelve and Twenty,* coming in second in 1958 on the bestselling nonfiction list to Art Linkletter's *Kids Say the Darndest Things!* and then claiming the top spot for itself in 1959. After that came televised holiday and patriotic specials, appearances on talk shows, and, with the advent of cable, Christian broadcasting celebrity.

But it remains for the movie careers to expand most vividly on the music story. With early experiments such as *Love Me Tender* and *Jailhouse Rock,* along with quick evolutions such as *Loving You* and *Kid Creole*—all of them done prior to enlistment in the army—Elvis not only found a new career in the movies. He invented a whole genre called the Elvis movie. When he came out of the service, he quickly capitalized with *G.I. Blues,* and then he played Elvis for an astonishing twenty-six more. More or less concurrently, Pat Boone tried movies too, with mixed success. He did musical love stories such as *Bernadine, April Love,* and *Mardi Gras* and a Disney adventure *Journey to the Center of the Earth,* where his occasional singing came off at least no worse than Kirk Douglas's breaking into sailor tunes in *20,000 Leagues under the Sea.* Boone's one original venture turned out to be the wholesome *State Fair,* a Rodgers and Hammerstein musical written for the screen. There, ironically, he was paired with Ann-Margret, eventually the quintessential Elvis-movie love interest in what might be the golden classic of Elvis movies, *Viva Las Vegas.* In the event, Boone was done with Hollywood star turns by the early 1960s, touring with his family in a gospel act and cultivating Christian celebrity, and most recently, as if to catch up on the grotesquerie of Elvis's later career, the jumpsuits and the scarves, the obesity and the drugs, having invested in bizarre self-parody, while appearing in the cult film *The Eyes of Tammy Fay,* about the freakish ex-wife of a disgraced televangelist, and producing a rap album, *In a Metal Mood.*

Just how complicated the musical competition had all been from the beginning may now be further reprised in the overnight ascendancy, even for the times, of a whole new second wave of rock names and celebrities. To be sure, young solo singing idols continued to be mainly male. Rick Nelson, for instance, seemed a kind of genetic recombination of favorable traits of both Elvis and Boone for middle-of-the-road audiences. Ditto the *American Bandstand* Philadelphia cluster, courtesy of Dick Clark, including Fabian, Frankie Avalon, and Bobby Rydell, along with a Canadian import, Paul Anka, specializing in adenoidal teen angst. Dion and the Belmonts were socially acceptable greasers. A black crossover favorite was Clyde McPhatter, with "A Lover's Question" and "Little Bitty Pretty One." Out of hillbilly came Roy Orbison with "Crying," "Running Scared," and the blockbuster "Pretty Woman." The Everly Brothers were the first country boys to make it as mainstream teen singers. Bobby Darin, in contrast, was all over the place with "Splish Splash," "Mack the Knife," and "Beyond the Sea." Although no solo female singers appeared for the moment of comparable celebrity or visibility, girl groups such as the Teddy Bears scored with "To Know Him Is to Love Him," the Poni-Tails with "Born Too Late," or the Shirelles with an early hit, "Dedicated to the One I Love." Here, too, there was the odd crossover soul singer, Dinah Washington, or a country newcomer like Brenda Lee. But mainly girl singers leaned toward novelty fare, like Connie Stevens and "Kookie, Lend Me Your Comb" or Dodi Goodman with "Tan Shoes and Pink Shoelaces." Lesley Gore did teenage hurt with "It's My Party" and "You Don't Own Me," and Connie Francis specialized in yearning ballads like "Where the Boys Are." The barest prediction of a future of female rock singing lay with outlaw mixtures of white and ethnic, with race image suppressed, such as the Ronettes and the Shangri-Las.

The third wave of rock in the 1960s took seriously musical origins, playing on the roots of legend. The Beatles, tremendously influenced by Elvis, as well as black pioneers such as Chuck Berry, succeeded in the beginning on their own mixture of adolescent rebellion and humorous good cheer. The Rolling Stones, trading from the outset on the outlaw darkness—"Their Royal Satanic Majesties," as one album title put it—made no pretense about where they cast their cultural lot. Elvis by now was tame, MOR (middle of the road). There were still movies and records. But mainly he had become the Las Vegas act seen round the world, the jumpsuits, sunglasses, bizarre sideburns and hair, the King going the way of Sinatra, Dean Martin, Sammy Davis Jr., Wayne Newton. He became the weird, bloated, overprescribed recluse, surrounded by retainers and flunkeys, making the world safe for Michael Jackson—whom, of all people, his own daughter, Lisa, would briefly marry. He was the weird, addled guy pictured with Nixon in the Oval Office, awarded a phony drug enforcement badge after having shown up unannounced in a limousine at the White House with a rambling pitch about drugs, communism, and other forces undermining America. It just wasn't supposed to end like that.

To go back to my own sense of where the music had begun—with 78 platters and then 45s, and WBAL from Baltimore on TV—I tried watching *Hairspray* (the 1988 version) some months ago. I couldn't find the music or Buddy Dean, the TV dance party guy on whom the movie disc jockey was modeled. It just didn't work. Maybe for the movie it was too much a John Waters thing. I was a goofy straight kid out there in the hinterlands, even though I did actually mingle once with the real Buddy Dean and a couple of members of his teen committee dragooned during a hop appearance at a local school. Or maybe it was too much a Baltimore thing, the way Dick Clark was a Philadelphia thing or Alan Freed was a New York deal with the payola and all the scandal.

The movies can play one false as well. When you wax nostalgic on a next viewing of *Rock around the Clock,* you need to check your memory and note that it was a 1956 movie. According to the divided plot, Bill Haley and the Comets shared the musical spotlight with the Platters. Ditto the crash that killed the Big Bopper, Richie Valens, and Buddy Holly: that was 1958. *American Graffiti,* set to a golden age rock 'n' roll sound track, was way too late to catch up. The music was right, but the people, the place, and the feelings were all too California. Somehow it winds up being downright provincial.

One touch from the movie that does call back the era, wherever one lived during the times, roughly speaking, was the clear-channel radio idea, where the Richard Dreyfus character goes looking for the tower and the studio from which all the top-forty music on all the car radios is emanating because he just knows there has to be a real Wolfman Jack. Well, there was, of course, a Wolfman Jack, just as there was a Cousin Brucie in New York, a Hugh Baby in Nashville, and a Dick Biondi in Buffalo, coming at us out of our car radios right in the places in America where we were in fact growing up. Another such realization helped by the movie is that in the late 1950s and early 1960s a lot of popular music was really rather regional. The South specialized in beach music, a dance called the shag, with songs by groups like the Tams and Maurice Williams and the Zodiacs; Detroit became the epicenter of Motown, the Temptations, the Miracles, the Supremes, the Four Tops. Black female singers began to hit it big, including Mary Wells, Dionne Warwick, the Chiffons, the Marvelettes, Martha and the Vandellas. The folk craze, in contrast, was more of a northeastern phenomenon. Odetta and Ian and Sylvia played urban clubs; one night at Newport (I know. I was there.) Joan Baez dragged Bob Dylan out onstage. He sang "Mr. Tambourine Man" unaccompanied, just his guitar and harmonica. The Beach Boys and Jan and Dean were the whole California car and surfing scene.

By the time I left college, the Beatles were the last big thing, and the next was the Stones, whom I saw on their first American tour in 1965—the same year, by strange synchronicity, I was back at Newport on the night Bob Dylan went electric. From there everything went fast-forward for a while. In the army my Vietnam playlist required an entire chapter in a book I wrote ten years ago. I drifted in with Otis Redding and "Sitting on the Dock of the Bay" and The Doors with "Light My Fire." A year of Vietnam combat was a time warp—old Stones, old Wilson Pickett, old Doors, old Eric Burdon and the Animals, along with new Janis Joplin, Jimi Hendrix, Country Joe and the Fish, and Jefferson Airplane. In 1969, while unavoidably detained on the Cambodian border, I missed Woodstock. (I also found out about the *Apollo* moon landing two weeks after it happened, somewhere around the time the armed forces papers also picked up on My Lai, which had taken place a year earlier.) When I got back from Vietnam, it was even more complicated. People in my English graduate student cohort parsed Don MacLean's *American Pie* in their freshman English and sophomore lit. courses, explaining what was lost on the Day the Music Died. But there was also Cream, the Who, Steppenwolf, and the Ike and Tina Turner Review. Jefferson Airplane updated to Jefferson Starship. People danced to all nineteen minutes of Iron Butterfly doing "Inna Gadda Da Vida" and nodded knowingly to the druggy profundities of the Moody Blues. Elton John was just starting out.

Then it all bled into the 1970s, surely the most awful of all times in the history of American popular music. Just naming some names tells the story: Seals and Croft, Loggins and Messina, Barry Manilow, the Bee Gees, Donna Summer. Disco. That was it for me, save possibly the Allmans, a little Jimmy Buffett, some early Bruce Springsteen.

Not surprisingly, I see as I look back, my music ended right in the middle of a decade I spent living without a TV in the house; my concert-going days were over, nor did I go to but an utter bare handful of movies—few enough that I can still remember specific occasions, with fleeting musical sound tracks. *Butch Cassidy and the Sundance Kid:* all the shooting, the whimsical, doomed, desperado, buddy and girlfriend sentimentality and slow-motion killing, to the sound of "Raindrops Keep Falling on My Head." In Charlottesville I saw *The Great Gatsby,* melodies lingering in my head long after of 1920s classics like "What'll I Do" and "Ain't We Got Fun." At the drive-in I was part of a pickup truckload of really stoned people for a double Disney musical bill of *Fantasia* and *Song of the South.*

Years later I finally saw a rock 'n' roll film that remains my choice for how it was according to the movies. It was *The Buddy Holly Story,* with Gary Busey in the title role, for much of the plot a strange, confused anachronism, the ultimate remake and Hollywood cover—a 1970s movie shot in color I actually remember to this day as having seen in black-and-white. A good bit of the time it seemed, if anything, a *Rock around the Clock* for nostalgists; but at the same time there was Busey as Buddy Holly, not an impersonation but more like reincarnation or inhabitation. Busey was channeling the voice, the music, the times, and the guy himself—the kind of jut-jawed, smart-mouthed, duck-tailed, what-the-hell kind of older teen rebel I idolized so fully in those days—and wanted so badly to be—with a beautiful, understanding, patient rah-rah girlfriend waiting for him and a good mom and a heart full of love for the world. The thing that will always remind me of the day the music died is the song they roll with the final credits. Throughout the movie we've heard the Big Bopper doing "Chantilly Lace" and Richie Valens doing "La Bamba," Buddy Holly and the Crickets doing "Peggy Sue," "Maybe Baby," and "That'll Be the Day." But now, one last time, we hear another Holly song, "True Love Ways," a strange, barely articulate teen ballad if there ever was one, with a full orchestra picking it up and carrying it through to the ending, the long slow fade. And without a hint of the banal or maudlin, you are at the prom again. In a white sport jacket, dark pants, a pressed white shirt with a black bow tie. Your date has on a rustling prom dress, with a wrist corsage. You hear it:

> Sometimes we'll sigh
> Sometimes we'll cry
> But you'll know why
> Just you and I
> Know true love ways.

And if you are a person who knows anything about early rock 'n' roll—about Elvis and Pat Boone, sure, but also about Del Shannon and Connie Francis, Dinah Washington and Sam Cooke—you'll know exactly what Buddy Holly means.

16
Let's Play Dien Bien Phu

"Let's play Dien Bien Phu." On a day I must now place as somewhere in 1954 or early 1955 at the latest, when I was nine or ten years old, I remember hearing one of my friends say this sentence, in exactly these words. The guy was one of our anointed ringleaders, admired for his easy athletic skills and Tom Sawyer–like ingenuity in inventing new adventures for the group. This was his way of suggesting that we vary our sideyard war games from the customary routines of exterminating Krauts, Japs, and, most recently, North Korean Gooks and Communist Chinese Chinks. That sounded good enough to me and the rest, although it occurs to me that we didn't know who the enemy was exactly. We just knew that they had to be opposed somehow to what Americans and other "Free-World Nations," as we used to call them, stood for. As I recall, we did not debate it much, nor did anyone offer any more than the usual objections to being consigned to play the bad guys. That they were "Communists" we may have understood vaguely; that they were Asians, perhaps, but despite this they were also somehow strangely different from North Koreans or Red Chinese. What we did know was that the French Foreign Legion was involved on the anticommunist side. These people, we knew from the newspapers, magazines, movies, and TV, were definitely the good guys—not to mention glamorous: dashing, hard-bitten, insanely brave, ready to go down with guns blazing and a cigarette hanging insouciantly from the lip. How we got to the particulars of the image remains a mystery. We were too young for *Beau Geste;* nor, along with anybody else in America, do we seem to have paid attention to a 1952 B-production Hollywood flop, *A Yank in Indochina.* On TV Buster Crabbe and his kid-sidekick in *Captain Gallant of the Foreign Legion* would not show up until a year later. *Rat Patrol* would be in the early 1960s. Perhaps partly it may have been our understanding that the French forces were paratroops. That certainly would have appealed to our American memories of the great World War II airborne formations, jumping into enemy-occupied terrain to undertake deadly behind-the-lines missions.

Since the latest war to offer a direct frame of reference was Korea, my guess is that we understood Dien Bien Phu pretty much the way we vaguely comprehended Panmunjom, which for three years or more had come to mean "dreadful stalemate." We had heard about the Pusan Perimeter, the Inchon Landing, the Chosin Reservoir (in the latter case without the foggiest notion that, for all the bravery of the Americans fighting their way out, the marines, Chesty Puller and the like, it had been one of the great disasters in American military history). On our parents' bookshelves we may have seen popular titles such as James Michener's *The Bridges at Toko-Ri* and S. L. A. Marshall's *Pork Chop Hill.* (The first would shortly show up also on movie screens, in glorious Technicolor, with William Holden and Grace Kelly; the latter would come years later in grim black-and-white with Gregory Peck.) What we had intuited was that Korea had come down to some kind of nasty endgame at Panmunjom. Panmunjom meant the good guys still going at it bravely on the battlefield while negotiators haggled over cease-fire regulations, geographic boundaries, prisoner exchanges, demilitarized zones, and the like.

Now, with Dien Bien Phu the latest word, the same sort of desperate thing seemed to be going on somewhere else, vaguely Asian, with walled mud forts, strings of beleaguered defensive positions, trenches, foxholes. Legionnaires were sharing scarce cigarettes, gathering up remaining ammo, getting ready for oncoming hordes of screaming, native guerilla fighters, with no regard for casualties, willing to be shot down in droves, the last ones getting through, then more coming behind them, then the positions gradually being surrounded, then . . . the screen going blank. Such enemies, we knew, had "no respect for human life." It was sort of like us against the Japs, and now the Chinks and the Gooks;

or the British in the Middle East, India and Pakistan, Ceylon and Malaya. It was hard to tell about the French. They were fighting somewhere out in Legion country, Africa, the Middle East, Asia. Wherever it was, it sounded a lot like Timbuktu.

At the time, "Indochina" would not have helped a great deal either. That was somewhere in Asia but hotter than Korea, down below China, on the other side of India, maybe like Burma. Nor did anyone except specialists understand that several countries were actually involved—French Indochina proper being composed of Viet-Nam (as it was usually spelled in those days), Laos, and Cambodia; abutted by China, also by Thailand, the former Siam, as in Rodgers and Hammerstein's *The King and I.* That even Vietnam itself was a composite of histories—Cham, Khmer, Chinese, Vietnamese—or a composite of ancient regions—Tonkin, Annam, Cochin China—would have stumped the most adept high school geographer—save, in the last case, one with enough Rodgers and Hammerstein experience to remember that the bawdy native woman Bloody Mary and her exquisite, virginal daughter, Liat, in *South Pacific* were "Tonkinese," whatever that meant.

Wherever Vietnam was, one was somehow encouraged to think of it as hot and rainy, with a lot of jungle. Given the current fighting at the place called Dien Bien Phu, that would have also been confusing, since the battle we saw in magazine pictures and newsreels seemed in a place far to the north—as in fact it was in Vietnam—way out in the fogs and mists of mountains, where it rained and looked cold. But maybe that was just some strange weather. (Actually, it was the nasty annual stuff that colonials called the *crachin.*) The French, we knew, somehow, were elite forces, special-operations troops, commandos in camouflage fatigues and jaunty berets who were certainly up to the task. At the time we could have had no idea how many of the Western combatants were German, Central European, Slavs, the occasional Scandinavian, many of them ex-Wehrmacht; or how many of the others, company after company, battalion after battalion, were colonial troops recruited from the corners of a dwindling empire—native Vietnamese, but also Laotians, Senegalese, Sudanese, Guineans, Moroccans, Algerians. Nor had we the remotest idea that the reason for Dien Bien Phu in the first place had to do with their all being hopelessly encircled in a great valley, cut off from both ground and aerial reinforcement and resupply, with the valley commanded by surrounding heights, all enemy occupied, somebody mysteriously called the Viet-Minh, where no one had ever imagined, in the fullness of colonialist arrogance, the latter would be able to assemble tens of thousands of troops for a siege, let alone emplace and supply vast amounts of heavy artillery.

We hadn't seen *Lost Command,* with Anthony Quinn, dealing with many of these things—taken from a contemporary French source, or Jean Lartéguy's *The Centurions,* actually dealing with Algeria and Vietnam—since none of us read French and since the movie would not be produced until 1966. We probably had some memory of Errol Flynn and *They Died with Their Boots On* from the late show or Saturday morning reruns, but that was about Custer. The newest Red hordes themselves were very hard to conceptualize. Although they seemed to rise up in great, charging, suicide formations, vaguely "oriental," as we would have phrased it at the time, they were not nasty little yellow Japs. Nor were they North Korean or Communist Chinese with their quilted uniforms, red-star winter caps, and tommy guns—with the latter, as in our *G.I. Joe* and *Fighting Marines* comics, on full automatic. Of Ho Chi Minh we seem to have known very little. To the best of my recollection, the "Viet Minh," whoever they were, had not seemed to be really Asian in any identifiable way. Above all, it could never have occurred to us that the people we were imaginatively playing war against were the enemy from a very real American war on the horizon that would nearly kill some of us.

As young Americans trying to stay abreast of "current events" as they were called in those days—my friend, apparently, being one of them—we knew a little background. French politics in 1954 were a mess; the premier, at least, had a relatively easy name to remember, Pierre Mendes-France, but not for long. The fall of his government was somehow further connected with the Geneva Conference, resolving whatever it was that had happened at Dien Bien Phu with the partition of Indochina into North and South Vietnam. The communists, known as the Viet-Minh, would control the North. The anticommunists would control the South. It would be like North Korea and South Korea or East Germany and West Germany—a brutal communist dictatorship on one hand, on the other a government of decent, striving, freedom-loving people like ourselves. South Vietnam would officially become part of the "Free World." As we had stood up against the Communists in Berlin during the blockade and the airlift, as we had supplied the main body of U.N. forces standing first against the invading North Koreans and then the Communist Chinese in Korea, we would do it again here in whatever way necessary. We even had a little knowledge and experience on how it might be done. We had applauded the success of the British in Malaya, and we had marshaled our own allegedly triumphant campaign against the Huks in the Philippines. A kind of Pacific Eisenhower, Magsaysay was definitely our guy, even if we didn't know much about the rest. If we could do it there, we could do it in the next place. We just had to find some right-thinking, freedom-loving, local patriot and make him our guy.

From there, somehow, it would all go fast-forward in Indochina. The figurehead rule in the South of the former emperor, Bao Dai, would be succeeded by the installation of the allegedly democratic regime of Ngo Dinh Diem, propped up in turn by the apparatus of an increasingly massive U.S. mission; in the early 1960s Kennedy would supply the glamorous and much-publicized Green Berets with high-powered military and civilian advisory assistance sufficient to prop up the publicity effort for a couple of years, if not the client government. Those of us who had played Dien Bien Phu a few years earlier were getting our driver's licenses in 1960, a crucial year in Vietnam. Most important was the formation in South Vietnam of the National Liberation Front (NLF) as an official revolutionary counterpart to the Ho Chi Minh government in the North and the political arm of the fighting guerilla formations in the South now called the Viet Cong—the latter a derisive term that had become serious, quite respectful military parlance. On the ground South Vietnamese forces proved repeatedly to be poorly led and nonbattleworthy. Most notable at the time was the Battle of Ap Bac, where American advisers were unable to get Vietnamese commanders to commit their large, comparatively well-armed troops to attacking a smaller, surrounded, Viet Cong force. Several American helicopters were shot down, an entire South Vietnamese armored cavalry regiment sat by as their infantry counterparts were chopped to pieces, and nearly all the enemy filtered out of the trap. Diem himself had become increasingly isolated, erratic, and intransigent, surrounding himself with intriguers and timeservers. That unhappy phase of cowardice and corruption ended with the Diem assassination, part of a military coup that Kennedy himself was said to have approved. Within a month Kennedy himself was dead at the hands of an assassin. Kennedy's successor, Lyndon Johnson, impelled to honor his predecessor's anticommunist legacy, felt constrained to honor the new military commitment. By 1964, after a confusing, largely contrived affair in offshore Vietnamese waters, allegedly involving Communist gunboats and a U.S. destroyer, Congress passed the Gulf of Tonkin Resolution, as it came to be called, authorizing presidential use of military force. Major commitments of U.S. Army, Navy, Air Force, and Marine units began in 1965. Beginning with Operation Rolling Thunder, major air-bombing campaigns were staged against the North. Marine and army ground units were rapidly fed in to secure South Vietnam air bases, port facilities, and major government centers. In the Ia Drang valley the First Air Cavalry fought major battles with North Vietnamese regulars. By the time my friends and I were finishing college, it was the Americans and not the French who were now in the old Dien Bien Phu thing all the way.

In retrospect, the general media had not kept us completely in the dark. Magazine journalism had kept up a certain amount of rah-rah stuff—Time-Life, of course, but also *Reader's Digest,* even *National Geographic.* The basic tone was always the same: "Plucky Vietnam Tries to Build Anti-Communist Democracy," or some such. Up to that point the Green Berets had been publicized as a kind of military Peace Corps. To be sure, there was Special Forces military mystique: elite, highly intelligent, schooled in various forms of specialty training, weapons, medicine, foreign languages, demolitions, civil affairs—an image enhanced by Robin Moore's garishly adulatory book and the best-selling 1965 top-forty ballad by Sergeant Barry Sadler. But they also suggested the kind of positive, savvy, internationally adept diplomat-soldier fit for a new, "youth" generation as we understood it, one that would, indeed, as Kennedy himself had put it, go anywhere, pay any price, bear any burden. Among civilian heroes, one of the most celebrated popular-culture figures at the time for young people was Dr. Tom Dooley, author of such inspirational texts as *Deliver Us from Evil* and *Promises to Keep.* Modeled on *Burma Surgeon,* the popular wartime text by Dr. Gordon Seagrave, here, written from the freedom's frontiers in Indochina itself was a staunchly anticommunist message delivered through the memoirs of an adventurous physician risking his own life every day at the hands of the Communists in order to save lives among brave, freedom-loving, allied peoples. In retrospect it stands as vintage medical missionary stuff, something of A. J. Cronin meets Norman Vincent Peale. Only decades later would a Catholic investigation reveal the hero to have been a promiscuous homosexual and an agent actively on the CIA payroll.

Other books proved more substantial and decidedly less happy and glowing. About Dien Bien Phu itself, and its centrality to the failure of the whole French enterprise, the journalist Bernard Fall published the 1956 classic *Hell in a Very Small Place.* Meanwhile, the U.S. newcomers to the Indochina scene underwent severe scrutiny in Graham Greene's *The Quiet American* (1953) and William Lederer's and Eugene Burdick's *The Ugly American* (1956). Both would quickly be made into movies. In the Hollywood *Quiet American* the titular character, Alden Pyle, would get a decidedly pro-American spin. Depicted by Greene as a naive ideologue, an idealistic meddler who gets a lot of people killed, not least, finally, himself, the movie Pyle, played by Audie Murphy, the nation's greatest combat hero of World War II, won a sacrificial victory over death as noble, patriotic, and selfless. *The Ugly American* barely had to wait for its movie version for the critical politics to become lost through misconstructions of the title into a popular culture cliché. In the world the ugly American became somebody who hates Paris or Prague because it is hard to find a McDonald's. In the book the titular character is in fact the best of the Americans abroad in South Asia, an agricultural engineer and field-worker named Homer Atkins who teaches the peasants of Sarkhan, an imaginary country in the throes of communist rebellion somewhere near Vietnam—which is depicted as a "real" place—to recycle broken bicycles into human-powered pumping machines for irrigation. Atkins is in fact so named because he is physically ugly to the point of being culturally notable. In the movie virtually all of this is subsumed in a political plot dominated by the smooth, mediagenic ambassador to the Sarkhanese, played with signature star power and mannerism by Marlon Brando.

Of a lot of epithets that have been attached to the American effort in Vietnam from the earliest days onward, one that still applies is "the secret war"—that is, the first major war that the U.S. government ever managed to get into up to its neck while keeping its vast commitments of money, materiel, and eventual manpower largely a secret from its citizens. Such was the thrust of Greene and of Lederer and Burdick in their early books; and, like many clichés, it would prove to be reasonably true in the first place, eventually bringing down two presidential administrations in the process and eventuating in a disordered withdrawal, dooming the South Vietnamese to a long agony of defeat. As important, even by the time of Dien Bien Phu, was the degree to which American policy makers had already managed to keep the real war a secret from themselves, in ways that would never improve. They would know nothing of the revolutionary struggle and the arduous, painful political organization, recorded in such texts as Tran Tu Binh's *The Red Earth,* that had been going on since the 1920s and 1930s, culminating in Ho Chi Minh's 1941 founding of Doc-Lap Dong Minh Hoi—the Revolutionary League for the Independence of Vietnam. They would somehow count it as nothing that, after World War II Japanese occupation, with the compliant Vichy French installed as political overseers, the return of India to the British would be paired with the return of Indochina to the French; that the proud Vietnamese, while this was effected, would suffer interim occupations by the British in the South and, of all people, the Chinese in the North; that Ho Chi Minh, by the late 1940s, under direction neither from Moscow nor Beijing, had formulated and established—as definitively related in Frances Fitzgerald's *Fire in the Lake*—a particular, syncretist, native brand of communist ideology and practice derived from a peasant socialism rooted in Vietnamese sensibility, cultural consciousness, with the village and community structure embodied in the national image of the great mandarinate, of the scholar-warrior-wise ruler. The leader is he who adjusts the administration of government, the rule of power, to the will of heaven. From the start, he, Ho Chi Minh, is that leader. He begins as Nguyen Ai Quoc—"Nguyen the Patriot"; he ends as Ho Chi Minh—"he who enlightens."

To be sure, at the other extreme, among the things we did not know must also be accounted the broad ignorance contained in the radical sentimentalizations of the American left, with Uncle Ho, the great leader himself, not in the least a figure to be so sanctified: as cynical as his

Korean counterpart, Kim Il-sung, playing off the Russians against Chinese, in the latter case with a millennia-long history of resistance against invasion and occupation; as ruthless as Lenin in consolidating power, eliminating rivals by state terror, arrest, exile, imprisonment, assassination, simple political murder; as without compunction as Stalin—albeit perhaps later with some remorse—in land redistribution schemes in the Red River delta eventuating in starvation, suffering, and deaths for hundreds of thousands; as clever as Khrushchev or Mao in calling for apologies and rectifications of methods. And above all, with triumph suddenly near, he proved quite ruthlessly like himself in accommodating the slaughter, during the 1968 Tet Offensive, of Viet Cong military cadres and the NLF infrastructure of southern political leadership as a welcome price of the assimilations the People's Republic of Vietnam would not have to pay after achieving full control over the country.

Meanwhile, in the South, the more common course of "current events" knowledge somehow wound up helping us miss all the bizarre feuds and factionalism. Those perplexed by Buddhist resistance, culminating in widely publicized self-immolations, were not able to anchor it in the general resistance of southern Vietnamese to an elite, colonial ruling class, French-educated and acculturated northern Catholics, brought south through the division of the country in 1954. On the government side the banana-republic lore of American adventurisms abroad made palatable, even comic, Diem and his conniving, dysfunctional palace clan, his stooges, his flatterers, his generals with their own palaces, concubines, secret bank accounts, padded false duty rosters, and constant assurances about combat readiness. But no one could really get to the bottom of all the attendant factions and sects, sometimes with their own idiotic governments and armies. The Cao Dai, as represented in Greene's novel, actually did hold the city of Tay Ninh as the papal site of a religion including among its primary saints Jesus, Buddha, Joan of Arc, and Victor Hugo. The Hoa Hao, their chief political and religious rivals, were formed around the cult of a Buddhist faith healer. The Binh-Xuyen were organized crime, a gangster organization allied with the Corsican mob, running nearly all illicit activity: drugs, smuggling, prostitution, extortion, and protection rackets. They had their own army, uniformed and armed, until it was systematically exterminated by Diem. Meanwhile, Diem was being done in by the Buddhists. And then eventually, of course, he was consigned to murder by the Americans. So, from the start, there was never the hope of what Alden Pyle in *The Quiet American*—relying on the foreign policy scriptures of his idol, York Harding—or Colonel Hillandale in *The Ugly American*—transparently modeled on the legendary early American democracy do-gooder Edwin Lansdale—and all the others theorized in Asia as a "Third Force." Somewhere around Dien Bien Phu, in good American fashion, we too would get there arrogantly in great, doomed force and only later realize it was not a game and we had gotten it all too wrong.

By the mid-1960s we were in it militarily for real, honest-to-god war—war by air, navy, and ground forces, with the latter consisting of a roll call of celebrated fighting units from the European and Pacific theaters in World War II: eventually the 1st, 4th, 9th, 25th, 101st Airborne, Americal Divisions, the 1st Marines, a Brigade of the 5th Mechanized, a Brigade of 82nd Airborne, the 11th Armored Cavalry. To show our smart flexibility, we also devised new, highly touted formations, gotten up for precision response to the new challenges of the "brushfire" or "guerilla" war—separate light infantry brigades, the 11th, 196th, 198th, 199th, 173rd Airborne. We had Rangers, Seals, Recondos, Land-Air-Sea and Combined Force outfits rigged out with the latest killing apparatus. At the height we counted around 550,000 in-country, roughly quadruple the current force in Iraq. Of these, 58,000 would eventually die.

At the end of the 1960s I was a member of one of those big maneuver units, serving a year as an armored cavalry platoon leader in the jungled III Corps tactical zone, centered on Saigon and stretching from the Cambodian border to the South China Sea. There, fifteen years more or less after that afternoon in the side yard, my new buddies and I came close to meeting our moment of ultimate truth in a mini–Dien Bien Phu—albeit actually of a sort that we had come by then to call the battle of the latest trail bend that happened everywhere in Vietnam on any given day. This one was an ambush along a much-traveled road, with a killing zone around a kilometer long. There were fifty or so of us; with trucks, tanks, armored personnel carriers, some shot up, others burning down to the road wheels, herringboned outward on both sides in a hasty defense. There were several hundred of the enemy, somehow having moved invisibly and silently into position overnight, firing from spider holes and bunkers. It was a trail bend we knew well. Now, with reinforcements being newly engaged as they were fed in, we spent the better part of the day stuck there, getting whittled down. They finally got a lot of us, including our brigade commander. Why they did not get all of us, I will never know. Maybe we just pounded them too hard with nonstop artillery and airstrikes. Maybe they thought they'd made their point. Maybe it was just that it was getting dark. In retrospect, among the things I marvel at is the pasting we gave them, maybe as much high explosive and tank and machine-gun fire in eight hours as any single day at Dien Bien Phu. The other is how they sullenly, invisibly withdrew, almost without a trace—figuring, I have to suppose now—that they had just killed enough of us for one day.

Later, in my academic career, where I had come to do a good bit of writing about the literature of the war, I got to know a retired U.S. general who as a young French-speaking officer had actually spent time at Dien Bien Phu in 1954, flying in as part of a U.S. inspection team under the official U.S. liaison representative to the French, a lieutenant general named Iron Mike O'Donnell. Ironically, my friend seemed to have known from the start many of the things we didn't know in many of the forms of military and geopolitical ignorance outlined here. When he got to be a general himself, still, he said he never got much of an audience, even though he counted "Westy" and "Abe," as he called them, trusted colleagues and friends. (On top of everything, he had also gone on to Geneva as a French-speaking military liaison to John Foster Dulles; to Cambodia, where he was head of the U.S. military mission until getting the golden handshake from Sihanouk; and then back in Vietnam in 1968, as chief of staff USARV [United States Army Vietnam], where he was the only member of the high command to predict the Tet Offensive.) He confirmed the story frequently reported as a historical anecdote about his realization of the deadly game the French had gotten themselves into. The general, apparently, had jumped out of the plane barely as it landed. Walking around it 360 degrees on the airstrip with the French greeting party in tow, he had pointed to surrounding mountain after surrounding mountain. "Who controls that ground?" he asked. "And that?" "And that?" He kept getting the same answer. "The Viet-Minh, mon Général." At some point, he said, "Well I'll be goddamned," got on the plane, and flew back out.

Apparently, this kind of thing really never seems to have stopped happening in Vietnam, either for generals or lieutenants and privates. Around the same time I met my friend, the older general, I was reading the memoirs of a younger one, roughly my contemporary in Vietnam, Colin Powell, the recently retired U.S. Army chief of staff and engineer of victory in Operation Desert Storm, who had served two tours in-country. He recalled one of his first experiences as an adviser officer there in 1963, when he had early come face-to-face, he later realized, with the siege-ridden absurdity of it all. It was one of those eye-blink things, he recalls, a vintage Vietnam epiphany, what Michael Herr, in *Dispatches,* would have called another mythopathic moment. In this case it involved Powell's first meeting with the Vietnamese captain he had been sent to advise. The two stood in a firebase deep in the A Shau Valley. "Laos," offered the Vietnamese helpfully, pointing to a nearby mountain that dominated every piece of the immediate landscape including the perimeter within which they stood. "Very important outpost," he added.

"What's its mission?" Powell asked.

"Very important outpost," his Vietnamese counterpart repeated.

Powell pressed on. "But why is it here?"

"Outpost is here to protect airfield," he said, pointing toward the dust cloud left by the helicopter on which Powell had just arrived.

"What's the airfield here for?" Powell asked.

"Airfield here to resupply outpost."*

Such a despairing flash—some simple matter of the moment suddenly rendered emblematic of a whole, grand, overarching idiocy—was a common experience among those of us who got to see the war from the far side of the U.S. enterprise, especially toward the end. Some of us saw it

*Colin Powell, with Joseph E. Persico, *My American Journey: An Autobiography* (New York: Random House, 1996), 79.

and did not come back. Some of us came back grievously wounded in body and/or spirit. Many of us think that we have never really come back at all.

In between, we all now have our particular names to remember: Ap Bac. Pleiku. Con Thien. Lai Khe. Loc Ninh. Qan Loi. Dong Ha. An Khe. The A Shau. The Ia Drang. For the marines Khe Sanh is a big one, basically a siege they were ordered to get themselves into up in the mountains, out toward the Laotian border. A memorable admonition of Lyndon Johnson to his advisers, civilian and military at the time, was, "We don't want no Din Bin Foos." We didn't get that, but almost. Some say the marines broke the siege; some say it was relieved only when Tet started breaking loose all over the South. That same year, we also got another name, something that would stand for us as our own shibboleth, a byword and a curse. The name was My Lai. It was something that happened out on bare ground, in the old VC cauldron of the Batangan Peninsula, in Quang Ngai Province; it too came of the folly, the frustration, the anger, the hate. My Lai became another name for our part of the action, one to gain immortality in American memory for all the wrong reasons.

In retrospect, it probably took that to show us how completely, brutally, and hopelessly we had worked ourselves into all those besieged spaces in the Vietnamese wilderness. We had a siege mentality to begin with; we just got the terms of besieger and besieged backward. The VC/NVA waged a sapper war, of probes, assaults, overrun firebases; they mortared and rocketed main camps. Around every corner was the ambush and the dreadful fear you'd be overrun, that this time they'd get every single one of you. We put out probes. Everyday missions were called search and destroy, search and clear, reconnaissance in force. The big ones were operation so-and-so or operation such-and-such. Big ones went into Cambodia and Laos. Repeatedly we pulled back into the siege-works, the cities and the big base camps. The borders were porous. The enemy supply lines remained not only unbroken but unbreakable according to conventional warfare. All the airpower in the world could not interdict the Ho Chi Minh Trail. All the naval interdiction in the world could not plug up Haiphong in the North and Sihanoukville in the South. All the energy, money, and goodwill in the world could not prop up a government that was hated by the vast majority of its people.

We lost the siege. We destroyed the cultural and political fabric of at least four countries. How many deaths we caused, we will never, ever know: fifty-eight thousand Americans for certain; with great likelihood, between 2 and 4 million Vietnamese. Cambodians died by the thousands during the 1970 invasion, with millions to follow later in the killing fields. We dropped millions of bombs on Laos. The Thais are still getting over us. A latest colonial incursion, by the Chinese, wound up with the Vietnamese kicking their butts. We have come and gone, taking our business now to other precincts, leaving behind, to use Michael Herr's trenchant phrasing, "the country that was the war."* All the while we never did find out where Dien Bien Phu really was, what actually happened there, or what the war in Indochina, as they used to say, was really all about.

*Michael Herr, *Dispatches* (New York: Knopf, 1977), 3.

Conclusion

Good-bye to All That

Although I did not know it at the time, I may have started writing this book the day I got home from Vietnam. That was the day I came "back to the world," as we used to say. The emphasis on Vietnam veterans' experience of forty years ago seemed to be that we were somehow profoundly different for having gone there. An equally compelling realization for many of us now is that the world we once knew, or thought we once knew before we went to Vietnam, had also become profoundly different. It is somewhere at the intersections of those two hypotheses, I might propose, that I have probably now spent the four decades in question trying to figure out how to say good-bye to myself and the world I grew up in. As to the particular title I have chosen for this conclusion, I actually did know something about Robert Graves back then, having studied in graduate school with a glamorous young professor at the time writing a book on the hermetic White Goddess mythology erected by Graves as a modernist poetic contemporary of Pound, Eliot, and others. Ironically, I knew nothing at the time of Graves's memoir of his experience as a World War I combat officer in the trenches, first published in 1929 and then revised and reissued in 1957. To be truthful, it is now impossible for me to recall when I first read *Good-bye to All That,* except to say that it must have been among the works of the post–World War I poets, memoirists, and novelists—Wilfred Owen, Siegfried Sassoon, Erich Maria Remarque—to whom I felt myself drawn in the years after my own experience of combat and return, who ratified my sense that a sojourn on death's gray landscape, as Owen phrased it, had brought me back to a world of popular attitudes and concerns I no longer recognized as the ones I had left behind. What I can say further is that *Good-bye to All That* remains the single book over the years that continues to mean more to me than any other.

On such matters literary and cultural, it is probably good how time and knowledge catch up with us and help us to demystify cherished notions of prophecy and context. Take Graves's title. One imagines a chastened, *Grand Illusions,* "been there, done that" sort of tone; or maybe something partaking of the dry stoicism of Jake Barnes's reply to Brett Ashley's suggestion that they might have been happy together save for the war. "Yes," says Jake. "Isn't it pretty to think so?" Graves's version of "Good-bye" is simple, firm, and final; the "All That" reference seems to hover somewhere between scorn and rueful affection—as in good-bye to all that rot, but also as in good-bye to all that once strangely seemed to have meant so much. Actually, in the case of *Good-bye to All That,* after years of reading, the kinds of strange, serendipitous library navigations and ransackings that English professors do, I have come to a happy suspicion that Graves took his 1929 title from an odd, distinctly British 1927 parody of history handbooks—a kind of H. G. Wells *Outline of History,* Monty Python–style, entitled *1066 and All That.* The latter, a short, funny text, is the strange sort of thing the British do so very well, with their conjoined mockery and reverence for England and all things English. It begins with Caesar invading Britain: "This was in the Olden Days, when the Romans were top nation on account of their classical education, etc."* After 1066 things go along pretty well until the Great War, which "lasted three years or the duration, the Americans being 100 percent victorious" (114). Most notable for my purposes here is how it abruptly comes to an end, with "A BAD THING" as far as any future English history was concerned. America became "clearly top nation, and History came to a ." (116). In just this vein the title I have chosen for the book at hand—*The Victory Album: Reflections on the Good Life after the Good War*—might as easily read "1945 and All That." It is the "all that"

*Walter Carruthers Sellar, Robert Julian Yeatman, and John Reynolds, *1066 and All That* (London: Methuen, 1930), 1.

that determines things for me also as a measure of memory and history, personal and cultural reflection. It dictates also where I stop the last predication to signify in my own case both the passage of a generation and the vanishing of a world.

I should say that, as an American combat veteran of the Vietnam War, along with such literary contemporaries as Tim O'Brien, Philip Caputo, Ron Kovic, and others, I am hardly alone in my identification with the Anglo European and American experience of the trenches from the World War I western front. Partly this is a peculiar identification, a certain kind of grunt solidarity. But it is also part of a palpable lost-generation mentality, an understanding one feels in connection with figures such as Graves, Sassoon, Owen, Remarque, Barbusse, the Anglo European British generation of 1914 to 1918, and by a certain extension Americans such as Hemingway, Dos Passos, and Fitzgerald. It is a palpable, lost-generation thing. As one contemporary of mine has put it, there is a wall ten miles wide and a hundred miles high between those of us who went to Vietnam and those who didn't, and it is never coming down. Like such writer-veterans as O'Brien, Caputo, and Kovic, I continue to find profound American analogies then and now about a lousy, grim, savage, forgotten nightmare place, a plane ride away from R&R or delivery back to the world, and what Paul Fussell has called "the Matter of Flanders and Picardy,"* of being part of a pointless, horrific, death-machine kind of war that, once it was set in motion, as Michael Herr says in *Dispatches,* could do everything but stop the killing.

This was the experience of combat and return to a familiar world forever rendered strangely alien. And while it is frequently the common fate of the soldier, in personal memory and history for many of us it does stand at some distance from the welcome accorded World War II veterans, their sense of having their duty and sacrifice acknowledged by people at home. As opposed to the Vietnam era, where people were often separated even from their age-cohort, there was a sense across post-1945 generations that something necessary and worthy had been done and that the world was going to be better for it. So writes Tim O'Brien, for instance, au-

*Paul Fussell, *The Great War and Modern Memory* (New York: Oxford University Press, 1975), x.

thor of *If I Die in a Combat Zone,* one of the great soldier memoirs of the Vietnam War: "I was the offspring of the great campaign of the tyrants of the 1940s, one explosion in the Baby Boom, one of millions come to replace those who had just died. My bawling came with the first throaty note of a new army in spawning. I was bred with the haste and dispatch and careless muscle-flexing of a nation giving bridle to its own good fortune and success. I was fed by the spoils of 1945 victory."* A Vietnam army nurse officer, Lynda Van Devanter notes her father's intense regret at being repeatedly rejected for World War II military service coupled with his sense of the tremendous obligation conferred by victory, "the obligation that we all had to be of service not only to our family, community, church, and country, but to all mankind."† With more specificity, if less reverence, Vietnam marine lieutenant Philip Caputo writes in *A Rumor of War:* "I was raised in Westchester, Illinois, one of the towns that rose from the prairies around Chicago as a result of postwar affluence, VA mortgage loans, and the migratory urge and housing shortage that sent millions of people out of the cities in the years following World War II. It had everything a suburb is supposed to have: . . . supermarkets full of Wonder Bread and Bird's Eye frozen peas; rows of centrally heated split-levels that lined dirtless streets on which nothing ever happened."‡ And thus it follows in narrative after narrative. What was called into question during the Vietnam era and the attendant tumults was not just the memory of the Good War but that of the Good Life after the Good War. Even on the far side of the Vietnam-era political spectrum in the generation of youth, Jerry Rubin, radicalized middle-American poster boy of the counterculture and antiwar movement, would concoct an autobiographical counternarrative, albeit with parallel phrasings. The account of his early boyhood he calls "Child of Amerika"; that of his adolescence is entitled "Elvis Presley Killed Ike Eisenhower."§

In the personal sphere the Elvis and Eisenhower notes are apt. Along with everyone else, I watched Elvis on Ed Sullivan and still remember go-

*Tim O'Brien, *If I Die in a Combat Zone* (New York: Random House, 1999), 11.
†Lynda Van Devanter, *Home before Morning* (New York: Beaufort, 1983), 27–28.
‡Philip Caputo, *A Rumor of War* (New York: Macmillan, 1996), 4–5.
§Jerry Rubin, *Do It! Scenarios of the Revolution* (New York: Simon and Schuster, 1970).

ing to the movies to see *Love Me Tender* and *Jailhouse Rock.* (I also owned a pair of blue suede shoes, which I wore until the soles separated hopelessly from the uppers.) By historical happenstance I grew up around Ike's grandchildren in Gettysburg, saw the president and Mamie in church, as I noted earlier, even shagged golf balls for him once at the country club. I, too, had come from a kind of Robert Graves world of upper-middle-class comforts and certainty—a world of stable relationships and certain privileges but also of a host of obligations resulting therefrom—of duty, hard work, self-discipline, a healthy abstemiousness—even, if required, a valiant self-sacrifice. In high school and college I was a good student, with time out for utterly unabstemious bad behavior; in Vietnam I almost got to do the sacrifice thing a couple of times, realizing increasingly that if I did die, I would be doing it out on the ass-end of nowhere for next to nothing. Somehow I already knew what I was saying good-bye to: 1945 and all that; and somehow I knew that if I ever lived long enough to write that book, it would be the one I am writing here.

So, in a vein very much like that in which Graves bids farewell to the world before the war, I now put a period to a comparable time in America—or at least, for someone of my middle-class social, educational, and cultural background, a world that seemed to be mine and that of many of my generational cohort in post-1945 America. Of course, it hadn't run the way the other had begun in 1066 and then marched along rather imperially until 1914–18. Our post-1945 world was, in significant ways, a true time of peace and prosperity, handed down to us from those who had undergone the experiences of World War II and the Depression, before that, World War I. In retrospect it is also really hard to say when it ended. A lot of people might specify November 22, 1963, the Kennedy assassination, as a good guess. Others might choose 1968, the year of the Tet Offensive and the riots at the Chicago Democratic Convention; or 1974, with the Nixon impeachment and Watergate. Or maybe it waited all the way until September 11, 2001, when the Twin Towers came down and the world entered the new age of terror.

Certainly people will have personal choices. For me, I might choose eight hours of nightmare on a dusty road bend somewhere up in Binh Thuy Province in early 1970. It might have been as early as the night I watched my father slump over in a chair, dying of a coronary occlusion, in

1957. It could have been somewhere around 1974–75, when I got my first job, bought my first house, when Watergate ran together with the fall of Saigon.

Ironically, in nearly every respect, after all these years America is still "top nation." But things have gone terribly wrong. Abroad, a militaristic administration brought a post–September 11, 2001, proliferation of the savage wars of American peace. At home, mortgage foreclosures, bank failures, and soaring gas prices brought meltdowns of financial and investment markets. It wasn't supposed to turn out this way. Accordingly, despite my pride in being a descendant of the greatest generation and a legatee of the good life after the good war, I am impelled to write a book that remains notably ambiguous about the alleged blessings of 1945 and all that. As to comprehensiveness, I acknowledge a lot of things I haven't written directly about, were this to be a sober, compendious, all-embracing attempt at social history argument or even popular-culture survey. There might be specific sections for instance on newspapers, magazines, books, radio, TV, movies; business and industry, banking and finance; medicine and health care; the armed forces; government domestic programs; diplomacy and international policy; the beginnings of globalization; American cultural imperialism. There are some important books in which some of those things have been done pretty well. From the standpoint of journalistic analysis the benchmark text remains David Halberstam's *The Fifties.* Numerous compilations of popular-culture lore exist as well, most notably Marion Nowak's *The Fifties: The Way We Really Were.*

In proposing a broader concept of post-1945 generational history, I make a conscious choice to go beyond decade-labeling, which, as in dealing with comparable eras, often seems to me reductive and simplistic; as far as my own generational perspective on the era is concerned, I have also wished to stake out a larger landscape of remembering somewhere between personal memory and cultural reflection. As a matter of both organization and perspective, my chief goal has been to register a sense of what happened—what it felt like to be a person living in the world at the time; a fairly average young American of the era, if not representative, certainly typical—and couple it with a larger, historically informed sense of how it has been frequently remembered and mythologized by the larger culture. The result is a certain kind of social history of growing up in post-1945 America, at once personal and cultural.

An academic way of saying this is that I have tried to use autobiography as a portal to ideology, to speak to the way in which certain matters of cultural assumption came to undergird the value and meaning systems of an era. Accordingly, if nothing else, honesty requires a brief summary elaboration and judgment on such matters. We finally critique ideology by making the effort to get it on the table. For good and ill, one needs to say, these were the articles of common wisdom—the basic propositions about life and culture that Americans generally believed or would have agreed to as characterizations of what Americans generally believed. These were the marching orders a victorious nation took from memory and history.

On the national and international scenes Americans conceived of the United States as a justly and rightfully victorious democracy, and the American system of politics, economics, and culture, while hardly perfect, as providing proof that the democratic way of life and capitalist free enterprise could triumph over economic depression, political dictatorship, military aggression, and all other ruthless schemes of world domination. At home the American people deemed themselves entitled to the material and spiritual rewards of their efforts and their sacrifices. American democracy and free enterprise were deemed manifestly the foundations of the best way of life, and it was simply assumed that all people, given their choice, would want a way of life similar to that enjoyed by postwar Americans.

At the everyday level—whether in rural areas, small and middle-sized towns, or suburbs and cities—Americans at least conceived of themselves as generally living together as married couples and/or as members of families. They got up in the morning together and went to bed at night together; in between they ate supper together, watched TV together, went to church together, took vacations together. Kids grew up together, went to school together, and played sports together, as brothers and sisters, as neighbors, as classmates, as fellow team members. In towns married couples and families started in apartments or duplexes—maybe part of their parents' or in-laws' houses or sometimes in part of a building shared with a business or store. In the country they lived in farmhouses or, out west, one imagined, on ranches. Eventually they found a way to rent or buy a family house—in a neighborhood where somebody needed to move on to something bigger or in one of the new suburbs springing up everywhere. Parents wanted only the best for their children and, it was believed, frequently did know best. Rebellion was part of being a teenager and not altogether a bad thing. Part-time or summer work for a young person was a good way of getting to know the value of a dollar. Extracurricular activities were a way of becoming socially and culturally well-rounded. A teenager who got badly out of line was considered a juvenile delinquent.

Americans felt justified and rewarded in partaking of a postwar bounty of domestic production. Owning a home and driving a new-model car were acceptable and even praiseworthy signs of economic success and arrival at social status. Here, as in the domain of what we would now call "big ticket" items—stoves, refrigerators, washers and dryers, televisions and vacuum cleaners—"Made in the U.S.A." meant what it said as far as unrivaled quality, value, and durability were concerned. In daily life a vast cornucopia of great American products, enjoyments, and conveniences were seen as the just rewards of average citizens who worked hard and earned their paychecks. At the same time, those who remembered what it had been like going through the Depression and who had experienced wartime shortages did well to keep in mind—and instruct their families accordingly—that hard times could always come again.

Abundant food, often local and regional, came from farms or from grocery stores and gleaming new supermarkets where shelves were also stocked with infinite varieties of canned and boxed goods. Frozen foods were a great symbol of American progress, "convenience items," a distinct advance over canned food, often as good as fresh. Fast food was a novelty and a treat. Among adult pleasures, no matter whether one personally smoked or drank, cigarettes and alcohol had a certain glamour.

Sex could get a person in trouble before marriage or after—marriage being, by definition, the only socially accepted venue for sex. Before marriage, girls who put out got a reputation, and boys bragged about their adventures. Girls got knocked up, and boys had to marry them. Extramarital sex was always grounds for scandal and sometimes divorce. Parents had talks with adolescents on the facts of life or gave them cursory little books, depending for the rest to come out in school during health class, where it might be discussed under the topic of Sexual Hygiene. Venereal diseases were things basic trainees were shown horrifying movies about in the military. Contraceptives could be found in vending machines in truck-stop bathrooms. The machines were marked, "For the Prevention of Disease Only." Homosexuality was considered so unspeakably deviant that respectable people simply did not talk about it.

Drugs were things sold at a drug store. Marijuana was for hipsters and musicians. Heroin was for addicts.

Rock 'n' roll was here to stay.

Hollywood movies were bigger and better than ever before, something for a great nation to be proud of. An epic production such as *The Robe* or *The Ten Commandments* was a great cultural event. Foreign movies were called "films," usually shot in black-and-white, and almost always complicated and intellectual.

Newspapers, magazines, and books, as well as regular news broadcasts, were important as ways of keeping up with cultural trends and gaining useful knowledge of what were called current events. Television was an important source of information and a culturally respectable form of entertainment. Big TV shows were things to look forward to and then talk about until the next week.

Education was important, and teachers and principals were respected community figures. The American public-school education was second to none, from the primary through the secondary grades, and people who got their high school degrees could hold good jobs and make a good living. For those who went beyond, American colleges and graduate and professional schools were also the best in the world and would supply the nation indefinitely with teachers, doctors, scientists, engineers, and business and political leaders at unparalleled levels of knowledge and expertise.

Military service was honorable and praiseworthy, and, for young men especially, a good way to learn discipline and get prepared for life.

It was generally believed that American women for the most part were satisfied with their traditional roles as wives and mothers, homemakers and domestic managers, by their own choice, and if they wanted careers or professional lives outside the home, it was their business. American girls were so instructed.

Segregation, like slavery a hundred years earlier, was for most people a southern problem that the south would eventually have to take care of—emphasis on the eventually. Negroes—as blacks were called at the time—who wanted to get ahead were supposed to go slowly and be a credit to their race.

By its nature, politics was going to throw up the occasional rotten apple, but most people who pursued public service as elected or appointed officials had a strong sense of civic responsibility and devotion to their work as leaders and public servants. Dwight Eisenhower won out over Douglas MacArthur for the presidency because people really did like Ike and sensed that MacArthur was a dangerous egomaniac. They caught on pretty quickly to Joseph McCarthy as well. In the case of Richard Nixon they formed a peculiar love-hate relationship with a clever politician they frequently understood as using an appeal to their own largely decent values to disguise his manipulation of the darker impulses in the national character.

Government, it was firmly believed, generally needed to stay out of business, because any attempt to control free enterprise was a step toward socialism, and socialism was a step toward communism. And one thing could definitely lead to another. As far as political policy and information were concerned, in a democracy leaders were generally open and truthful, but they also had a right to keep certain matters secret. This was particularly true in their dealings with the Communists, who were secretly out to rule the world but could be stopped by a strong national defense and, when necessary, limited wars of containment and other intelligence and security operations.

The use of the atomic bomb on Hiroshima and Nagasaki, coupled with American and Soviet developments of advanced weaponry such as the hydrogen bomb, had made future nuclear warfare unthinkable. Communism was a threat, but the people who lived under it, especially Russians and Central Europeans, were mainly people like us, just tremendously unfree and unfortunate. The United Nations promised to offer a way of eliminating full-scale war as a means of resolving world conflict, with authority to conduct, as in Korea, police actions.

A little religion—or in some cases a lot—never hurt anyone, as long as people kept it their own business. America was a Christian nation, with *Christian* acknowledged as meaning mostly protestant. Catholics were Irish and Italians and descendants of other immigrants who ate fish on Friday and went to "parochial school" and then college at Notre Dame, Villanova, St. John's, and places like that. While Hitler had done terrible things to the Jews, in big cities they still often seemed pushy people who liked to make money. A lot of Communist-blacklist artists and intellectuals were Jews, and of course the Rosenbergs were Jews. In public religion, big religious leaders stressed their sincere belief in the compatibility of Americans belonging to the major religions, and most Americans believed them. Religion was important, and ministers were respected community figures, but most people didn't wear religion on their sleeves and tried to get along with those of other denominations and creeds. Sectarian religious strife, at home or abroad, would become a thing of the past.

In reciting these articles of common belief, components of popular ideology, call them what you will, from life in post-1945 America, I hope I have made it clear that many of them were unworthy of personal or cultural assent then or now. As provisions of meaning and value held by "thinking" people in any time or place, notions that once seemed simple and well-intentioned—right down to the banality of the phrasings in which they were cast—they now turn out to be not just misguided but stupid and wrong. As regards historical specifics, it should also be clear that America after World War II was no more post Georgian and Edwardian England than I am Robert Graves, than Tim O'Brien and Philip Caputo are Edmund Blunden and Siegfried Sassoon, or than the late Lynda Van Devanter was Vera Brittain. Beyond the slaughter, the numb violence, the disdain for patriotic lies, it is always the fate of generations to record the crumbling, breakdown, annihilation of a society, a culture. Finally, at the same time, I hope I have made it clear that I am not remotely a nostalgist for some fondly reimagined postwar idyll. Back with mom and dad, the house you grew up in, a high-school sweetheart, and the golden era of rock 'n' roll were great colliding cultural vectors of belief and doubt, complacency and bigotry, immense goodwill and astonishing bad faith. *Pleasantville* is a creepy movie that keeps switching back and forth between Technicolor and black-and-white; it also remains the name of a postal station allowed by the government to be maintained as a mailing address for the *Reader's Digest.* Still, for many of us, banal and stupid as it may seem, our place of memory will always lie in a great, beckoning sense of cultural sureties and sentimental attachments, of an America that was once a place of hot cars, dates at the drive-in, summer picnics, winter sledding parties, TV, top-forty radio, high school sports, and college plans. The post-1945 America described here remains a lost world in just this sense. It is a world to which I now simply, like Robert Graves, take "an opportunity for a formal good-bye to you and to you and to you and to me and to all that."*

*Robert Graves, *Good-bye to All That: An Autobiography* (New York: Jonathan Cape, 1930), 1.

Index